The
LEADER'S GUIDE
to Storytelling

The LEADER'S GUIDE to Storytelling

MASTERING THE ART AND DISCIPLINE
OF BUSINESS NARRATIVE

Revised and Updated

STEPHEN DENNING

JOSSEY-BASS
A Wiley Imprint
www.josseybass.com

Published by Jossey-Bass
A Wiley Imprint
989 Market Street, San Francisco, CA 94103-1741—www.josseybass.com

Jossey-Bass books and products are available through most bookstores. To contact Jossey-Bass directly call our Customer Care Department within the U.S. at 800-956-7739, outside the U.S. at 317-572-3986, or fax 317-572-4002.

Jossey-Bass also publishes its books in a variety of electronic formats. Some content that appears in print may not be available in electronic books.

Library of Congress Cataloging-in-Publication Data
Denning, Stephen, 1944–
    The Leader's Guide to Storytelling : Mastering the Art and Discipline of Business Narrative / Stephen Denning.—Revised and updated edition.
        p. cm
    Includes bibliographical references and index.
    ISBN 978-0-470-54867-7 (cloth); ISBN 978-1-118-00876-8 (ebk); ISBN 978-1-118-00877-5 (ebk); ISBN 978-1-118-00878-2 (ebk)
    1. Communication in management. 2. Public speaking. 3. Business communication.
4. Communication in organizations. I. Title.
    HD30.3.D457 2011
    658.4′5—dc22

                                                                                                2010048700

Printed in the United States of America
REVISED AND UPDATED EDITION
C10004180_091718

CONTENTS

this—a springboard story—are the story's foundation in a sound change idea, its truth, its minimalist style, and its positive tone.

Communicating who you are and so building trust in you as an authentic person is vital for today's leader. The type of story that can accomplish this typically focuses on a turning point in your life. It has a positive tone and is told with context. Sometimes it is appropriate to tell your story, but sometimes it isn't.

Just as a story can communicate who you are, a story can communicate who your company is. Stories that the company tells about its brand are becoming less important than stories that customers tell. The products and services that are being offered are often the most effective vehicle to communicate the brand narrative to external stakeholders.

Values differ: there are robber baron, hardball, instrumental, and ethical values; there are personal and corporate values, and espoused and operational values. Values are established by actions and can be transmitted by narratives like parables that are not necessarily true and are typically told in a minimalist fashion.

Different patterns of working together include work groups, teams, communities, and networks. Whereas conventional management techniques have difficulty in generating high-performing teams and communities, narrative techniques are well suited to the challenge.

Knowledge-sharing stories tend to be about problems
and have a different pattern from the traditional well-told
story. They are told with context, and have something
traditional stories lack: an explanation. Establishing the
appropriate setting for telling the story is often a central
aspect of eliciting knowledge-sharing stories.

Stories form the basis of corporate culture, which is a
type of know-how. Although conventional management
techniques are generally impotent to deal with the rumor
mill, narrative techniques can neutralize untrue rumors
by satirizing them out of existence.

Future stories are important to organizations, although
they can be difficult to tell in a compelling fashion since
the future is inherently uncertain. The leader can tell a
future story in an evocative fashion or use a springboard
story as a shortcut to the future. The differences among
simulations, informal stories, plans, business models,
strategies, scenarios, and visions are reviewed.

None of the traditional approaches to transformational
innovation actually works. Solving the paradox
of innovation requires rethinking the whole concept
of management. Storytelling has a major role to play.

Effective use of the full array of narrative techniques
entails becoming an interactive leader, that is, a kind of

leader quite different from a conventional command-and-control manager. The interactive leader is someone who participates, connects, and communicates with people on a plane of equality and is relatively free of ego.

PREFACE

Much has happened in the five years since the first edition of this book provided the basic building blocks of leadership storytelling.

Since the first edition, the importance of storytelling as a leadership tool has become generally accepted, even in big organizations. The days are gone when I would be recruited by a nervous executive to hold a storytelling workshop for a major corporation with a euphemistic label like "strategic change management." Now executives tell me, "Let's call it what it is: storytelling!"

This reflects the fact that storytelling has gained recognition as a core competence of leadership. It is now standard practice to include a section on storytelling in books on leadership and change management, such as *A Whole New Mind* (2006) by Dan Pink, *The Leadership Challenge* (2008) by Jim Kouzes and Barry Posner, *Made to Stick* (2008) by Chip Heath and Dan Heath, and *Getting Change Right* (2010) by Seth Kahan.

The concept of leadership has itself also evolved. Chapter Twelve of the first edition of this book argued that storytelling is more than simply a communication tool and implied the emergence of a different kind of leader—someone who engages in interactive conversations rather than merely telling people what to do. It suggested that storytelling goes beyond the use of individual stories for specific purposes and implied a different way of thinking, speaking, and acting in the workplace.

I developed these ideas further in my book *The Secret Language of Leadership: How Leaders Inspire Action Through Narrative* (2007), which examined what this different way of thinking, speaking, and acting entailed. It explored in more detail how storytelling tools could be deployed to meet the specific challenges of leadership. It showed how the leadership communication triad, "get attention–stimulate desire for change–reinforce with reasons," could be used as a template to deal with virtually any leadership challenge. Chapter Two of this edition has been updated to reflect these discoveries.

Since 2005, a massive rethinking of management itself has also gotten under way. In 2009, the Shift Index quantified with startling clarity the long-term decline of management: the rate of return on assets of U.S. firms is now only a quarter of what it was in 1965; the life expectancy of a firm in the Fortune 500 has declined to less than fifteen years and heading toward five years unless something changes; executive turnover is accelerating; only one in five workers is fully engaged in his or her work.[1] The dysfunctionality of traditional management was further underscored by the Kauffman Foundation's discovery that established firms in the United States created no net new jobs between 1980 and 2005; virtually all net new jobs were created by firms that were five years old or less.[2]

The standard practices of management are increasingly seen as anachronistic. "Tomorrow's business imperatives," Gary Hamel wrote in *Harvard Business Review* in 2009, "lie outside the performance envelope of today's bureaucracy-infused management practices . . . Equipping organizations to tackle the future would require a management revolution no less momentous than the one that spawned modern industry."[3]

Chapter Eleven of the first edition of this book began to explore through the lens of disruptive innovation what this management revolution might involve. I argued that leadership storytelling is part of the answer. Since then, I have come to see more clearly what management actions in addition to storytelling are needed to create an organization that promotes continuous innovation on a sustained basis. In effect, storytelling is not just a core competence of leadership: it is also central component of management itself. My new book, *The Leader's Guide to Radical Management: Reinventing the Workplace for the Twenty-First Century* (2010), spells this out in more detail, and Chapter Eleven of this book has been updated to reflect these insights.

This book thus provides the building blocks of storytelling for two of my other books. *The Secret Language of Leadership* (2007) shows how storytelling is a central component of leadership. *The Leader's Guide to*

Radical Management (2010) shows how storytelling is a core competence of management itself.

The importance of storytelling in branding and marketing has also been reinforced by the explosion of social media. In 2005, when the first edition of this book was published, Facebook and YouTube had just been created, and Twitter did not exist. Today these three Web sites have hundreds of millions of participants, who are telling stories about their lives and the products and services that they use. This phenomenon has had a dramatic impact on practices in branding and marketing, as the ongoing shift in power from seller to buyer has dramatically accelerated. Understanding and mastering the elements of interactive storytelling in this sphere has become even more important than before. Chapter Five of this edition has been updated to incorporate the implications of these developments.

Stories are trapdoors, escape hatches, portals through which we can expand our lives and learn about other worlds. They offer guideposts to what is important in life. They generate meaning. They embody our values. They give us the clues from which we can discover what ultimately matters. In the past five years, I have learned much from studying both the power and the limits of storytelling. I am happy to have the opportunity to share those learnings here with you.

o   o   o

December 2010   Stephen Denning
Washington, D.C.

The
LEADER'S GUIDE
to Storytelling

INTRODUCTION

This book is an account of a simple but powerful idea: the best way to communicate with people you are trying to lead is often through a story. The impulse here is practical and pedagogical. The book shows how to use storytelling to deal with the most difficult challenges that leaders today face.

THE DIFFERENT WORLDS OF LEADERSHIP AND STORYTELLING

Storytelling and leadership are both performance arts, and like all other performance arts, they involve at least as much doing as thinking. In such matters, performers always know more than they can tell. I have tried to convey here as much as I can of what works—and what doesn't—at the intersection of the two different worlds of leadership and storytelling.

For the first several decades of my working life, I remained firmly in the world of leadership and management. I was a manager in a large international organization. The organization happened to be the World Bank, but had it been any other large, modern organization, the discourse would have been essentially the same: rates of return, cost-benefit analyses, risk assessments, performance targets, budgets, work programs, the bottom line—you name it.

The organization happened to be located in the United States of America, but the talk would have been the same if it had been situated in any other country. The forces of globalization have rendered the discourse of management and organizations thoroughly international. It's a world almost totally focused on analysis and abstractions. The virtues of sharpness, rigor, clarity, explicitness, and crispness are everywhere celebrated. It's a world that is heavy with practical import: the fate of

1

nations and, indeed, the economic welfare of the entire human race are said to rest on the effectiveness of the discourse.

It was the force of circumstance rather than temperament that led me away from the world of the boardroom, the negotiation table, and the computerized spreadsheet to a radically different world: the ancient performance art of storytelling. At the time, I was facing a leadership challenge for which the traditional tools of management were impotent. In trying to communicate a new idea to a skeptical audience, I found that the virtues of sharpness and rigor weren't working. Having spent my life believing in the dream of reason, I was startled to find that an appropriately told story had the power to do what rigorous analysis couldn't: to communicate a strange new idea and move people to enthusiastic action.

Initially the idea that storytelling might be a powerful tool for management and leadership was so counterintuitive and contrary to my entire education and work-life experience that I had difficulty in believing the evidence of my own eyes. In fact, it took me several years to admit to myself that I was being successful through telling stories.

"Soft." "Fuzzy." "Emotional." "Fluffy." "Anecdotal." "Irrational." "Fantasy." "Fairy stories." "Primitive." "Childish." These were just some of the terms that the advocates of conventional management hurled at leadership storytelling. They saw it as contaminating the world of pure reason with the poison of emotions and feeling, thereby dragging society back into the Dark Ages. It took a certain amount of intellectual courage to brave this disdain and suggest that the world of rational management might have much to learn from the ancient tradition of narrative.[1]

To build up intellectual stamina to face these challenges, I spent time in the radically different world of storytelling. Not that I was made to feel particularly welcome there. On the contrary, I was initially greeted as an interloper—someone who risked sullying the noble tales of glorious heroes and beautiful heroines, the figures who made the imagination soar and the heart leap, with the shallow, mean, and dirty world of business, commerce, and making money. To some, I was borrowing the magic language of narrative to accomplish something for which a tersely worded "fit-in-or-you're fired" memo might be more suitable. Not everyone could see that I was trying to subvert the "fit-in-or-you're-fired" approach to solving human problems.

What made my reception worse was that I didn't enter the world of storytelling on bended knee in a mood of respectful submission to drink from the ancient fonts of wisdom and accept without question what had been known for millennia about the elements of a well-told story. Instead I arrived with an iconoclastic attitude, suggesting that perhaps it was time to reexamine the Aristotle's eternal verities of storytelling. I implied that it might be healthy to throw back the curtains and open the windows and get some fresh air and light on some of these dusty old traditions. To the world of storytelling, this was heresy of the gravest kind. The suggestion that the ancient world of storytelling might actually have something to learn from organizations was as absurd as it was horrifying.

THE INTERSECTION OF LEADERSHIP AND STORYTELLING

The result was that for some years, I found myself uneasily inhabiting these two different worlds—each profoundly suspicious of the other, each using discourse that supported the validity of its own assumptions and conduct, each seemingly unable or unwilling to grapple with what it might learn from the other. Storytellers could talk to storytellers and managers could talk to managers, but managers and storytellers couldn't make much sense of one another. And what little they did understand of the other side's discourse, they didn't much like. As I gradually learned to converse, more or less successfully, in both worlds, I found myself in the role of go-between—someone who reported back from the other world, much as in the thirteenth century Marco Polo reported on his trip to China, telling astonished Venetians that there were strange and wonderful things in that distant world if you took the trouble to go there and check it out. Just as Marco Polo discovered, the very strangeness of my tale rendered my credibility questionable.

Occasionally when I would make a report to managers of what was going on in the world of storytelling, or to storytellers what was happening in the land of management, one of them would say, "How interesting!" And that is one of the points of this book: to point out matters of profound interest to both the world of storytelling and the world of leadership. So when in this book I take potshots of various kinds at both the world of management and the world of storytelling, please see that they are fragments of a lover's quarrel. If I didn't care deeply about both these worlds, it wouldn't be worth the hassle to undertake the role of dual ambassador.[2]

One of the factors driving me was the awareness that the average manager was not having extravagant success in meeting current leadership challenges. Let me cite just a few statistics:

- Study after study concludes that only 10 percent of all publicly traded companies have proved themselves able to sustain for more than a few years a growth trajectory that creates above-average shareholder returns.[3]

- Repeated studies indicate that somewhat less than 10 percent of major innovations in large corporations—the ones on which the future is said to depend—are successful.[4]

- The multibillion-dollar activity of mergers and acquisitions enjoys a success rate, in terms of adding value to the acquiring company, of around 15 percent.[5]

- The rate of return on assets of U.S. firms has declined by 75 percent since 1965.[6]

- The life expectancy of firms in the Fortune 500 has declined to fifteen years and is heading toward five years if trends continue.[7]

- Only one in five workers is fully engaged in his or her work.[8]

To grasp the significance of these figures, you need only ask yourself this: If your airline's flights arrived only 10 to 15 percent of the time, would you be getting on that plane? If your surgical operation was successful only 10 to 15 percent of the time, would you be undergoing that operation?

Managers thus have little reason to be complacent about their current mode of getting results.[9]

Nor was it obvious that the storytellers I met had any reason to be happier with their overall situation. Many of them were entangled in one way or another with the world of organizations. Often storytelling for them was a part-time avocation because it didn't generate sufficient revenue to make ends meet: they had day jobs to fill the gap. And those few who were involved full time in storytelling found themselves willy-nilly in the world of commerce.

But storytellers tended to keep the two worlds separate. They were just as unhappy as anyone else with the command-and-control management practices widespread in organizations, but the storytellers had no idea how to change them. They tended to live bifurcated lives: left-brained workers by day, right-brained storytellers by night. They couldn't see a way to bring their right-brained storytelling capacity into the workplace, and it was not clear that they even wanted to.

Just as the left-brained managers were reluctant to contaminate the rationalism of management with impassioned narratives, so storytellers were reluctant to risk dirtying the world of storytelling by immersing it in the world of commerce.

As I moved uneasily between these two different worlds, it was apparent to me that each of them had something to offer to the other. When I saw how storytellers could hold an audience totally engrossed in what was being said, I could see that this capacity is what analytical managers often lack: their brilliant plans often leave audiences confused and dazed. I also saw how slighted storytellers felt when the world of organizations didn't take them seriously. By clarifying the theory and practice of storytelling, I felt that I could show that storytelling had much to offer to organizations. By taking a clear-sighted view of what storytelling could and couldn't do, I believed I could help it assume its rightful place as an equal partner with analysis as a key leadership discipline. Storytellers would get the respect they want and deserve. Leaders would be able to connect with their audiences as human beings.

And of course what both worlds of storytelling and organization have been overlooking is that storytelling already plays a huge role in the world of organizations and business and politics today. One has only to glance at the business section of the newspaper to see that organizations are chockablock with stories that have massive financial impact.[10] Stories are the only way to make sense of a rapidly morphing global economy with multiple wrenching transitions under way simultaneously.

The choice for leaders in business and organizations is not whether to be involved in storytelling—they can hardly do otherwise—but whether to use storytelling unwittingly and clumsily—or intelligently and skillfully. Management fads may come and go, but storytelling is fundamental to all nations, societies, and cultures and has been so since time immemorial.

And it's not just leaders in business and politics who can benefit from a greater capability to use story. Anyone who has a new idea and wants to change the world will do better by telling stories than by offering any number of reasons. It is equally applicable to those outside organizations, such as schoolteachers, health workers, therapists, family members, professional colleagues—in short, anyone who wants to change the minds of those around them.

THE ROLE OF STORYTELLING

In one sense, telling a story is simply giving an example. The common-sense view is that it is "glaringly obvious, and something we all know instinctively. A good example may make something easier to understand, and easier to remember."[11]

So what? We can, the thinking goes, recognize the power of giving an example and go on managing the way we've always been managing without significant change. No big deal.

And yet it turns out to be a very big deal indeed, with storytelling being such a sizable part of the modern economy. Deidre McCloskey has calculated that persuasion constitutes more than a quarter of the U.S. gross national product (GNP).[12] If storytelling is—conservatively—at least half of persuasion, then storytelling amounts to 14 percent of GNP, or more than $1 trillion. But it's not just the size of the phenomenon. There's something qualitatively different going on here.

WHAT'S NEW IN STORYTELLING

To clear away some of the underbrush, let me start with some basics. In my experience, the following propositions do not seem particularly controversial to most people:

- Storytelling is an ancient art that hasn't changed much in several thousand years.

- The effective use of storytelling in organizations involves crafting and performing a well-made story with a hero or heroine, a plot, a turning point, and a resolution.

- A storyteller catches and holds the attention of an audience by evoking the sights and sounds and smells of the context in which the story took place.

- A well-made story is effective regardless of the purpose for which the story is being told.

- Storytelling is a rare skill in which relatively few human beings excel.

All these propositions, widely regarded as noncontroversial, are wrong. They constitute some of the popular misconceptions about storytelling. One of the purposes of this book is to explode these myths and expose what's really involved in using story for leadership in organizations.[13]

For one thing, it turns out that different narrative patterns are useful for the different purposes of leadership. Knowing which pattern is suitable for which task is a key to the effective use of storytelling. Ignorance of the different narrative patterns makes it likely that aspiring leaders will stumble onto an inappropriate narrative pattern for the task at hand and fail to attain their chosen goal.

It also transpires that some of the most valuable stories in organizations don't fit the pattern of a well-made story. For instance, a springboard story that communicates a complex idea and sparks action generally lacks a plot and a turning point. A story that shares knowledge is about problems, solutions, and explanations and often lacks a hero or heroine. The stories that are most effective in a modern organization do not necessarily follow the rules laid down in Aristotle's *Poetics*. They often reflect an ancient but different tradition of storytelling in a minimalist fashion, which is reflected in the parables of the Bible and European folk tales.[14]

Just as the human race began to make rapid progress in the physical sciences when people stopped believing what Aristotle had written and started observing with their own eyes whether two stones of different weights fall at the same or different speeds, so in the field of organizational storytelling, we begin to make progress when we stop looking at the world through the lens of Aristotle's teaching and start using the evidence of our own eyes and ears to examine what stories are actually told in organizations and what effect they have.

Moreover, the idea that storytelling is a kind of rare skill possessed by relatively few human beings is utter nonsense. Human beings master the basics of storytelling as young children and retain this capability throughout their lives. One has only to watch what goes in an informal social setting—a restaurant, a coffee break, a party—to see that all human beings know how to tell stories. Storytelling is an activity that everyone practices incessantly. It is so pervasive that it is almost invisible. We are like fish swimming in a sea of narratives. It is usually only when we are asked to stand up before an audience and talk in a formal setting that the indoctrination of our schooling takes over and a tangle of abstractions tumbles from our mouths. Learning to tell stories is less a task of learning something new and more one of reminding ourselves of something we already know. It's a matter of transposing the skills we apply effortlessly in a social situation to formal settings.

This book is about providing leaders at all levels in the organization with usable tools for communication—narratives that help tackle the most difficult challenges of leadership. The book has a strong focus on what works, but it also conveys enough theoretical background to give you an understanding of why some stories work for some purposes but not for others.

THE EMERGING LEADERSHIP DISCIPLINE OF NARRATIVE

Five years ago, when I published *The Springboard*, I was thinking of springboard stories as a tool, a remarkably useful tool but no more than a single tool.

By 2003, when I was finishing writing *Squirrel Inc.*, I could see that storytelling was more than one tool: it was at least a whole array of tools that could help achieve multiple purposes such as sparking people into action, communicating who you are or what your company is, transmitting values, sharing knowledge, taming the grapevine, and leading into the future.

In 2005, writing the first edition of *The Leader's Guide to Storytelling*, I sensed that narrative was even more than that. But what? A clue came recently when I was rereading Peter Senge's *The Fifth Discipline*.[15] At the end, Senge hints at the possibility of a sixth discipline—"perhaps one or two developments emerging in seemingly unlikely places, will lead to a wholly new discipline that we cannot even grasp today." The sixth discipline would be something invisible to conventional management thinking because it would be at odds with its fundamental assumptions.

Thus, it would be not a single gadget or technique or tool but rather a discipline, that is, "a body of theory and technique that must be studied and mastered to be put into practice. A discipline is a developmental path for acquiring certain skills or competencies. As with any discipline, from playing the piano to electrical engineering, some people have an innate 'gift' but anyone can develop proficiency through practice."[16]

Given the limited progress being made on innovation even using the five disciplines Senge talked about, this passage got me wondering whether storytelling might not be the missing sixth discipline. Certainly it has the characteristics that Senge envisaged for a discipline: something "where new and expansive patterns of thinking are nurtured, where collective aspiration is set free and where people are continually learning how to learn together." And it has to do with "how we think, what we truly want, and how we interact and learn with one another."[17] So could narrative be the missing sixth discipline?

Five years ago, I simply didn't know enough to call organizational storytelling a discipline: an emerging practice maybe, but not a discipline. Now I can draw on the work of practitioners like Madelyn Blair, Evelyn Clark, Seth Kahan, Gary Klein, Doug Lipman, Carol Pearson, Annette Simmons, Dave Snowden, and Victoria Ward, among many others. I can also see the wonderful work emerging from academia.[18] As I become more and more aware that I'm just scratching the surface of a subject that is broad and deep, I'm inclined to think that narrative is indeed an emerging discipline.

THE NATURE OF LEADERSHIP

This book talks more about leadership than management. Traditional management has focused more on means than on ends. Traditional managers usually take an agreed-on set of assumptions and goals and seek to implement efficient and effective ways of achieving those goals. They decide what to do, on the basis of agreed-on hypotheses, generally proceeding deductively.

Leadership deals with ends more than means. It concerns issues where there is no agreement on underlying assumptions and goals—or where there is a broad agreement, but the assumptions and goals are heading for failure. In fact, the principal task of leadership is to create a new consensus about the goals to be pursued and how to achieve them.

Leadership is essentially a task of persuasion—of winning people's minds and hearts. Typically it proceeds inductively by argument from one or more examples toward a more general conclusion about the goals and assumptions we should adopt toward the matter in question. Storytelling is thus inherently suited to the task of leadership.

THE MARRIAGE OF NARRATIVE AND ANALYSIS

This is not to say that abstract reason and analysis aren't also important. Storytelling doesn't replace analytical thinking. It supplements it by enabling us to imagine new perspectives and is ideally suited to communicating change and stimulating innovation. Abstract analysis is easier to understand when seen through the lens of a well-chosen story.

The physical sciences have had an aversion to anything to do with storytelling in part because it deals with such murky things as intentions, emotions, and matters of the heart. Yet in the past couple of decades, most of the human sciences have grasped the centrality of narrative to human affairs. Narrative has come to be influential in vast regions of psychology, anthropology, philosophy, sociology, political theory, literary studies, religious studies, psychotherapy, and even medicine.[19] Management is among the last of the disciplines to recognize the central significance of narrative to the issues that it deals with.

THE PERFORMANCE OF THE STORY

The basics of leadership storytelling can be mastered quickly. Mastery of the discipline, however, takes a lifetime. Storytelling is a performance art. It's one thing to realize that you need to link the story with the change idea; it's another thing to do it, time after time without fail, like the swing of a professional golfer who always performs flawlessly. You will not become a master storyteller simply by reading this book. You will have to put the ideas into practice so that you get into a groove.

Finally, keep in mind that the stories in this book are for the most part intended to be performed. Some of the stories included here, when read on the printed page, may seem so brief and bland that it is hard to imagine how they could have impact. Remember that everything is transformed in performance. Small things make a big difference. The look of the eye, the intonation of the voice, the way the body is held, the import of a subtle pause, the teller's response to the audience's responses—all these aspects make a huge contribution to the meaning of a story for audiences. Chapter Two discusses how to perform a story for maximum effect.

A DIFFERENT KIND OF LEADER

Throughout this book, I make the case, step by step, that if you consistently use the narrative tools described here, you will acquire new capabilities. Because you communicate who you are and what you stand for, others come to know you and respect you for that. Because you are attentive to the world as it is, your ideas are sound. Because you speak the truth, you are believed. Because you make your values explicit and your actions are consistent with those values, your values become contagious and others start to share them. Because you listen to the world, the world listens to you. Because you are open to innovation, happy accidents happen. Because you bring meaning into the world of work, you are able to get superior results. Chapter Twelve explores the implications of this kind of leadership for organizations.

LET'S GO!

The challenges of leadership are difficult, volatile, and sometimes daunting. This book doesn't shy away from those difficulties. And yet it offers a note of hope. Leadership is not an innate set of skills that a few gifted individuals receive at birth. Narrative patterns can be learned by anyone who wants to lead from whatever position they are in—whether CEO, middle management, or on the front lines of an organization, or outside any organizations altogether—anyone who sees a better way to do things and wants the organization to change.

Organizations often seem immovable. They are not. With the right kind of story at the right time, they are stunningly vulnerable to a new idea. And this book provides you with a guide to finding and telling the right story at the right time.

A DEFINITION OF *STORY* AND *NARRATIVE*

In this book, *narrative* and *story* are used as synonyms, in a broad sense of an account of a set of events that are causally related. Such a simple, commonsense notion is, however, controversial. Here I have space only to allude to some of the issues.

The Definition of "Story" and "Narrative"

What is a story? What is a narrative? Are they the same or different?

This book follows common usage and treats *story* and *narrative* as synonyms, to mean *an account of events that are causally connected in some way.*

Some practitioners have suggested different definitions. Some suggest that *story* should be defined in the narrower sense of a well-told story, with a protagonist, a plot, and a turning point leading to a resolution, while *narrative* might be a better choice in the broader sense I use. According to this view, locutions that lack the traditional elements of a well-told story are not so much stories as ideas for possible stories yet to be told or fragments of stories.[20]

Others have suggested that *story* should be used in a broader sense, while *narrative* should be restricted to the narrower sense of "a story as told by a narrator." According to this view, "narrative = story + theme": the theme is a layer added to the story to instruct, provide an emotional connection, or impart a deeper meaning.[21]

In common usage, both *story* and *narrative* are inclusive. Polkinghorne and others have suggested that we accept this broad meaning and treat the two terms as synonyms.[22] Within the broad field of story, it's possible to distinguish classically structured stories, well-made stories, minimalist stories, antistories, fragmentary stories, stories with no ending, stories with multiple endings, stories with multiple beginnings, stories with endings that circle back to the beginning, comedies, tragedies, detective stories, romances, folk tales, novels, theater, movies, television mini-series, and so on, without the need to get into theological discussions as to what is truly a story.

In common usage, *story* is a large tent, with many variations within it. Some variations are more useful for some purposes than others. There are probably many variations that haven't yet been identified. If we start out with predetermined ideas of what a "real story" is, you may end up missing useful forms of narrative.

The Internal and External Aspects of a Story

It is also important to keep in mind that story has an external and an internal aspect. Story in its external aspect is something to be observed, analyzed, and dissected into its component parts. In its internal aspect, it is something that is experienced, lived as a participant. This book explores both dimensions of story. The value of the external view of story is that it is stable and clear. Its drawback is that it stands outside the experience of the story itself. The value of the internal view of story is that it is fresh and immediate and participative. Its weakness is that it is elusive and kaleidoscopic and vulnerable to abuse.[23]

The Position Adopted in This Book

This book sees story as independent of the media by which it is transmitted. A story can be transmitted by words, pictures, video, or mime. While recognizing the suitability of language to communicate narrative, it is possible to study narrative in its nonverbal manifestations without requiring verbal narration.[24]

In examining the phenomenon of story and storytelling, both the external and internal aspects of story need to be taken into account.[25]

Part 1

---•---

THE ROLE OF
STORY IN ORGANIZATIONS

1

TELLING THE RIGHT STORY

Choosing the Right Story for the Leadership Challenge at Hand

" Storytelling is fundamental to the human search for meaning. "

Mary Catherine Bateson[1]

In 1998, I made a pilgrimage to the International Storytelling Center in Jonesborough, Tennessee, seeking enlightenment. As program director of knowledge management at the World Bank, I'd stumbled onto the power of storytelling. Despite a career of scoffing at touchy-feely stuff—like most other business executives, I knew that analytical was good, anecdotal was bad—my thinking had started to change. Over the past few years, I'd seen stories help galvanize an organization around a defined business goal.

In the mid-1990s, that goal was to get people at the World Bank to support efforts at knowledge management—the idea of sharing knowledge horizontally across an organization and even beyond. It was an unfamiliar notion at the time. I offered people cogent arguments about the need to gather the knowledge scattered throughout the organization. They didn't listen. I gave PowerPoint presentations that compellingly demonstrated the value of sharing and leveraging our know-how. My audience merely looked dazed. In desperation, I was ready to try almost anything.

Then in early 1996, I began telling people a story:

> In June 1995, a health worker in a tiny town in Zambia went to the Web site of the Centers for Disease Control (CDC) and got the answer to a question about the treatment of malaria. Remember that this was in Zambia, one of the poorest countries in the world, and it was in a tiny place six hundred kilometers from the capital city. But the most striking thing about this picture, at least for us, is that the World Bank isn't in it. Despite our know-how on all kinds of poverty-related issues, that knowledge isn't available to the millions of people who could use it. Imagine if it were. Think what an organization we could become!

This simple story helped World Bank staff and managers envision a different kind of future for the organization. When knowledge management later became an official corporate priority, I used similar stories to maintain the momentum. So I began to wonder how the tool of storytelling might be put to work even more effectively. As a rational manager, I decided to consult the experts.

At the International Storytelling Center, I told the Zambia story to a professional storyteller, the late J. G. "Paw-Paw" Pinkerton, and asked the master what he thought. Imagine my chagrin when he said he didn't hear a story at all. There was no real "telling." There was no plot. There was no building up of the characters. Who was this health worker in Zambia? And what was her world like? What did it feel like to be in the exotic environment of Zambia, facing the problems she faced? My anecdote, he said, was a pathetic thing, not a story at all. I needed to start from scratch if I hoped to turn it into a "real story."

Was I surprised? Well, not exactly. The story *was* bland. I did have a problem with this advice, though. I knew in my heart it was wrong. And with that realization, I was on the brink of an important insight: Beware the well-told story!

THE POWER OF NARRATIVE

But let me back up a bit. Do stories really have a role to play in the business world? Believe me, I'm familiar with skepticism about them. When you talk about storytelling to a group of hard-headed executives, you'd better be prepared for some eye rolling. If the group is polite as well as tough, don't be surprised if the eyes simply glaze over.

That's because most executives operate with a particular mind-set. Analysis is what drives business thinking. It seemingly cuts through the fog of myth, gossip, and speculation to get to the hard facts. It purports to go wherever the observations and premises and conclusions take it, undistorted by the hopes or fears of the analyst. Its strength lies in its objectivity, its impersonality, its heartlessness.

Yet this strength is also a weakness. Analysis might excite the mind, but it hardly offers a route to the heart. And that's where you must go if you are to motivate people not only to take action but to do so with energy and enthusiasm. At a time when corporate survival often requires transformational change, leadership involves inspiring people to act in unfamiliar and often unwelcome ways. Mind-numbing cascades of numbers or daze-inducing PowerPoint slides won't achieve this goal. Even logical arguments for making the needed changes usually won't do the trick.

But effective storytelling often does. In fact, in certain situations, nothing else works. Although good business cases are developed through the use of numbers, they are typically approved on the basis of a story—that is, a narrative that links a set of events in some kind of causal sequence. Storytelling can translate those dry and abstract numbers into compelling pictures of a leader's goals. I saw this happen at the World Bank—by 2000, we were increasingly recognized as leaders in the area of knowledge management—and have seen it in scores of other large organizations since then.

So why did I have problems with the advice I'd received from the professional storyteller in Jonesborough?

A "Poorly Told" Story

The timing of my trip to Tennessee was fortunate. Had I sought expert advice two years earlier, I might have taken the master's recommendations without question. But I'd had some time to approach the idea of organizational storytelling with a beginner's mind, free of strictures about the right way to tell a story.

It wasn't that I couldn't follow the Jonesborough storyteller's recommendations. I saw immediately how to flesh out my modest anecdote about the health worker in Zambia: you'd dramatically depict her life, the scourge of malaria that she faced in her work, and perhaps the pain and suffering of the patients she was treating that day. You'd describe the extraordinary set of events that led to her being seated in front of a computer screen deep in the hinterland of Zambia. You'd delineate the false leads she had followed before she came across the CDC Web site. You'd build up to the moment of triumph when she found the answer to her question about malaria and vividly describe how that answer could transform the life of her patient. The story would be a veritable epic!

This traditional, or maximalist, account would be more engrossing than my dry anecdote. But I had learned enough by then to realize that telling the story in this way to a corporate audience would not galvanize them to implement a strange new idea like knowledge management. In the hectic modern workplace, people had neither the time nor the patience—remember executives' general skepticism about storytelling in the first place—to absorb a richly detailed narrative. If I was going to hold the attention of my audience, I had to make my point in seconds, not in minutes.

There was another problem. Even if my audience did take the time to listen to a fully developed tale, telling it in that fashion would not allow listeners the mental space to relate the story to their own very different worlds. Although I was describing a health worker in Zambia, I wanted my audience to focus not on Zambia but on their own situations. I hoped they would think, *If the CDC can reach a health worker in Zambia, why can't the World Bank? Why don't we put our knowledge on a Web site?* If my listeners were immersed in a saga about that health worker and her patient, they might be too preoccupied to ask themselves these questions—or to provide answers. In other words, I didn't want my audience too interested in Zambia. A minimalist narrative was effective precisely because it lacked detail and texture. The same characteristic that the professional storyteller saw as a flaw was, for my purposes, a strength.

On my return from Jonesborough, I educated myself on the principles of traditional storytelling. More than two thousand years ago, Aristotle, in his *Poetics*, said stories should have a beginning, a middle, and an end. They should include complex characters as well as a plot that incorporates a reversal of fortune and a lesson learned. Furthermore, the storyteller should be so engaged with the story—visualizing the action, feeling what the characters feel—that the listeners become drawn into the narrative's world. Aristotle's formula has proved successful over the ages, from Ovid's *Metamorphoses* to *The Arabian Nights* to *The Adventures of Tom Sawyer* and most Hollywood screenplays.

Despite the narrative power of this kind of story, I knew that it probably wouldn't spark action in an organization. My insight blinded me to something else, though. Believing that this wonderful and rich tradition had no place in the time-constrained world of modern business was as wrongheaded as thinking that all stories had to be full of detail and color. Later I would see that the well-told story is relevant in a modern organization. Indeed, a number of surprises about the use of storytelling in organizations awaited me.

Tales of Success and Failure

In December 2000 I left the World Bank and began to consult with companies on the use of leadership storytelling. The following year, I found myself in London with Dave Snowden, then a director of IBM's Institute of Knowledge Management, teaching a storytelling master class to around seventy executives from private and public sector organizations.

In the morning, I spoke about my experience at the World Bank and how a positive orientation was essential if a narrative like the one about Zambia was to have its intended effect. But in the afternoon, to my dismay, my fellow presenter emphatically asserted the opposite.

At IBM and elsewhere, Dave had found purely positive stories to be problematic. They were, he said, like the Janet and John stories told to children in the United Kingdom or the Dick and Jane stories in the United States: the characters were so good they made you feel queasy. The naughtiest thing Janet and John would do was spill a bottle of water in the yard. Then they would go and tell their mother about it and promise never to do it again. Janet would volunteer to help with the cleanup and John would offer to help wash the car. These stories for children reflected a desire to show things as they should be rather than as they actually are. In a corporate environment, Dave told his audience, listeners would respond to such rosy tales by conjuring up negative antistories about what must have actually happened. His message: Beware the positive story!

After the workshop, Dave and I discussed why his stories focused on the negative while mine accentuated the positive. I could see he had a point. I'd used negative stories myself when trying to teach people the nitty-gritty of any subject. The fact is, people learn more from their mistakes than from their successes.

Eventually, however, it dawned on me that our points of view were complementary. We were talking about organizational stories used for different purposes: my stories were designed to motivate people, and Dave's were designed to share knowledge. His stories might describe how and why a team failed to accomplish an objective, with the aim of helping others avoid the same mistakes. (To elicit such stories, however, Dave often had to start by getting people to talk about their successes, even if these accounts were ultimately less useful vehicles for conveying knowledge.) It was then that I began to realize that the purpose of telling a story might determine its form.

Granted, even optimistic stories have to be true and believable, since jaded corporate audiences know too well the experience of being presented with half-truths. Stories told in an effort to spur action needed to make good on their promises and contain sufficient evidence of a positive outcome. But stories intended mainly to transfer knowledge must be more than true. Because their objective is to generate understanding and not action, they tend to highlight the pitfalls of ignorance; they are meant not to inspire people but to make them cautious. Just as my minimalist stories to spark action were different from traditional entertainment stories told in a maximalist fashion, so an effective knowledge-sharing story would have negative rather than positive overtones.

A Collective Yawn

Once I saw that different narrative forms can further different business goals, I looked for other ways that managers could make stories work for them. A number of distinct story types began to emerge—ones that didn't necessarily follow Aristotelian guidelines but were nonetheless used to good effect in a variety of organizations. (For descriptions of some of them and the purposes for which they might be used, see "A Storytelling Catalogue" later in this chapter.) And I continued to come across unexpected insights about the nature of storytelling within organizations.

For one thing, if negative stories have their place, so do apparently boring ones. In *Talking About Machines*, Julian Orr recounts a number of stories that have circulated among photocopy machine repair technicians at Xerox.[2] While rich in detail, they are even less storylike than my little anecdote about the health care worker in Zambia. Most of these tales, which present solutions to technical problems faced by the technicians, lack a plot and a distinct character. In fact, they are hardly stories at all, with little to hold the interest of anyone except those close to the often esoteric subject matter. Nevertheless, they are compelling even to this limited audience because they are driven forward by a detailed explanation of the cause-and-effect relationship between an action and its consequence—for example:

> You've got a malfunctioning copy machine with an E053 error code, which is supposed to mean a problem in the 24-volt Interlock Power Supply. But you could chase the source of that 24-volt Interlock problem forever, and you'd never ever find out what it is. If you're lucky enough, you'll eventually get an F066 error code, which indicates

the true source of the malfunction—namely, a shorted dicorotron. Apparently this is happening because the circuitry in the XER board has been changed to prevent the damage that would otherwise occur when a dicorotron shorted. Before the change in circuitry, a shorted dicorotron would have fried the whole XER board. Changing the circuitry has prevented damage to the XER board, but it's created a different issue. Now an E053 error message doesn't give you the true source of the machine's malfunction.

This story, paraphrased here, doesn't just describe the technician's accurate diagnosis of a problem; it also relates why things happened as they did. This makes the account, negative in tone and almost unintelligible to an outsider, both informative and interesting to its intended audience.

As I continued my investigation, one area of particular interest for me was the link between storytelling and leadership. I already knew from personal experience that stories can be used as a catalyst for action. And I had seen in several influential books—*Leading Minds* by Howard Gardner, *The Leadership Engine* by Noel Tichy, and *The Story Factor* by Annette Simmons—that stories can help leaders define their personality, boosting confidence in their integrity and providing some idea of how they might act in a given situation.[3]

I also had seen leaders using narrative to inculcate a positive set of corporate values and beliefs in the hearts and minds of employees. Think, for example, of Tyco's effort to repair its battered value system. The company began by developing a straightforward guide setting forth new rules in such areas as harassment, conflicts of interest, and fraud. But Eric Pillmore, senior vice president of corporate governance, soon learned that in this form, the booklet would merely gather dust on people's shelves. So he threw out what he had done and started again in an effort to bring the principles alive through stories. Here is one of them:

The entire team jokes about Tom being gay. Tom has never complained and doesn't seem to mind, but when Mark is assigned to work with Tom, the jokes turn on Mark. Now that Mark receives the brunt of the jokes, he tells his supervisor he wants to be reassigned. His supervisor complies with Mark's request.[4]

This story serves as a sidebar for the section of the guide that deals with sexual harassment and other forms of intimidating behavior. While the company's policy on harassment is clearly laid out in the guide, the simple narrative helps bring the policy to life and provides a starting point for thinking about and discussing the complex issues involved. Dozens of similar stories illustrate an array of company policies.[5]

An Enticing But Hazy Future

Although these types of stories furthered leadership goals in a relatively predictable way, others I came across were more quirky—particularly ones used to communicate vision. Noel Tichy writes about the importance of preparing an organization for change: "The best way to get humans to venture into unknown terrain is to make that terrain familiar and desirable by taking them there first in their imaginhations."[6] *Aha!* I thought. *Here is a place where storytelling, perhaps the most powerful route to people's imaginations, could prove indispensable.*

But as I looked at examples of such stories in a number of arenas, I discovered that most of the successful ones were surprisingly sketchy about the details of the imagined future. Consider Winston Churchill's "We Shall Fight on the Beaches" speech and Martin Luther King Jr.'s "I Have a Dream" speech. Neither of these famous addresses came close to describing the future in enough detail that it became familiar terrain in listeners' minds.

Over time—and in part through work I did that incorporated scenario planning—I realized the reason. Specific predictions about the future are likely to be proved wrong. Because they almost inevitably differ in major or minor ways from what eventually happens, leaders who utter them risk losing people's confidence. Consequently a story designed to prepare people for change needs to evoke the future and conjure up a direction for getting there—without being too precise. Think of the corporate future laid out in a famous mandate by Jack Welch: General Electric will be either number one or number two in the field, or it will exit the sector. This is a clear but broad-brush description of where Welch wanted to take the company. Like my Zambia story, it doesn't convey too much information, though for different reasons.

I also came across stories used in somewhat unusual situations that called for reactive rather than proactive measures. These stories counteracted negative ones that circulated like viruses within an organization and threatened to infect the entire body. Dave Snowden of IBM first pointed out to me how stories could be used in this manner. His hypothesis was that you could attach a positive story to a negative one and defuse it, as an antibody would neutralize an antigen.

For example, at an IBM manufacturing site for laptop computers in the United Kingdom, stories circulated among the blue-collar workers about the facility's managers, who were accused of not doing any real work, being overpaid, and having no idea what it was like on the manufacturing line. But an additional story was injected into the mix. One day a new site director turned up in a white coat, unannounced and unaccompanied, and sat on the line making ThinkPads for a day. He asked workers on the assembly line for help. In response, someone asked him: "Why do you earn so much more than me?" His simple reply: "If you screw up badly, you lose your job. If I screw up badly, three thousand people lose their jobs."[7]

Although this isn't a story in the traditional sense, the manager's words and actions served as a seed for the story that eventually circulated in opposition to the one about managers' being lazy and overpaid. You can imagine the buzz: "Blimey, you should've seen how he fumbled with those circuit boards. I guess he'll never work on the line. But you know, he does have a point about his pay." The atmosphere at the facility began improving within weeks.

A STORYTELLING CATALOGUE

Storytelling is an increasingly accepted way to achieve management goals. But leaders need to employ a variety of narrative patterns for different aims. The following sections sketch the kinds of stories I've found, following the general outline of Part Two of the book.

Sparking Action

Leadership above all is about getting people to change. To achieve this goal, you need to communicate the complex nature of the changes required and inspire an often skeptical organization to enthusiastically carry them out. This is the place for what I call a springboard story—one that enables listeners to visualize the large-scale transformation needed in their circumstances and then to act on that realization.

A springboard story is based on an actual event, preferably recent enough to seem relevant. It has a single protagonist with whom members of the target audience can identify. And it has an authentically happy ending, in which a change has at least in part been implemented successfully. (It also has an implicit alternate ending—an unhappy one that would have resulted had the change not occurred.)

The story has enough detail to be intelligible and credible but—and this is key—not so much texture that the audience becomes completely wrapped up in it. If that happens, people won't have the mental space to create an analogous scenario for change in their own organization. For example, if you want to get an organization to embrace a new technology, you might tell stories about individuals elsewhere who have successfully implemented it, without dwelling on the specifics of implementation.

Communicating Who You Are

You aren't likely to lead people through wrenching change if they don't trust you. And if they are to trust you, they have to know you: who you are, where you've come from, and why you hold the views you do. Ideally they'll end up not only understanding you but also empathizing with you.

Stories for this purpose are usually based on a life event that reveals some strength or vulnerability and shows what the speaker took from the experience.

Unlike a story designed to spark action, this kind is typically "well told," with colorful detail and context. So the speaker needs to ensure that the audience has enough time and interest to hear the story.

For example, Jack Welch's success in making General Electric a winner was undoubtedly aided by his ability to tell his own story, which includes a tongue-lashing he once received from his mother after he hurled a hockey stick across the ice in response to a disappointing loss. His mother chased young Jack into the locker room where the young men on the team were changing and grabbed him by the shoulders. "You punk!" he reports her saying in his memoir. "If you don't know how to lose, you'll never know how to win."[8]

On the face of it, this is a story about Jack Welch's youth, but it's also a story about the Jack Welch of today. From this story, we get a good idea of the kind of person Jack Welch became as CEO of GE—obsessed with winning, strong on loyalty, and with an aggressive style of behavior, someone who is very much in your face.

Communicating Who the Company Is—Branding

In some ways, the stories by which companies communicate the reputation of themselves and their products so as to establish their brand are analogous to leaders' stories of who they are.

Just as individuals need trust if they are to lead, so companies need trust if their products and services are to succeed in the marketplace. For customers to trust a company and its products, they have to know what sort of company they are dealing with, what kinds of values it espouses, and how its people approach meeting customers' needs.

Strong brands are based on a narrative—a promise that the company makes to the customer, a promise that the company must keep. It's a story that the customer has about the company and its products and services. The brand narrative is owned by the customer, not the company.

Once you have settled on the brand promise and made sure that the organization can deliver on it, communicating that to customers is most effectively done not through electronic advertising (which today has limited credibility) but rather through having the product or service tell its own story or by customers' word of mouth.

Transmitting Values

Stories can be effective tools for ingraining values within an organization, particularly those that help forestall future problems by clearly establishing limits on destructive behavior. A story of this type ensures that the audience understands "how things are done around here."

These narratives often take the form of a parable. Religious leaders have used them for thousands of years to communicate values. The stories are usually set in some kind of generic past and have few context-setting details—though the context that is established needs to seem relevant to the listeners. The facts of such tales can be hypothetical, but they must be believable. For example, a story might tell the sad fate of someone who failed to see the conflict of interest in not disclosing a personal financial interest in a company supplier.

Of course, narratives alone cannot establish values in an organization. Leaders need to live the values on a daily basis.

Fostering Collaboration

Every management textbook talks about the value of getting people to work together. But most don't offer advice on making that happen in real-life work environments except for generalities like, "Encourage conversations." Yes, but how?

One approach is to generate a common narrative around a group's concerns and goals, beginning with a story told by one member of the group. Ideally that first story sparks another, which sparks another. If the process continues, group members develop a shared perspective that enables a sense of community to emerge naturally. The first story must be emotionally moving enough to unleash the narrative impulse in others and create a readiness to hear more stories. It could, for example, vividly describe how the speaker had grappled with a difficult work situation.

For this process to occur, it is best if the group has an open agenda that allows the stories to surface organically. It is also desirable to have a plan ready so that the energy generated by the positive experience of sharing stories can be immediately channeled into action.

Taming the Grapevine

Rumors flow incessantly through every organization. "Have you heard the latest?" is a whispered refrain that's difficult for managers to deal with. Denying a rumor can give it credibility. Asking how it got started may ensure its spread. Ignoring it altogether risks allowing it to grow out of control. Rumors about issues central to the future of the organization—takeovers, reorganizations, major managerial changes—can be an enormous distraction (or worse) to the staff and to outside stakeholders.

So as an executive, what can you do? One effective response is to harness the energy of the grapevine to defuse the rumor, using a story to convince listeners that the gossip is either untrue or unreasonable. This kind of story highlights the incongruity between the rumor and reality. You could use gentle satire to mock the rumor, the rumor's author, or even yourself in an effort to undermine the rumor's power. For example, you might deal with a false rumor of "imminent corporate-wide reorganization" by jokingly recounting how the front office's current struggles involving the seating chart for executive committee meetings would have to be worked out first. Keep in mind, though, that humor can backfire. Mean-spirited ridicule can generate a well-deserved backlash.

The trick is to work with, not against, the flow of the vast underground river of informal communication that exists in every organization. Of course, you can't ridicule a rumor into oblivion if it's true or at least reasonable. If that's the case, there is little that can be done except to admit the rumor, put it in perspective, and move on.

Sharing Knowledge

Much of the intellectual capital of an organization is not written down anywhere but resides in the minds of the staff. Communicating this know-how across an organization and beyond typically occurs informally through sharing stories.

Knowledge-sharing narratives are unusual in that they lack a hero or even a detectable plot. They are more about problems, and how and why they got—or didn't get—resolved. They set out a description of the problem, the setting, the solution, and the explanation. Because they highlight a problem—say, the challenge employees face in learning to use a new system—they tend to have a negative tone.

And because they often focus in detail on why a particular solution worked, they may be of little interest outside a defined group of people. But although they lack most elements of a conventional story, they are nonetheless the uncelebrated workhorse of organizational narrative.

They present a difficulty, however. In a corporate setting, stories about problems don't flow easily, not only because people fear the consequences of admitting mistakes, but also because, in the flush of success, they tend to forget what they learned along the way. As a result, the knowledge-sharing story cannot be compelled; it has to be teased out. That is, a discussion of successes may be needed to get people to talk about what has gone wrong and how it can be fixed.

Leading People into the Future

An important part of a leader's job is preparing others for what lies ahead, whether in the concrete terms of an actual scenario or the more conceptual terms of a vision. A story can help take listeners from where they are now to where they need to be by getting them familiar and comfortable with the future in their minds. The problem, of course, lies in crafting a credible narrative about the future when the future is unknowable.

Thus, if such stories are to serve their purpose, they should whet listeners' imaginative appetite about the future without providing detail likely to prove inaccurate. Listeners should be able to remold the story in their minds as the future unfolds with all its unexpected twists and turns. And clearly the stories should portray that state in a positive way because people are more likely to overcome uncertainty about change if they are shown what to aim for rather than what to avoid.

Note that telling an evocative future narrative requires a high degree of verbal skill, something not every leader possesses. But the springboard story provides an alternative. Hearing about a change that has already happened can help listeners to imagine how it might play out in the future.

USING THE STORYTELLING CATALOGUE

The catalogue of narratives constitutes a handy menu of options that can be consulted by executives weaving together a set of stories for a full-scale presentation. Table 1.1 lays out the uses of the various types of stories.

The point is that there is no single right way to tell a story. Instead, narrative comprises an array of tools, each suitable to a different purpose. Different combinations of story can be woven together as an integrated narrative tapestry. Some examples:

- A presentation to introduce a new idea might first involve telling a story to get the audience's attention by talking about a problem of concern to the audience, followed by a springboard story to communicate a new idea and spark action related to it, and then, if the response is positive, concluding with knowledge-sharing stories showing how to deal with the issues of implementation.

- A presentation about the strategic direction of an organization might begin with a personal identity story ("who I am") followed by the company identity story ("who we are") eventually leading on to a future story ("who we are going to be").[9]

With the catalogue in hand, you can also avoid some of the most frequent mistakes in organizational storytelling:

- Using a story with negative tonality will generally fail to spark action. However useful such a story might be to share understanding, it is unlikely to inspire and move anyone.

- Telling a personal story in a traditional fashion is also unlikely to spark action. It might entertain the audience and communicate who the speaker is, but it is unlikely to galvanize people to action.

- Using success stories typically fails to communicate knowledge because it risks missing the nitty-gritty of how things actually get done in the world.

TABLE 1.1   Eight Narrative Patterns

If your objective is …	You will need a story that …	In telling it, you will need to …	Your story will inspire such phrases as …
Sparking action	Describes how a successful change was implemented in the past, but allows listeners to imagine how it might work in their situation.	Avoid excessive detail that will take the audience's mind off its own challenge.	"Just imagine …" "What if …"
Communicating who you are	Provides audience-engaging drama and reveals some strength or vulnerability from your past.	Provide meaningful details but also make sure the audience has the time and inclination to hear your story.	"I didn't know that about him!" "Now I see what she's driving at!"
Transmitting values	Feels familiar to the audience and will prompt discussion about the issues raised by the value being promoted.	Use believable (though perhaps hypothetical) characters and situations, and never forget that the story must be consistent with your own actions.	"That's so right!" "Why don't we do that all the time!"
Communicating who the firm is—branding	Is usually told by the product or service itself, or by customer word of mouth or by a credible third party.	Be sure that the firm is actually delivering on the brand promise.	"Wow!" "I'm going to tell my friends about this!"

continued

TABLE 1.1 *Continued*

If your objective is …	You will need a story that …	In telling it, you will need to …	Your story will inspire such phrases as …
Fostering collaboration	Movingly recounts a situation that listeners have also experienced and prompts them to share their own stories about the topic.	Ensure that a set agenda doesn't squelch this swapping of stories—and that you have an action plan ready to tap the energy unleashed by this narrative chain reaction.	"That reminds me of the time that I …" "Hey, I've got a story like that."
Taming the grapevine	Highlights, often through the use of gentle humor, some aspect of a rumor that reveals it to be untrue or unreasonable.	Avoid the temptation to be mean-spirited—and be sure that the rumor is indeed false!	"No kidding!" "I'd never thought about it like that before!"
Sharing knowledge	Focuses on problems and shows in some detail how they were corrected, with an explanation of why the solution worked.	Solicit alternative—and possibly better—solutions.	"There but for the grace of God …" "Gosh! We'd better watch out for that in the future!"
Leading people into the future	Evokes the future you want to create without providing excessive detail that will only turn out to be wrong.	Be sure of your storytelling skills. Otherwise use a story in which the past can serve as a springboard to the future.	"When do we start?" "Let's do it!"

34

- Denying untrue rumors often just accelerates them, although a satire can ridicule an untrue rumor out of existence.

- Using detailed scenarios to instill belief in a different future is generally ineffective. Even if believable when disseminated, such scenarios quickly become discredited as the future unfolds in unexpected ways.

THE RETURN ON INVESTMENT OF STORYTELLING

"What's the ROI of storytelling?" is a question I am often asked when addressing a business audience on the topic of storytelling. In dealing with such a question, the first thing to consider is whether it is genuine. Often the request to quantify benefits is merely a pretext for taking no action or a polite way of making a negative statement. When the response to a request for measurable benefits is followed by a request for additional measurements and studies, then beware. Measurement has value only when it is prompted by a genuine attempt to achieve understanding and is backed by willingness to act on the basis of the findings.[10]

Talk Is Work

Storytelling is about making managers and leaders more effective in what they do. So what do managers do? The first point to realize is that for managers—and indeed most people in the knowledge economy—talk is work. If you can learn how to talk more effectively, you can become much more productive.

The contrary view is of course still prevalent and still emerges today even in leading business publications.[11] But it flies in the face of serious research such as Henry Mintzberg's classic *Nature of Managerial Work*, which showed that talking comprises 78 percent of what managers actually do with their time.[12]

Where storytelling gets the message across more effectively, its incremental cost is zero, or close to zero, and so its ROI is massive.[13] Moreover, communicating through stories usually means talking more succinctly, so that the cost in terms of executive and staff time is actually lower than for ineffective talk.

Impact of Storytelling on Implementing Change

Assessments of the effect of storytelling on performance have emerged. A study explored the experience of some forty companies undergoing major change, including banks, hospitals, manufacturers, and utilities.[14] Each of these projects was initiated by senior management and involved changes such as implementing a Six Sigma program, optimizing business processes, and adopting a new sales strategy. All the programs could potentially have had a large economic impact on the organization, and all required major companywide changes in behavior, tasks, and processes.

Two things are striking about the study's findings. First, it's remarkable how little success the companies had with their change programs. The team gauged the difference between the expected value of a project (essentially calculated in the business case for it) and the value the company claimed to have achieved when it was completed. In all, 58 percent of the companies failed to meet their targets; 20 percent captured only a third or less of the value expected. And the overall differences between the winners and losers were huge. The successful 42 percent of these companies not only gained the expected returns, in some instances they exceeded them by as much as 200 to 300 percent.

Second, one of the key success factors was storytelling. The study rated each company's strength in twelve widely recognized factors for managing change effectively, including the ability to tell a simple, clear, and compelling story with no mixed messages. The researchers found a high correlation between the success factors, including storytelling, and the outcome of the change program. Storytelling wasn't the only success factor, of course; other elements included the company's project management skills, training, and incentives for promoting change. But without a storytelling capacity, the chances of success were significantly lower.

Narrative Is the Foundation of an Organization's Brand

Some progress has been made in quantifying the impact of narrative in brands. A strong brand generates benefits in terms of raising capital, launching new products, acquiring new assets, or attracting new partners.

Although strong brands reflect the immense value that can be generated by narrative—the top ten global brands are together worth some $380 billion—the phenomenon of advertising illustrates how extraordinary quantities of money can be wasted in the ineffective use of narrative.[15] And what narrative creates, narrative can also take away: the narrative-generated value of brands is vulnerable to attack by narrative. The advent of social media has led to public relations crises of astonishing scale and rapidity. When companies don't live up to their brand values, the consequences can be devastating.

The Emerging Microstudies on the Impact of Storytelling

Research in speech communications has begun to clarify why stories are effective in stimulating responses from listeners. Stories excite the imagination of the listener and create consecutive states of tension (puzzlement and recoil) and tension release (insight and resolution). Thus, the listener is not a passive receiver of information but is triggered into a state of active thinking.[16] The listener must consider the meaning of the story and try to make sense of it. By this process, the listener is engaged; attention and interest are fostered.[17]

Studies in social psychology show that information is more quickly and accurately remembered when it is first presented in the form of an example or story, particularly one that is intrinsically appealing.[18] One study compared the effectiveness of four different methods to persuade a group of M.B.A. students of an unlikely hypothesis: that a company really practiced a policy of avoiding layoffs. In one method, there was just a story. In the second, the researchers provided statistical data. In the third, they used statistical data and a story. In the fourth, they offered the policy statement made by a senior company executive. The most effective method of all turned out to be the first alternative: presenting the story alone.[19]

Storytelling Is an Amplifier

How consistently does storytelling work? Is it effective 100 percent of the time? Or 50 percent? Or 10 percent of the time? This question can't be answered yet because the body of research simply doesn't include enough longitudinal studies. Nevertheless, it is possible to infer the eventual findings by comparison with an area on which a great deal of research work has been done: teams. The amazing reports from the field about the benefits of specific teams contrast sharply with the gloomy picture that emerges from scholarly research on the impact of teamwork on performance across many organizations: overall, no net improvement in performance can be detected. How can the two be reconciled? Richard Hackman makes several helpful points in *Leading Teams*.[20]

First, in organizations, there is no simple cause-and-effect relationship between introducing a management technique and getting an improved business result. This contrasts with other spheres of activity where simple causal relationships do seem to operate. Hit the nail with the hammer, and it goes into the wood. Show a dog food, and it salivates. This kind of simple cause-and-effect logic can be misleading if applied to the complex world of organizations, where it is difficult to trace single effects to single causes. Uncontrollable outside factors can sink a wonderfully designed team (a hurricane just swept the entire inventory out to sea) or rescue one whose design was so bad that failure seemed assured (the firm that was competing for the contract just went belly-up). In organizations, multiple causes are operating at the same time and interacting with each over an extended period of time.

Second, the apparent paradox of zero improvement in performance from teams in organizations overall—along with extraordinary gains reportedly made in specific instances—reflects the fact that teams are found at both ends of the effectiveness spectrum. While some extraordinary teams outperform any traditional units, other teams do so poorly that they are easily outperformed by traditional units. So the absence of an overall benefit from the impact of all teams doesn't mean that teams are irrelevant to performance.

I won't be surprised to find a similar result with storytelling. Thus, you may continue to see case studies indicating improved performance in some instances.[21] You will also see instances where storytelling didn't work at all: compare, for example, Chapters Five and Six of *The Springboard*, which describe how a story that was highly effective in one context got derailed in a different context as a result of extraneous factors.

It remains to be seen whether overall assessments across many organizations will detect a major correlation between the use of storytelling and organizational performance—or not, as in the case of teams. In any organizational change, many factors play a role in achieving organizational performance: a good story may be undermined by other factors (such as counterproductive managerial behavior in other areas), while a story that appeared to fail with most of the audience may be rescued by external events that make the change inevitable (for example, the firm is taken over by a company that is already implementing the new approach).

The effectiveness of storytelling is related to the nature and consistency of the leadership involved, a point I'll explore further in Chapters Eleven and Twelve. It is by no means clear whether any correlation between storytelling and performance will emerge. Nevertheless, as in the case of work teams, it seems probable that storytelling will operate like an amplifier: whatever passes through the device—whether signal or noise—comes out louder. If care is taken to ensure the quality of the signal, the effect can be extraordinary.[22]

2

TELLING THE STORY RIGHT

Four Key Elements of Storytelling Performance

> " Who knows why certain notes in music
> are capable of stirring the listener
> deeply, though the same notes
> slightly rearranged are impotent? "
>
> **Strunk and White[1]**

Knowing the right story to tell is only half the battle. The other half is telling the story right. Storytelling is a performance art, and the way a story is performed can radically change its emotional tone, and hence its impact on the listener. Thus, a leader may have an excellent story to tell and may possess highly developed verbal skills, and yet perform poorly as a storyteller because the story is told as a monologue rather than as a conversation. Conversely, a leader may have very limited verbal skills but a firm grasp of the idea of reciprocity that lies at the heart of effective storytelling and so deliver a very effective performance. "Telling the story right" entails having all of the elements of storytelling mesh together to form the social act known as storytelling.[2]

In performance, the story, the storyteller, and the audience interact to form a meaningful ensemble. In the world of organizations, there's often a preoccupation with what is said, while in the world of pure storytelling, the focus is more often on how the story is performed. In leadership storytelling, the story's form and content, the storyteller, and the audience are all inseparably intertwined with each other.

Because storytelling is a performance art, reading this chapter will not by itself enable you to tell a story right. Just as you learn how to ski by actually skiing or to sing a song by actually singing, so you will learn how to tell the story right through telling stories. This chapter can explain to you the principles, but you alone can master them through practice. Nevertheless, a guide can help. By knowing what to look for and which pitfalls to avoid, you can accelerate the learning involved in developing your storytelling skills.

The suggestions fall under four headings:

- Style
- Truth
- Preparation
- Delivery

STYLE

Among the many styles of storytelling, the one most suitable for modern organizations is a style that is plain, simple, and direct. This will be the foundation that you can customize for particular settings and requirements.

DIFFERENT STYLES OF STORYTELLING

The plain, simple, and direct style of storytelling advocated in this book obviously isn't the only possibility. Here are some other styles:

- *The raconteur:* The raconteur is polished, glib, even elegant—someone who is always in performance, someone who looks and sounds so polished that every story comes across as a performance, not as sincere. In a corporate context, the raconteur is usually too good to be true.

- *The stand-up comedian:* The comedian is crisp, witty, sardonic, and topical, with the principal objective of keeping the audience amused. The organizational storyteller may tell jokes, but the principal objective is not to amuse and entertain.

- *The orator:* The orator revels in the explicit stance of talking to a large crowd rather than talking to an individual—for example: "And so we see, ladies and gentlemen, in this instance, as so many other instances that have occurred and are likely to occur, that what our organization does will improve the lives of billions of people around the world, and so let us pledge our lives to nurturing that cause." It is a style of speaking that lives on in the political speech, but is out of place in the organizational context.

- *The reflexive, self-conscious academic:* The academic speaks with endless qualifications and reservations, all aimed at protecting against the potential objections of academic colleagues—for example: "Subject to what others have said, and with all due respect to what my colleague has said on the subject, a different point of view can possibly be argued here if we weigh the various conflicting pieces of evidence." Academics cover themselves against all criticism, but in the end, they often obscure the very message they intend to convey.

- *The romantic:* The romantic storyteller wallows in the explicit emotions of the story rather than simply telling the story. Thus, at the start of the Macintosh era, Steve Jobs used stories based on the conflict of good and evil to invigorate his team, describing the world in terms similar to those used in the movie *Star Wars:* "'If we do not succeed,' forecast Steve Jobs, 'IBM will be the master of the world'" (Roche and Sadowsky, n.d.).

These styles may work in various social or professional settings or for the purposes of entertainment. But in a purpose-driven organizational setting, they often get in the way of the business at hand, which is to reveal the truth of the matter under discussion, simply, clearly, and directly.

Here's an example. It happens to be Lou Gerstner, talking at a press conference in New York City on June 5, 1995, about the events that led to IBM's purchase of Lotus. As a story, there's nothing unusual or remarkable about it. It's a typical example of business storytelling: plain, simple, and direct. As a story, it would not be considered brilliant. Nor is there anything that would draw attention to Gerstner as the storyteller. Listen:

> I think it is useful to step back and look at the evolution of this industry to really understand the strategic rationale of this transaction. The industry began as a very centralized model of computing. It was the world of mainframes, large central processors.
>
> And while there will be the need for central processors for many, many years to come, that first phase ended a decade or so ago—and the second phase began, which is the era of the PC.
>
> And so powerful, stand-alone computers were put in the hands of workers around the world, and we had the PC revolution. It provided enormous personal productivity benefits to workers in enterprises, small businesses, and even at home.
>
> But it's clear to me and to many others that the industry is now entering a new phase of the information technology industry. And it is a phase in which all of the computing power of an enterprise is linked together—so that the mainframes or servers and the PCs become linked in a network . . . .
>
> . . . but not just a hierarchical network, so that the PCs can talk to the mainframes or servers—but very importantly, a world in which all of the users can talk horizontally to each other, and to work together in what is known as "collaborative" or "team" computing. That is a very, very powerful need of our customers around the world.[3]

Gerstner's story is not in any way remarkable, yet it illustrates a number of important characteristics of a style of storytelling that is effective for leaders in organizations.

Tell Your Story as If You Were Talking to a Single Individual

Gerstner's idiom is the voice of conversation. The model is that of one person speaking to another. The style appears to be spontaneous and motivated by the need to tell the listeners about something of interest.

It's as if it has just occurred to Gerstner to tell his audience about what has been going on in the computer industry, and so he begins to do so. What he has to say doesn't feel like a set piece. There's no sign that Gerstner has labored over the language beforehand, systematically refining and arranging his thoughts, editing their expression, checking with the corporate lawyers, and then reading the final cleared text aloud. It's as if something has just occurred to him, and so he says it.[4]

As it happens, Gerstner is talking to a crowd of journalists, but he might just as well be talking to each person in the audience, one on one. His voice is the voice of dialogue.

Gerstner says one thing, and after another moment, something else occurs to him, and so he says that too. It happens to be a useful progression from his former thought, so the listeners follow along. His speech has the rhythm of conversation. It's a series of movements, each one brief and crisp, beginning at the beginning and ending with a suitable conclusion.

The appearance of spontaneity is of course an illusion. Gerstner has carefully rehearsed the story and knows exactly where it is heading. In retrospect, the audience may see that these movements of thought are in fact organized into a flawless order, but at the time, the illusion is created that this order is simply the consequence of Gerstner's logical, penetrating, uncluttered mind. His words appear to come out the way they do without any special effort. The order is never referred to. Its existence is not even acknowledged. Everything that is dispensable has been edited out, but the result doesn't sound edited.

Avoid Hedges

Gerstner avoids indicating that he is doing anything other than presenting the situation as it actually is. Thus, he avoids the kinds of hedges that writers often adopt to protect themselves against possible objections.[5]

Gerstner has banished from his vocabulary phrases like, "As we shall see ..." and "Before I move on to my next point ..." and "As far as I know ..." He doesn't bother with disclaimers that he doesn't have time to tell the whole story or that he has skipped over important events.

In telling his story, Gerstner presents the situation as being obvious to anyone who will take a hard look: "It is clear to me and to many others ..." He refrains from indicating alternative points of view. He doesn't, for instance, say, "My predecessor in IBM took an entirely different view of the situation and was on the verge of breaking up the company."

Keep Your Storytelling Focused, Simple, and Clear

The virtues of Gerstner's story, like most other good organizational storytelling, are clarity and simplicity. These are also its vices. Gerstner doesn't acknowledge ambiguities, qualifications, or doubts. He has made hard choices silently and out of the listeners' sight. He presents the story on the basis that this is what happened. Once made, the choices are presented as if they are inevitable.

Gerstner's language doesn't draw attention to itself; rather, it serves as a window that reveals the content of the story he is telling. If the audience were to notice Gerstner the person, through a dazzling use of language or some unusual mannerisms or some striking gestures—rather than the content of the story—then he would have been less effective. He tells the story in an understated manner. At the end of his presentation, no one says, "My heavens, that Lou Gerstner is a wonderful storyteller!" Instead, the focus is on what he says. The audience is more likely to exclaim, "How fascinating!"

Gerstner presents his story in a way that is seemingly transparent, as if the listeners are looking at his subject through a perfectly clean and nondistorting window. The window doesn't draw attention to itself.[6]

Present the Story as Something Valuable in Itself

Gerstner doesn't spend time justifying the telling of his story. As storyteller, he presents his story as something that is inherently valuable. The value comes from the story itself and from its role as part of a larger whole. He has selected elements that are common knowledge and put them together in a way that gives them broader significance. In so doing, he gives the events a meaning that the audience might not otherwise have grasped.

Be Yourself

Style isn't something separate from the person or detachable from the content of what is said. Gerstner performs his story in a style that lets the content shine through. He stands behind what he has to say because he has seen it, experienced it, and thought it out independently. He may be stating what is a common conclusion among experts in the industry at the time, but in expressing it, he is neither joining a chorus nor embracing a platitude.[7]

Instead, he presents his story as if it has the freshness of a discovery. He talks as though what he is saying doesn't come from following what he has been told to say by his public relations team or from a briefing by his technical experts.

As a storyteller, Gerstner presents himself as a thinking human being, not the head of a large bureaucracy or the construct of his handlers. In the apparent absence of these encumbrances, his utterances have a freshness that no committee of speechwriters can give.[8]

He speaks not as if he is trying to persuade, but rather as though he is presenting reality as it is. The implication is that listeners are free to draw their own conclusions, but if they were to draw any other conclusion than Gerstner's, they would be in error. He is inviting them to conclude, just as he already has, not only that the experience has a bearing on the future but also that there is a need to update their previously held views.[9]

TRUTH

As storyteller, Gerstner proceeds on the basis that all listeners have what is essential to identify the truth, whether or not they have any special education. The implication is that failure to identify truth comes from not seeing reality clearly.

Gerstner places his listeners where he was when he examined what was happening in the computer industry, and he does what he can to make what has happened intelligible to them. He proceeds on the basis that once received opinion, custom, and prejudice have been cleared away, what is true will be immediately apparent because of its distinctness and clarity.

In telling his story, Gerstner assumes parity between himself and his listeners. Although he may have a wider experience than his listeners and he may have access to inside information, he trusts the listeners to know exactly what he knows as if they had seen what he has seen. His purpose is to put the listeners in a position to achieve that parity.

Proceed on the Basis That It Is Possible to Tell the Truth

Is it possible to tell the truth? In telling his story back in June 1995, Gerstner was proceeding as if it is possible to know the results of disinterested thought and to present them without significant distortion. These assumptions may be hard for a philosopher to justify, but they contribute to a form of communication that is immensely useful. The assumptions constitute in effect a set of enabling conventions. Whether Gerstner believes in the enabling conventions—for example, that truth can be known—telling a story in this way requires no lifelong commitment to the belief, only a willingness to adopt this position for a limited time and purpose.[10]

Similarly, playing the game of tennis doesn't necessitate adopting the position that your lifelong aim is to defeat your opponent. But if you want to play a good game of tennis on a particular day, it does require that you adopt the conventions of tennis and try to defeat your opponent on that particular day. You cannot play an excellent game of tennis if you are all the time questioning the conventions of the game. After the game is over, you may sit back and have such discussions. But for the duration of the game, you have to set these questions aside in order to play an excellent game of tennis. Then the game can proceed.

So it is with storytelling. The performance of storytelling requires the storyteller to accept the conventions of storytelling at least for the duration of the performance. In performance, the storyteller is certain, fearless, and relentless in presenting things "as they really are." The role can be useful and even thrilling, but it can hardly be permanent.

For better or worse, human beings cannot remain in a permanent state of certainty, fearlessness, and relentlessness. No reliable evidence supports the storyteller's claim to the disinterested expression of truth. The insouciance required to ignore what everyone knows cannot be maintained for very long, and master storytellers know the limits. The storytelling performance is thus a sprint, not a marathon.[11]

Tell the Truth as You See It

Telling the truth as best we can isn't easy. In fact, it's terrifying to think how many things can go wrong in an effort to present something clearly and accurately. Our memory may be playing tricks on us. We may have difficulty expressing what we see. Our insights may lack edge. We may have been misled.

These concerns stop some people from ever opening their mouths to tell an effective story. For others, it causes them to allow the doubts to become the centerpiece of what they say, since the doubts are the only things that seem certain.

The enabling convention that it is possible to tell the truth frees the storyteller from these concerns. Presenting the truth as you see it is a capability that is available to everyone. Such competence is no more problematic than being able to see what you see with your own eyes.

PREPARATION

The preparation for a storytelling performance is laborious and repetitive, but the actual performance is like white-water rafting. In rehearsal, myriad options must be considered, tried out, and evaluated for their possible impact. In performance, you have no time for thought, for reflection, for second thoughts. You hurtle forward, swept on by the rush of events, the thing finished in a matter of seconds, the lips moving faster than the mind. If you have done the preparation and are ready for the performance, then the self—and the story—will flow effortlessly. But if you have not thought through what you are trying to say and are not comfortable with who you are or how this relates to the story you are telling, then the audience almost certainly will feel those discords, which will get in the way of your performance. Careful preparation is of the essence.

Good organizational storytelling is perfect performance, with no hesitation, revision, or backtracking. Its implicit fiction is that this perfection happens at the first try. The story appears as though it could not have been told in any other way. This is an illusion, but it is powerful. The storyteller may seem to have been born with a unique ability that other human beings lack. As a result, listening to perfectly told stories can be intimidating to a beginner, who does not see the care and preparation that have gone into the presentation.

With effort and discipline, anyone can get the essential things right. Effective storytelling is accessible to all who are willing to make the effort. It is the result not of natural endowment but of meticulous preparation, ending in achievement.

Be Rehearsed But Spontaneous

Perhaps the most impressive aspect of good storytelling is its combination of perfection and spontaneity. The performance has no mistake, no false step or deficiency, and it looks inevitable. And yet it also looks fresh and spontaneous, almost improvised.

How is this possible? The perfection comes from practice, while the spontaneity comes from reliving the story mentally for each retelling. Even if you are telling the story for the seventeenth time, you relive it afresh in your mind as if you were experiencing it for the first time. You feel the emotions of the original participants yet again, and the audience will also feel those emotions. Because the story is fresh each time for the storyteller, it's also fresh for the audience.

Choose the Shape of Your Story, and Stick to It

Design is the backbone of effective storytelling. As the storyteller, you will both build on your design and add to it as a result of the unexpected events that occur with every live performance. The audience laughs, and you dwell on the point for a moment to take advantage of the resonance. The audience fidgets, and you move on swiftly to an element that is more likely to be appealing. But in the midst of these adjustments, you stick to the basic design of the story.

The key is to get the right balance between structure and spontaneity. If the performance follows a rigid advance plan too closely, then the story will sound false and programmed. If we allow the story to ramble aimlessly as we recall events as they occur to us in a somewhat haphazard fashion, then we risk becoming a garrulous windbag, and the audience will stop listening. To achieve the requisite balance of structure and spontaneity, it's necessary to foresee the overall shape of what is to come and to pursue that shape, no matter how many enticing side roads open up along the way.[12]

DELIVERY

In any oral communication, much depends on the nonverbal aspects of performance—the tone of voice, the facial expression, and the accompanying gestures. Exactly how much do these nonverbal aspects contribute? In 1971, Professor Albert Mehrabian stunned the world of communications with his conclusion that only 7 percent of the meaning of a communication is in the content of the words that are spoken, while 93 percent of meaning comes from nonverbal communication.[13] His widely cited conclusion was, however, based on artificial laboratory studies involving the use of single, mostly ambiguous words, and Mehrabian didn't claim that his findings were applicable beyond the resolution of simple, inconsistent messages. As L. Michael Hall points out, you can tell that content must be more than 7 percent of communication just by trying to watch and understand movies on planes when you don't have the headphones or by trying to communicate any simple abstract statement nonverbally.[14]

But just as clearly, the way a story is performed can radically change its emotional tone in the mind of the listener. So Mehrabian is right in thinking that how an oral communication is performed is important, even if determining exactly how important would require separating content from performance—which is precisely what cannot be accomplished in the social act of communication, where story, storyteller, and audience are inseparably intertwined.

Be Ready to Perform

Once you have the shape of your story and have made your selections as to what to include and exclude, you must be ready to perform. In writing, you have the leisure of composition over a sustained period of time. If you are not in the mood for writing or have no energy or inspiration on any particular day, you can postpone the act of writing until conditions are more propitious.

As storyteller, you have no such luxury. Storytelling is a performance art, and you must be ready to deliver your peak performance at the appointed hour, without misstatements, errors, omissions, or unintended effects.

When you open your mouth, make sure you are ready to speak—that you are fully there for the audience. You may be suffering from all sorts of worries, tensions, and difficulties. Nevertheless, now is the time to put these out of your mind and make yourself totally available for the audience. If you are there for them, they will be there for you.

If necessary, pause a moment and collect your thoughts. If you're not feeling calm and relaxed, take a few deep breaths before you start to speak. There's no need to rush. An opening pause can be a dramatic focusing of the audience's attention on what you are going to say.

Get Out from Behind the Podium

Because you are presenting your story as an individual in a conversation, the more you can arrange the physical setup of the room so as to reflect that of a conversation, the better.

Don't hide behind podiums or microphones or use notes. In fact, get rid of anything between you and the audience. Notes are a huge distraction for the audience, which will take them as a signal that this is not a conversation but rather a one-way communication. You risk being seen as uninterested in the people you're talking to.

Connect with All Parts of the Audience

Use body movement to show your interest in the entire audience. Don't always talk to the same part of the audience. Move toward the audience so as to show your eagerness to speak to everyone.

Keep an open body stance, evincing your willingness to be open with the audience. Maintain direct eye contact so as to get attention and facilitate interaction.

Use Gesture

Appropriate gestures can emphasize key elements of your story as well as demonstrate that you believe the story—not just in your mind but with your whole body.

Your gestures should be natural and flowing and communicate your pleasure in speaking to this audience at this time. Avoid abrupt facial expressions or jerky gestures, which reflect lack of composure and a sense of unease in speaking to the audience. If you as the speaker feel unease, your audience will experience an equal or greater unease.

Be Lively

Since you are the one doing the talking, keep the audience's interest. It is through reliving the story that you are telling that will stimulate the audience's interest. Vary the pace and tone of your story to keep people alert.

Raise and lower the tone of your voice appropriately. Figure out the parameters of what is permissible in the specific setting. If you're in a board meeting, the parameters might be quite narrow. But if you are in an off-site retreat or conference, you can establish very broad parameters so as to make what you say entertaining. The parameters that are permissible in any context may be wider than you think.

Use Visual Aids Judiciously

It's fashionable to complain about PowerPoint, but that's like complaining about the English language. PowerPoint is an infinitely flexible tool. What people are complaining about is the bad use of PowerPoint. Use it intelligently: to convey images and support your storytelling. PowerPoint can reinforce the story and serve as a prompt to you as the storyteller so that you don't lose the thread.[15]

Remember also that human responses to linguistic and visual messages are not gender neutral. On average, women do better with words, and on average, men do better with the visual. These are averages, and of course there are vast numbers of individual exceptions. But the bell curves of men and women don't overlap exactly.[16] So if you want to increase your chances of reaching everyone in the audience, use both words and images.

Making your slides available electronically to your audience—for example, on the Web or an intranet—at the time of the presentation can be an effective way of disseminating the story. Thus, if listeners like the presentation, they can use the downloaded PowerPoint slides to retell the story to their own teams and communities. In this way, a lively presentation can cascade rapidly through a large organization just like a juicy rumor.

Be Comfortable in Your Own Style

You can present any story in many different ways, but you must feel comfortable in the particular style that you have chosen. You may prefer to sit down rather than stand up. You may prefer to use visual aids or avoid them. These are choices that you make, conscious of the costs and benefits of each. For instance, if you decide to talk sitting down rather than standing up, you may be less mobile in terms of holding yourself accessible to all the members of the audience in different parts of the room, but you may gain the benefit of seeming more approachable and collaborative. And if you decide to forgo visual aids, you may concentrate attention on yourself as the storyteller, but you risk having a less powerful impact on listeners whose preferred learning style entails the reception of visual images.

These are the trade-offs. In the end, choose a style that is suitable for you. Once you are at ease with your own style of telling the story, the audience will be at ease with you.

Know Your Audience

The more you know about the audience, the better. Mingle with them and find out what makes them tick, what their hopes and fears are, what their current priorities are as opposed to yesterday's news. This information is vital to making your presentation sound fresh and up-to-date.

One key area to focus on is the audience's interests: What's in it for them? How do they stand to gain or lose? When as a leader you come to make a proposal for change, many in the audience will be asking themselves, *What does it mean for me?* It is therefore crucial to tell a story that draws attention to benefits in terms of interests, roles, and goals for the audience and is frank about risks. The audience will want to know what role they are going to play in the change process and how it will affect them. And perhaps the most important question is, What's the audience's story? What's the larger story in which they see themselves living?

In any audience, you will need to take account of the propensities of listeners to certain approaches. Some listeners may prefer numerical results, detailed reasoning, and evidence of what has worked in the past, while others may be more interested in getting the sense of the idea. Some may be attracted to what is new and different, while others may be more concerned about risk.[17]

Robert Nisbett has also suggested the presence of geographical differences between audiences, with East Asians (a term that Nisbett uses as a catch-all for Chinese, Koreans, Japanese, and others) being measurably more holistic in their perceptions (taking in whole scenes rather than a few stand-out objects), while Westerners (a term Nisbett uses to refer to those brought up in Northern European and Anglo-Saxon-descended cultures) tend to have a "tunnel-vision perceptual style" that focuses much more on identifying what's prominent in certain scenes and remembering that.[18]

More striking, however, than the differences between the listeners are the similarities: in all countries and all cultures, stories have a universal appeal.

Connect with Your Audience

You connect with your audience by approaching the task of story-telling interactively and modeling your behavior on the concept of conversation—a dialogue between equals. You proceed on the basis that the relationship between you and your listeners is symmetrical. You talk as if the listeners could take the next turn in the conversation.

In practice, the differences in status or power between the storyteller and the audience may be vast. You may be a boss talking to your subordinates or a subordinate talking to your boss or bosses. You may be someone with great wealth and power talking to people who have neither, or it may be the reverse—you may be a supplicant requesting the rich and powerful to change their ways. As an interactive storyteller, you ignore these differences and talk to your listeners as one human being to another. In this way, you slice through the social and political barriers that separate individuals and humanize the communication.

Nevertheless, if you are presenting bold new ideas that will turn your listeners' working lives upside down, those ideas will come across as profoundly disturbing. The audience may be skeptical or even hostile. How do you tell a story that will ignite their enthusiasm for doing something radically different? It is to this fundamental challenge of leadership that I turn in Chapter Three.

Part 2

EIGHT NARRATIVE PATTERNS

3

MOTIVATE OTHERS
TO ACTION

Using Narrative to Ignite Action
and Implement New Ideas

> " It is useless to attempt to reason a man
> out of what he was never reasoned into. "
>
> **Jonathan Swift**

If I was a leader and could choose to tell only one kind of story, that story would be a springboard story. That's because a springboard story performs the most useful thing a leader can do: communicate a complex new idea and inspire action to implement it. That's what leadership is centrally about—inspiring people to implement new ideas in the future. And not just grudgingly but enthusiastically, because they believe in it.

THE CHALLENGE OF IGNITING ACTION
AND IMPLEMENTING NEW IDEAS

The conventional management approach to this challenge is to give people reasons.[1] Sadly, this faith in reason isn't borne out in practice. Asking people to stop doing the things they know and love doing and start doing things that they don't know much about amounts to asking them to adopt new identities. The usual result? Skepticism. Hostility. Sitting on the fence. Anything but enthusiastic implementation.

Then what happens? Leaders in their desperation drift toward more directive methods: "You've got to do it or you're fired!" This generates an adversarial relationship—the exact opposite of what a leader needs to achieve.

Fortunately, there's a solution at hand in a particular form of story. Better yet, it's one of the easiest kinds of stories to tell. It's a story about the past that is told without a great deal of embellishment. It has the advantage of getting the listener to do the hard work of inventing the future. Even better, as the future evolves, the listener keeps updating the story as the future changes. The story doesn't become stale because the listeners keep seeing new meaning in it—which they themselves provide.

I call this type of story a *springboard story* because it springs the listeners enthusiastically into a new future.[2] I've already presented one example of a springboard story in Chapter One: the Zambia story. This was a story that I told in 1996 when I was trying to introduce the World Bank to the idea of knowledge management as a strategic thrust. This simple story helped World Bank staff and managers envision a different kind of future for the organization.

Now let me give you another example of a springboard story and then discuss the ingredients that make it work and why.

An Example of a Springboard Story: Pakistan

Once knowledge management had become an official corporate priority in the World Bank, I used stories to maintain the momentum. September 1998 was a moment of particular difficulty. The effort to implement knowledge management had been under way for almost two years and, as with any major innovation, implementation had been far from smooth. Communities of practice were sprawling untidily all over the organization, and their purpose was not well understood by top management. Moreover, there was a feeling that the external world was at the brink of a global financial crisis. Russia had just defaulted. East Asia was in financial ruins.

Brazil was teetering on the brink. The currency and stock markets were gyrating wildly. Inside the World Bank, people were asking: "Why are we bothering with knowledge when the world is on the brink of crisis?"

I was asked to make a presentation to the president and senior managers about the status of the knowledge-sharing program. Here is one of the stories that I told to show why knowledge management and communities of practice were crucial to our future:

> Let me give you an example of how knowledge management is working in practice. Just a few weeks ago, on August 20, the government of Pakistan asked our field office in Pakistan for help in the highway sector. They were experiencing widespread pavement failure. The highways were falling apart. They felt they could not afford to maintain them. They wanted to try a different technology, a technology that our organization has not supported or recommended in the past. And they wanted our advice within a few days.
>
> I think it's fair to say that in the past we would not have been able to respond to this kind of question within this time frame. We might have proposed to send a team to Pakistan. The team might send the report to the government, and eventually—perhaps three, six, nine months later—might provide a response. But by then, it would have been too late. By then, things would have moved on in Pakistan.
>
> What actually happened was something quite different. The task team leader in our field office in Pakistan sent an e-mail to contact the community of highway experts inside and outside the organization (a community that had been put together over time) and asked for help within forty-eight hours. And he got it. The same day, the task manager in the highway sector in Jordan replied that, as it happened, Jordan was using this technology with very promising results. The same day, a highway expert in our Argentina office replied and said that he was writing a book on the subject and was able to give the genealogy of the technology over several decades and continents. And shortly after that, the head of the highways authority in South Africa—an outside partner who was a member of the community—chipped in with South Africa's experience with something like the same technology. And New Zealand provided some guidelines that it had developed for the use of the technology. And so the task manager in Pakistan was able to go back to the Pakistan government and say: this is the best that we as an

organization can put together on this subject, and then the dialogue can start as to how to adapt that experience elsewhere to Pakistan's situation.

And now that we have discovered that we as an organization know something about a subject we didn't realize we knew anything about, now we can incorporate what we have learned in our knowledge base so that any staff in the organization anywhere at any time can tap into it. And the vision is that we can make this available externally through the World Wide Web, so that anyone in the world will be able to log on and get answers to questions like this on which we have some know-how, as well as on any of the other myriad subjects on which we have managed to assemble some expertise.

The story worked to spring the listeners to a new level of understanding as to what is knowledge management and refresh their memories as to why sharing knowledge is fundamental to the future of the World Bank. Immediately following the presentation, the president decided to push forward with accelerated implementation of knowledge management, and by the year 2000, the World Bank had met the stretch objective it had set for itself in 1997: the organization had been benchmarked by several organizations as a world leader in knowledge management.[3]

The Role of the Springboard Story

With the wisdom of hindsight, this successful outcome may seem inevitable. Today, it's a no-brainer that an organization like the World Bank needs to share its knowledge. But at the time, the situation was agonizingly fragile. Knowledge management was only half implemented. Benefits were emerging but still limited to a few parts of the organization, and costs were perceived as significant. As in any other major new initiative, implementation had proved more difficult than had been expected. Was the glass half empty or half full? The opponents of knowledge management, including some at the highest levels of the organization, viewed the glass as half empty and wanted to rethink everything.[4] Our contention was that the glass was half full: we felt we had made good progress and should press on to complete the job. The decision could have gone either way. Management could have set out on a witch hunt to find out why knowledge management hadn't already been fully implemented. Or it could focus on the fact that much progress had been made and push forward with a whole new spurt of energy to make knowledge management the major strategic thrust that it became. The Pakistan story was one of the factors that led to the latter result.

On the surface, the Zambia and Pakistan stories might not seem very similar. But in fact they share a common narrative pattern. That pattern makes it possible to find similarly effective stories in virtually any context. Understanding the narrative pattern is one of the steps necessary to move leadership from the realm of an arcane and mysterious art that only a few people possess to a skill that anyone can understand and learn.

Thus, in the late 1990s, leadership books—for example, Noel Tichy in *The Leadership Engine* and Howard Gardner in *Leading Minds*—began mentioning that storytelling is central to leadership. In the past ten years, storytelling has been a frequent theme in books on change and leadership, such as Jim Kouzes and Barry Posner in *The Leadership Challenge* and *Made to Stick* by Chip Heath and Dan Heath. Books like Annette Simmons's *The Story Factor* and Jim Loehr's *The Power of Story* have expanded our understanding of the impact of storytelling in various organizational settings.[5] What has been less clear in these books is that most stories do not result in people embracing major change. A story that can inspire people to change—a springboard story—has particular characteristics. Systematic success in using storytelling to spark change requires an understanding of those characteristics and the mechanisms underlying them.

THE MAIN ELEMENTS
OF THE SPRINGBOARD STORY

The springboard narrative pattern has the following main characteristics:

- The change idea being communicated by the story is clear and worthwhile.

- The story is based on an actual example where the change was successfully implemented—that is, it's a true story.

- The story is told from the point of view of a single protagonist.

- The protagonist is typical of the audience.

- The story gives the date and place where it happened.

- The story makes clear what would have happened without the change idea.

- The story is told in a minimalist fashion with little detail.

- The story has a positive tone and an authentically happy ending.

- The story is linked to the purpose to be achieved in telling it.

Of all the elements, the four most important are that the idea must be clear and worthwhile and the story must be true, positive, and told in a minimalist fashion. The following sections focus on the elements in the order in which they generally occur in crafting a springboard story.

Have a Clear and Worthwhile Purpose

The first step in crafting a springboard story is getting clear on the change idea that you are trying to get across. What are you trying to change in the world? What is the specific idea that you are attempting to get others to understand and implement? What are they not doing now that you want them to do in future?

The idea must be a worthwhile one that has the potential to resonate with people's hearts. An idea that merely imitates what others have achieved or focuses on the organization's numerical goals is unlikely to inspire anyone. Instead, the company needs a genuinely new and superior idea for a product, a quality standard, a technology, or a managerial model.[6]

Having a clear and worthwhile idea is one of the principal differences between organizational storytelling and entertainment storytelling. When you're telling a story to entertain, you may get the audience to laugh or to cry, and that in itself is enough. But when you're telling a story in an organization, particularly a springboard story, you are telling it with a purpose, and you must keep that purpose steadily in mind.

Getting clear on the change idea is also important because it is the basis for all the other steps in crafting a springboard story. You refer back to this purpose in terms of deciding what to include and what to exclude from the story. For each of the other steps in the process, you ask, Is this part of the story relevant to communicating my purpose? If it is, it may stay in. But if it's not relevant to purpose, you have to ask yourself, Why is it in this story? If it's not relevant, it must be deleted, no matter how entertaining it may be.

If the storyteller isn't clear on the purpose, the story usually fails. For instance, when people start crafting a story, and I ask them, "What's the purpose?" they sometimes reply: "I want to change the world." I reply, "That's fine, but could you give us a hint as to which specific part of the world you want to change?" The change idea has to be specific enough so that people could see whether they are making progress to implement it.

In other cases, people are very clear on what's wrong with the current situation, but they haven't thought through what things would be like if the problems were resolved. The problem might be absenteeism at work, or the lack of healthy food choices in a fast food chain, or the lack of a common approach among the various parts of a global consulting company. Unless the storyteller has thought through what the organization would look like once those problems were resolved, it's going to be hard to tell a powerful story that will help the organization get there.

Not being clear on the change idea is one of the most frequent mistakes people make in crafting springboard stories. If you're having persistent difficulty in coming up with a powerful story to communicate a change idea, check the clarity of the idea!

Find an Example

The second step in the process is to think of an incident where the change idea has already happened. You want an example where the change has already taken place, at least in part. It may be in your own organization or community. Or it may be in another organization or community, preferably similar to yours. A place where this piece of the future has already happened.

Here's another example from a company that I'll call Global Consulting, a company that was trying to energize the staff around the idea of becoming a truly global corporation. To communicate the idea, the change agent crafts a story based on an example where the change has already happened:

> As you know, Global Consulting aspires to become the leading provider of consulting services in its field. So we're trying to implement lots of changes to make that happen. Let me tell you about one recent example of how this is working out.
>
> It's about James Truscott, who works for us in London. A few months ago he heard about an invitation to bid on a large consulting engagement for one of the biggest industrial firms in the U.K.—British Engines. What had been happening even as recently as a couple of months ago is that we weren't winning many of those big consulting engagements, because our staff from different countries would compete among themselves for the same engagement and end up totally confusing the client.
>
> What James did in this case, when he heard about the invitation to bid for this worldwide account, was that he contacted all the people in Global around the world who deal with British Engines. He brought them all together as a team and together they developed Global's pitch to British as a global team.
>
> As it turned out, a competitor undercut us with a lower price, but James went back to British. He didn't lower the price. Instead he went back to British with other experts from the firm to explain why we were more expensive, so that in fact British could see that they were getting a better deal.
>
> And guess what? We won that multimillion-pound engagement with British. It was a huge thing. It showed to us the power of acting together as a global organization, rather than acting from individual country perspectives. Just think what a company Global could be if all of us would join together and think about the client from a global

perspective, so that we could serve the client better as a whole. Just imagine the impact that would have!

The story is thus based on a specific example where the change has already taken place—in this case, in the same organization.

When I ask people to think of an example where the change idea has been successfully implemented, the reply that I often get is: "I can't think of one." To which my response is invariably, "Think harder!"

If in fact you think harder and you can't find any example where change has been successfully implemented, at least in part, either in your organization or somewhere else, then I have a different set of questions: "Is this idea ready for prime time? If this idea hadn't been successfully implemented anywhere, even in part, is it really ready for implementation across your organization? Maybe it should be tested before you start trying to inflict it on your entire organization."

So almost by definition, if your idea is ready for prime time, there must be a case where it has been implemented at least in part somewhere in the world—preferably in your organization, but if not, in some other organization, preferably an analogous or similar organization.

Tell a Story That Is Authentically True

A springboard story is about something that has actually happened—not an imaginary story about something that might happen. It's something that has already occurred, something of which the veracity can be checked. It's the truth of the story that can shake the skeptics out of their complacency.

When I say a true story, it's not enough to tell a story that's true as far as it goes. You must tell an *authentically* true story: a story that once people check it out—and they will check it out—and all the facts are known, people will still say, "Yes, that's pretty much what happened."

Here's an example of a story that is factually accurate as far as it goes but is not authentically true:

Seven hundred happy passengers reached New York after the Titanic's maiden voyage.

That story is factually accurate as far as it goes. But it leaves out the detail that the ship sank and fifteen hundred other passengers drowned. And when those facts become known, if they aren't already known, then the negative backlash on the story and the storyteller is massive.[7]

Although this is a bad way to tell a story, ironically corporate communications often fall into this pattern. They paint a rosy picture of a situation, but just around the corner is lurking some hidden negative element. Once that element becomes known, if it isn't already known, there is a massive negative backlash on the story and the storyteller.

Give the Date and Place

In storytelling, little things can make a big difference. Here's one. For a springboard story, you state the date and place where the event happened. This may sound trivial, but it's critical. In fact, it's one the secrets that can make the difference between success or failure.

Giving the date and place is important because it signals to listeners that this is a true story. This story actually happened!

If I announce, "I'm going to tell you a true story ..." there's likely to be pushback from the audience. When someone tells you he's an honest man, you tend to reach for your wallet to make sure it's still there. So announcing that your story is true may lead the audience to conclude that something is amiss. The better way to signal that you are telling a true story is to give the date and place.

So the story begins, "In June 2010 in London ..." In one sense, it doesn't really matter whether the story happened in June 2010 in London or September 2010 in Paris. The gist of it is that it was somewhere recent in Europe. But what the opening does is signal to the listeners the truth of the story.

Pick a Single Individual as the Story's Protagonist

Who is the hero or heroine of your story? It's not a group, not a team, not a company, not a country. You are looking for a single individual—perhaps an anonymous individual who carries out or facilitates implementation of the change idea.

Here you are plugging into an archetypal narrative pattern—the hero's journey. You are taking your audience on the journey of someone who set out to accomplish something that is difficult, someone who met obstacles along the way but finally triumphed. Ta-dah! Everyone has heard this kind of story thousands of times. Sound corny? But it works. This kind of story has deep roots in the human psyche. All of us tend to see our own life as a journey with goals and obstacles that get in the way of attaining those goals. So when we hear a story in the form of a hero's journey, we respond from the deepest reaches of our psyche.[8]

It's a good idea to link the date, the place, and the single protagonist at the start of your story. In this way, the listeners, who are likely to be searching for someone to identify with, will be grateful. They will understand that here is a storyteller who understands their need for a protagonist. If you introduce the protagonist further on in the story, after you've laid the scene for instance, the audience will be wondering all along, *Who is this story about? Where is it heading? Who's the hero?*

Remember that in oral storytelling, you've got only seconds to draw in your audience. You're not writing *War and Peace.* You don't have the luxury of hundreds of pages to lay out the scene and gradually introduce a vast cast of characters. Make it easy on both the audience and yourself: start out with the date, the place, and the protagonist:

In September 2009, a software developer in Denmark ...

That's the simplest and easiest way to start your story. Later, when you've mastered the basics of storytelling, you can be creative and do something different. But when you're getting started, make it easy on yourself. Use a pattern that has worked for your predecessors: begin with the date, the place, and the protagonist, all three, right at the start.

Pick a Protagonist Who Is Similar to the Audience

Tell the story from the perspective of a single individual who is typical of your audience. This makes it easy for the audience to identify with the hero or heroine of your story. It will be one tiny step for the audience to put themselves in the shoes of the protagonist and think to themselves, *That could be me! I could be doing that!* If you are talking to an audience of economists, the hero is likely to be an economist. If you are talking to a global consulting company, the hero is likely to be a team leader in a consulting firm. And if you are talking to oil drillers, the hero is likely to be an oil driller.

You tell the story from the perspective of someone who will inspire your audience to say, "I know that situation! I've been there! I've had that problem!" And so they identify with that protagonist. In effect, they start to imagine themselves a new story in which they become the hero. In their minds, they begin to undertake the hero's journey in which they encounter obstacles, overcome them, and eventually attain the goal. In this way, your story becomes their story.

Fully Embody the Change Idea

In telling the story, make sure that the narrative fully embodies the change idea. If necessary, extrapolate the story—for example:

> In 2009 in Paris, the head partner of a law firm noticed that the staff of the IT department became markedly more productive when they arranged the work in self-organizing teams that worked in short cycles and delivered value to their clients at the end of each cycle. He then introduced the approach to the paralegal staff and got a similar result: the work got done much more quickly and the people doing the work were much happier. So then he began exploring with the other partners: Why wasn't all the work in the firm done in this manner? Just think what the impact would be if everyone in the firm was working in an agile fashion.

Here the narrator is talking about a situation where the change has happened in part of the organization—the IT department and the paralegals. But the idea is larger than that: it's to have the whole firm operating this way. The narrator invites the audience to make a leap in their imaginations: if software developers and paralegals could become more agile in this way, why not the rest of the firm? This is not just a better way of developing software or doing paralegal work; it's a better way of doing work for the entire company. Because people are already in a narrative mode of thinking, it is easy to make the imaginative leap from one kind of experience to another. So even if the example that you have discovered is only a fragment of the overall change idea, you can extend the story so that it fully embodies the entire change idea. In this way, you get the audience to embrace the larger idea in their narrative imaginations.

Spell Out the Alternative

Spelling out what would have happened without the change idea helps make clear that the story isn't about "the way things normally happen around here."

Now you might think that it would be obvious to your audience what would have happened without the change idea in the absence of your mentioning it. But strange to say, that's often not the case. In the heat of the moment, when you're telling them about something different, it's likely that many of the audience will have forgotten—at least momentarily—how things normally happen. They may be thinking: *So what? What's unusual about that? This sort of thing happens all the time.* You need to remind them of what would have happened without the story.

The following story was used by authors W. Chan Kim and Renée Mauborgne in their book *Blue Ocean Strategy* to communicate the complex new strategic concept of competing in an arena where there is no competition.[9]

> In 1984, Guy Laliberté, a former accordion player, acrobat and fire-eater in Montreal, looked at the existing circus industry and saw a losing proposition. The shrinking circus industry was dominated by two entrenched players—Ringling Bros and Barnum & Bailey—whose shows appealed primarily to children. "Star performers" tended to call the shots. Relatively inexpensive alternative forms of entertainments were emerging. Animal rights activists were agitating against the treatment of animals by circuses. If Laliberté had followed conventional strategy analysis, he would have concluded that starting a circus company had little prospect of success.

> Instead Laliberté developed a new business model in which he sidestepped competition with the existing players and created a market space where there was no competition. He founded the Cirque du Soleil which eliminated animals and deemphasized individual stars. He combined extreme athletic skill with sophisticated dance and music. He created a new form of entertainment that appealed to upscale audiences of all ages around the world. Its shows have now been seen by more than 40 million people in ninety cities around the world.

Not only was the Cirque du Soleil a huge business success, but also the story *about* the Cirque du Soleil was a huge success for Kim and Mauborgne in terms of communicating their complex idea of a blue ocean strategy. The story helped sell more than 1 million copies of their book and communicate their strategic concept to a vast audience.

The story they told contrasted what would have happened without the change idea with what actually happened. It compares the conventional strategy of competing with the existing dominant players in a shrinking industry (a "red ocean" of sharks) with the successful "blue ocean" strategy of creating a new market where there is practically no competition. Why swim in the red ocean with all those sharks when you can have the blue ocean all to yourself? It is like night and day. Black and white. The contrast is painted in such stark terms that everyone can grasp that what is being discussed is different. The contrast enhances the probability of communicating the change idea.

Strip Out Unnecessary Detail

A springboard story is told in a minimalist fashion. It's quite unlike the way that anyone would tell a story for the purpose of entertainment.

In this respect, the springboard story is a descendant of the minimalist tradition of storytelling of which the biblical parables and the European folktale laid the foundation. In these stories, there is what Max Luthi calls "depthlessness."[10] The persons depicted in these stories have no psychological richness or complexity. The subjective plane of the feelings and viewpoints of the characters is limited. The story typically has none of the sights and sounds and smells that Aristotle's *Poetics* considered essential for creating the reality of the story.

In springboard storytelling, there are good reasons for this strategy. In the first place, the listeners in a business setting don't have time or the patience to listen to a fully detailed account of the situation. More important, the minimalist style leaves plenty of space for the audience to imagine a new story in their own context. In fact, it's the listener's story that is crucial because it springs the listener into a new future.

Thus, for each member of the audience, there are two listeners: the physical person you see in front of you and a second listener known as "the little voice in the head." You know what the little voice in the head is. And if you're asking yourself, "What on earth do you mean by 'the little voice in the head'?" that is exactly the little voice that I mean!

You are talking to the audience about one subject. But the little voice in the head of each listener may well be focusing on something else, such as: *I've got all these problems back in my office, my in-box is filling up, I've got e-mail to answer. If only I could slip out of here!* So the little voice may be distracting the listener from paying real attention to what you're saying.

The conventional view of communications is to ignore the little voice in the head and hope that the message will somehow get through. Unfortunately, the little voice often doesn't stay quiet. Often the listener is getting a new and possibly unwelcome perspective on what the speaker is talking about.

So you do something different. You don't ignore the little voice in the head. Instead you *work in harmony with it*. You engage it by giving it something to do. You tell a story in a way that elicits a second story from the little voice in the head.

When this occurs, the little voice is already racing ahead to figure out how to implement the change idea in the organization. And because the listeners have created the idea, they like it. It's their own wonderful idea!

And this can happen very quickly. The first time I noticed this was back in April 1996 in the World Bank.

After pounding the corridors and talking to anyone I could find about the strange new idea of knowledge management, I finally got ten minutes in front of the change management committee of the World Bank. This was a committee of the most senior managers, the ones who were supposed to be orchestrating change in the organization. It wasn't obvious to anyone that this was what they were doing, but certainly they were an obstacle on my path to persuading the World Bank to adopt knowledge management as a strategy. Up to this point, no one in senior management was willing to give me the time of day, let alone pay attention to my idea.

So when I got ten minutes in front of the change management committee of the World Bank, I told the Zambia story. And what happened? Two of those executives raced up to me after the presentation and started asking why wasn't I doing this or that to get the program off the ground. And I thought to myself: *This is a very strange conversation. Up 'til ten minutes ago, these people weren't willing to give me the time of day, and now I'm not doing enough to implement their idea. This is horrible! They have stolen my idea!* And then I had a happier thought. *How wonderful! They have stolen my idea. Now they own the idea. It's become their idea!* And indeed, it was one of those executives who was able to get to the president of the World Bank and explain to him that knowledge management was the very future of the organization.

What makes the minimalist story so powerful is that it resolves a fundamental paradox of transformation. Transformation must be *both* personal to all participants *and* centrally directed in order to be coherent.

Thus, on one hand, everyone involved needs to internalize the change. All the participants must undergo a kind of identity transition. Getting thousands of people to move across that threshold is the hardest task facing a leader aiming to spark transformational change. Yet on the other hand, if the change is to have any coherence, there must be some way of achieving a common direction. Without some capacity to set direction, the transformation risks splintering into multiple factions.

The paradox is that transformation must proceed with some central direction and yet ultimately individuals must make this decision for themselves.[11] A springboard story told in a minimalist fashion resolves the paradox by creating a vehicle that encourages listeners to craft similar stories, each of which is the listener's own story. The result is personalized coherence across large numbers of people.

Have a Happy Ending

Here's some unusual news. Hollywood is right! Yes, in a story aimed at sparking action, you have to have a happy ending. Springboard stories thus differ from knowledge-sharing stories, which tend to have a negative tone. But to spark action, the positive tone of the story is an essential element. And not just a positive tone but an authentically positive tone. This isn't spin. This isn't about whitewashing problems. This is about telling a story that is at once authentically true and ends well: this is the way it actually happened.

Thus, when Adrian Hosford had to communicate why British Telecom, a private organization, should be devoting a large sum of money—23 million pounds sterling—for social and environmental causes, he used the following example of the impact of the program, with an authentically happy ending:

> On the 25th December 2001, an operator with the charity Childline took this call. We'll call the child Julie—although this is not her real name.
>
> Julie is thirteen. She's ringing from a payphone, from a back street in Deptford. She is very upset.
>
> It's Christmas Day and Julie is desperate, in tears. She feels that nobody cares about her.
>
> Julie lives in a children's home. She's run away. She hates being on her own—hates it "in there."
>
> Julie received a Christmas present. Just the one.
>
> She says, "No one cares. I'm on my own."
>
> She says, "I feel like jumping in the river so nobody will find me."
>
> The operator and Julie talk. They discuss what might happen after Christmas when Julie is due to move in with new foster parents.
>
> Julie accepts that things might improve, although she's worried they won't like her.
>
> The Childline operator spends thirty-five minutes talking to Julie.

After thirty-five minutes Julie says she feels better and is going to return to the care home.

The postscript is dated April 2002.

Julie rings Childline to say thank you for being there and listening when she desperately needed to be heard.

Julie says she is getting on well with her new foster parents.

For now at least, Julie is happy.

Julie's story is rooted in communications breakdown. It shows very clearly that everybody needs to have the ability and means to communicate effectively. Because everyone—and particularly young people—deserves to be heard. Everybody wants to be understood; to have their contribution recognized.

Ultimately everyone wants to make a difference.

So, what if BT could help everyone benefit from improved communication—starting with young people who are in real distress? Because although Childline does an incredible job, handling three thousand calls every day, at the moment twelve thousand more calls go unanswered. That's 80 percent. How many children like Julie do you think go unheard in those twelve thousand unanswered calls? This is a tragedy which we have to fix, urgently, and with the help of our customers and staff, we can fix it. What if we were to support Childline, so they could answer every call from every child that needs to be heard?

What if we were to work in the education system to teach basic human skills of talking and listening in thousands of schools, to millions of children?

And support teachers by deploying thousands of BT volunteers to use their communication skills in the classroom, and by volunteering in the community?

What if we were to work in some of our country's most economically deprived areas—to see what can be achieved when we act to energize communication within communities?

And what if BT were to take its responsibility to society seriously, and practice what it preaches by using better communications to run its business more effectively, at less cost to the environment, and to engender a better work-life balance for its employees?

The story was successful in communicating to a wide range of British Telecom's managers and staff, as well as outside stakeholders, the rationale for British Telecom's social and environmental program. British Telecom calculated that its social and environmental performance accounts for more than a quarter of its overall business and reputation, which is the second biggest factor driving change in its customer satisfaction rates.[12]

It might sound melodramatic to ask for an ending that makes people want to stand up and cheer. But for stories aimed at inspiring action, there are solid reasons for insisting on it.

If I tell a story with a happy ending, the limbic system kicks in with something called an "endogenous opiate reward" for the human brain, the cortex. It pumps a substance called dopamine into the cortex. Basically it puts the human brain on drugs. This leads to a mild sense of euphoria, the kind of warm and floaty feeling that you have after a wonderful movie. This is the perfect frame of mind to be thinking about a new future, a new identity for yourself or your organization.

This is not to say that all stories need a happy ending. Stories to share knowledge typically have a negative tone because they deal with issues and problems and difficulties. Other stories—for example, stories to communicate to transmit values—can be either positive or negative in tone: the tone is less relevant because those stories are not aimed at getting people into rapid action. But if your goal is inspiring people to action, then Hollywood is right: you have to have a happy ending.

Link the Change Idea to the Story

Finally, it's critical to link the change idea to the story with one of these magic phrases:

"What if ... "

"Just imagine ... "

"Just think ... "

If you don't have any link at all, then the listeners are likely to say, "So what?" They may ask, "Why do you bother us with the anecdote about a health worker in Zambia? What relevance was that to us? We don't work in Zambia. We don't work in health." And they are likely to miss the point.

So you need to give them a hint, a suggestion, some guide-rails as to where to go, as to what's the point. But if you are too directive, it will backfire. For example, suppose you tell your springboard story and then go on:

> *This is what that story means for you. This is what it means for you tomorrow morning when you go into the office. You need to do the following sixteen things...*

Of course, if you say anything like that, you are back in command-and-control mode. You will have lost all of the energizing impact of narrative. You will have switched from the listener's story back to your own ideas, your own decisions, your own instructions, and so the listener becomes another passive disgruntled employee, waiting for the next management directive. Ramming home the point is counterproductive.

So how do you give enough guidance but not too much? These phrases—"What if..." and "Just think...," and "Just imagine..."—reflect a middle way of neither too little nor too much guidance. They're like Goldilocks's porridge: just right.

By asking, "What if?" you are inviting the audience to dream. You're issuing an invitation to imagine. The listeners have to make the decision as to whether to dream and whether to decide to live that dream. You point them in the direction. And with luck, some or even most of the audience will dream the dream and start planning their own implementation of it.

There's an old Brazilian proverb that when you dream alone it's just a dream, but when you dream together, it's already the beginning of a new reality. So these little phrases have just the right balance to inspire audience to dream together: "What if..." and "Just imagine..." and "Just think..."

> *Just think what it would be like if this incident was happening here, not just in this instance, but all across our division. All across the region. All across the company. All across the world.*

You're inviting the audience to make a leap of the imagination—and they are usually willing to do it if you provide them with the right guide-rails for them to dream.

AVOIDING THE MAIN PITFALLS

The elements of the springboard story look relatively obvious and straight-forward when expressed as performance criteria. But implementing these elements in performance isn't as easy as it seems.

Embody the Right Idea

You might think that being clear on the change they are pursuing would be something that leaders routinely do. And yet on a daily basis, the business world is full of CEOs who are telling stories that don't embody the change idea they are trying to communicate. Here's a spectacular example:

> On September 4, 2001, Carly Fiorina, CEO of Hewlett-Packard (HP) announced her plan to buy Compaq for the equivalent of some $25 billion, which was a significant premium over the market price at the time. For two days, Fiorina talked to the major financial institutions in New York and Boston explaining the reasons for the acquisition. The implications of whether Wall Street accepted her proposal were significant. Unfortunately for Fiorina, the news on September 6, 2001, wasn't good. The headline in the Wall Street Journal summed it up: "Wall Street still doesn't buy Fiorina's story." In just two days the market had erased some $13 billion off the combined share value of the two companies. Eventually, five months later, after a massive and divisive proxy battle, Fiorina won a slim majority of shareholders in favor of her plan.

What went wrong? In retrospect, it's clear from an interview that Fiorina gave on CNN on the afternoon of September 4, 2001, that one factor was telling the wrong story. In those first few critical hours when the merger was being presented to the world, interviewer Lou Dobbs asked a simple question: "Why is HP taking over Compaq?" Here is what Fiorina said:

> Well, I think, as you point out, we've been thinking about this for some time, beginning with the recognition that our companies shared a strategic vision. And I think Michael [Capellas, CEO of Compaq] and I first began to figure out twelve to eighteen months ago both when we would get together in industry kinds of events, and share notes but also importantly, as we watched each other move in the marketplace. Then what we saw was, each company making similar technology decisions. Both companies have signed up for the Itanium platform with Intel. We've also made some similar organizational moves. Both companies have organized themselves in similar ways about how to go to market and in product development. And we have cultures that have a lot in common, particularly around engineering discipline and a spirit of invention and innovation.

The gist of Fiorina's story was that HP and Compaq were two very similar companies. Her argument for the merger of the two companies was that they would enjoy significant synergy, which justified a premium over the current share price. Now, corporate synergy doesn't come from partners being alike. It comes from firms being different, so that the sum of the two firms together is greater than the sum of their parts. The more alike the firms are, the less likelihood of synergy there is, and the less reason to pay the premium that HP was offering to make the deal work.

Fiorina's story didn't embody the change idea that she was trying to communicate. In fact, her story had the opposite meaning. As one analyst put it, "Tying two stones together won't make them float." The response of the market was devastating.

How did Fiorina, normally a savvy, charismatic communicator in one of the most critical interviews in her entire career, come to be telling the wrong story? The fact is that in the heat of the moment, Fiorina forgot to make sure that the story she was to tell embodied the idea she was trying to get across.

Storytelling is a performance art. It's not enough to know intellectually what you're meant to do. You actually have to do it in the heat of the moment, when the whole world is hanging on your every word. You have to ensure that in performance, the story being told embodies the idea that you are trying to get across.

Find an Uplifting Ending

The idea of a happy ending is much misunderstood. In a broader philosophical sense, some would argue that there are never any happy endings. In the end, we are all dead.

The happiness of a story's ending relates to the narrative as told and the point of view of the narrator, not necessarily to the events that actually happen. Some endings that are regarded as happy include disastrous outcomes for the "bad" characters in the story. Take, for example the fairy stories "Snow White" and "Cinderella," which are generally seen as having happy endings, even though Snow White's stepmother is forced to dance herself to death in red-hot shoes and Cinderella's sisters have their eyes pierced by doves. The question isn't whether the events in the story are happy for all concerned; the question is whether the story is told in such a way as to convey a satisfactory ending for the character we care about, that is, the protagonist.[13]

It also depends on when the story ends. Cinderella's story ends with her marriage to the prince, with the implication that they live happily ever after. The story could have a very different tone if it continued to tell the tale of, say, her difficult marriage with the prince and ended with her premature death in a tragic car accident in Paris.

And it bears repeating yet again: a positive ending is needed for a story to spark action, not for all stories. Stories that get attention or transfer knowledge typically have a negative tonality. A frequent mistake is to try to spark action with a negative story.

Don't Use the Negative to Spark Enthusiasm

There is much talk in business circles of the need for a "burning platform" to create a "sense of urgency" that will catalyze change. Thus in

1993, IBM was going through a "near-death" experience, which made it easier for the new CEO, Lou Gerstner, to make the case that change was needed. This sometimes leads to the misunderstanding that a negative story will itself spark change. Negative stories get people's attention, but they don't spark action. The action comes from a positive story that shows the way forward.

Creating fear in your audience with negative stories, combined with hierarchical sanctions, may provoke grudging compliance—but not the enthusiastic implementation that transformational change requires. So use the negative knowledge-sharing a story to convey the message that the situation is indeed grim—but follow it with the positive story that shows how to solve the problem.

How to Deal with Bad News

Sometimes people tell me that there are no happy endings in their organization. Everything is terrible. It's as if they work for the Doom Channel. This isn't entirely plausible, but if you are in a situation where things are genuinely bad, then there is a way to deal with the bad news and still have an authentically positive ending. The secret is to get all of the bad news up front and then go on to your positive story.

If you were telling a story that occurred during the sinking of the *Titanic,* you could proceed as follows:

> I'm going to tell you about something that happened when the ocean liner Titanic sank, way back in 1915. It was a horrible thing. The ship sank. Fifteen hundred people drowned. It was a massive engineering disaster for a ship that was supposed to be unsinkable. Gross incompetence and stupidity on the part of the captain of the ship. Criminal negligence in not supplying the ship with enough lifeboats. This was a catastrophe—one of the worst naval disasters of the twentieth century. It continues to reverberate even today. But within that tragic scene, something rather wonderful happened to a young man on that ship. Let me tell you about it.

And then you go on to tell the wonderful, positive story of what the young man did on board the *Titanic*. You continue with that soaring positive arc of the young man's story with an uplifting end.

When you tell a story in this manner, you will have got all the bad news out of the way before you tell your positive story. You've leveled with the audience and told them the harsh truth of the disaster. But within that disaster, there was something positive, something wonderful. This isn't hype or spin. It combines the triumph with the tragedy.

So if you do have a generally grim situation, the key is to get all the bad news up front, and then tell your positive story.

Make Sure Your Listeners Are Listening

To tell a successful springboard story, you need listeners' undivided attention. If they are thinking about what they did at the party last night, or how they are going to answer the e-mail waiting for them in their in-trays, then the springboard story will have no effect.

In *The Secret Language of Leadership*, I discuss many different ways in which you can get the audience's attention. Here are two of the easiest and most effective. One is to talk about the audience's problems. You start talking about the issues that are keeping them awake at nights and describe those problems more starkly than they have ever heard in their lives. This catches their attention. Suddenly they're not just interested in what you have to say: they're riveted. Then you tell your springboard story.

The other way is to tell them who you are and how you dealt with some adversity that is relevant to the subject under discussion. One reason they're not listening to you may be that they don't know what sort of a person you are or why you might be relevant to their future. In this setting, communicating who you are through a story can begin to generate the interest and trust that you will need as a platform to spring them into the future. How do you tell such a story? It is to this issue that I turn in the next chapter.

INCORPORATING THE SPRINGBOARD STORY
INTO AN ENTIRE PRESENTATION

This chapter has focused on the springboard story as a kind of narrative that is particularly useful to leaders—a story that can spark change. My book, *The Secret Language of Leadership*, discusses in more detail how to weave the springboard story into an entire presentation.

Thought has to be given as to what precedes the springboard story. Thus, springboard stories are aimed at stimulating desire for action. But if the audience isn't paying attention, the springboard story risks falling on deaf ears. Hence, a preparatory step may be necessary: get the audience's attention, which is typically done with a story that is negative in tone.

Similarly, thought must also be given as to what follows the springboard story. Merely stimulating desire for change may prove ephemeral unless the change is reinforced with reasons. This is typically done with stories that are neutral in tone.

These three steps—getting attention, stimulating desire for change, and reinforcing the desire for change with reasons—are the same whatever the leadership setting (Figure 3.1). Of the three steps, the middle step—stimulating desire for change—is the most important. Without a desire for change, people will have no energy or enthusiasm. So if transformational leaders do only one thing, they should make sure they stimulate desire for change.

FIGURE 3.1   The Secret Language of Leadership

Effective presentation to get action

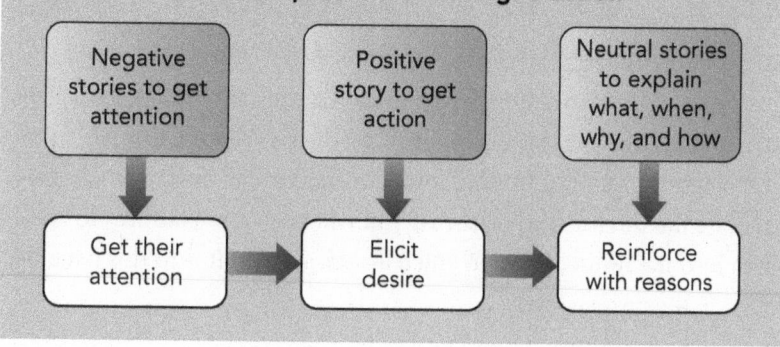

84

The three-step template is flexible. It offers a generic model for any leadership presentation. If resistance in the audience is particularly high, the speaker may need to spend a great deal more time getting attention than when the audience is already somewhat interested. By contrast, in an elevator speech, there may be time only for the critical middle step—a story that kindles desire for change. Where generous time is available, the speaker may be able to give a large number of reasons in favor of change. The template can be tailored to meet the needs of the specific audience and the time available.

Preparatory Step: Getting the Audience's Attention

In many business settings, people are not listening in any attentive way. So how do you get their attention? One study showed that the factors most highly associated with getting attention are, in rank order, the message is personalized, it evokes an emotional response, it comes from a trustworthy source or respected sender, and it is concise.[14]

Social scientists have also shown that negative messages are more attention getting than positive messages. Stories about the audience's problems or stories about how the author dealt with adversity similar to the audience's problems are well adapted to get the audience's attention. Questions, challenges, a striking metaphor, an unexpected exercise, something of value, or vulnerability admitted are other ways of getting attention.

Chapter Eight of *The Secret Language of Leadership* provides a detailed discussion of the different ways of getting the audience's attention.

Closing Step: Reinforcing with Reasons

Stimulating desire for change is important, but it's not enough. The desire for change may wane unless it is supported and reinforced by compelling reasons why the change makes sense. Where the reasons are placed in a presentation is crucial.

If reasons are given before the emotional connection is established, they are likely to be heard as so much noise. Worse, if the audience is skeptical, cynical, or hostile, the reasons tend to flip and become ammunition for the opposite point of view. By contrast, if the reasons come after an emotional connection has been established with the change idea, then the reasons can reinforce it, because now listeners are actively searching for reasons to support a decision they have in principle already taken.

The most effective way to present reasons that will resonate with your audience is to give the reasons in the form of stories—for example:

- The story of *what* the change is, often seen through the eyes of some typical characters who will be affected by the change
- The story of *how* the change will be implemented, showing in simple steps how we will get from here to there
- The story of *why* the change will work, showing the underlying causal mechanism that make the change virtually inevitable

Instead of relying on pure reason, or facts and figures and arguments, stories give reasons an emotional punch. Stories appeal to the heart as well as the mind and make the reasons memorable.

Chapter Ten of *The Secret Language of Leadership* provides more detailed discussion of how to use story to reinforce with reasons.

TEMPLATE FOR CRAFTING
THE SPRINGBOARD STORY

Finding the Right Story

1. What is your change idea?

2. Who is your audience?

3. What action do you want your audience to take?

4. Think of an incident where the change idea has been successfully implemented, at least in part.

5. In that incident, can you find a single individual who is similar to your audience and could be the protagonist of your story?

6. Does the story have an authentically positive ending for the protagonist?

7. Will the audience see it as an authentically positive ending for them?

8. Does the story fully embody the change idea? If not, can it be extrapolated so that it does?

Assembling the Story

1. Begin with:

   - The date

   - The place

   - The protagonist

2. What obstacles was the protagonist facing?

3. What would have happened without the change idea?

4. What did the protagonist do to overcome the obstacles?

5. What was the happy ending for the protagonist?

6. Check that the story has the right level of detail.

7. Link the story to the change idea, by "What if ... " or "Just think ... " or "Imagine ... "

Practicing the Story

1. Practice telling the story a number of times and observe the audience reaction.

2. Amend the story in the light of experience before telling it to your target audience.

4

BUILD TRUST

Using Narrative to Communicate Who You Are

> " Our fundamental tactic of self-protection,
> self-control, and self-definition is ...
> telling stories, and more particularly
> concocting and controlling the story we
> tell others—and ourselves—about
> who we are. "
>
> **Daniel Dennett**[1]

When I go into a new organization or encounter a new audience and start talking about an idea that is often seen as strange and counterintuitive, such as leadership storytelling or radical management, people are often wondering who I am. Who is this man? Where does he come from? Why is he talking about this subject? Should I listen to him? I respond to these issues in the following way:

> I was born in Sydney, Australia. I grew up there. I went to Sydney University. I studied psychology. I studied law. I worked for several years in a big corporate law firm. And then I went to Oxford University in England and studied some more law. And then I came to Washington, D.C., and joined the World Bank, this big international organization that lends billions of dollars to developing countries to help eliminate global poverty.

Now I was a quintessential left-brained, analytical kind of person. Clear, crisp, succinct, bottom line: that was me. And as you know, big organizations just love that kind of person. So I climbed up the managerial ladder in the World Bank. And by February 1996, I was actually the director of the Africa Region. The Africa Region handled about a third of the operations in this big international organization. So I was beginning to think that this was a pretty important kind of position.

But then the scene changed. The president of the World Bank suddenly died. My boss unexpectedly retired. Somebody else was appointed to my position.

Now, things weren't going too well for me in the World Bank. I went to see one of the top managers and asked him, "Do you have anything in mind for me?"

He replied, "Not really."

I pressed him quite a bit, and eventually he said, "Why don't you go and look into information?"

Now information in the World Bank in 1996 had the status of the garage or the cafeteria. So I was not being offered a promotion. I was being sent to Siberia.

But I was interested in information. So I went and looked into information and saw that we were wasting a lot of money there. But our real problems lay elsewhere: we needed to share our knowledge with all the millions of people who made decisions about poverty.

So I set out to persuade the World Bank to start sharing its knowledge. To my surprise, no one was interested. I gave the reasons. They didn't listen. I showed them charts. They looked dazed.

Then I stumbled on something else—a story that somehow had the capacity to communicate the idea of knowledge management and get people rapidly into action. One of my early listeners was high enough in the organization to get the ear of the president, and the president announced my idea as a major organizational initiative at the annual meeting of the World Bank in front of 170 finance ministers. Suddenly, the man from Siberia was back!

I was appointed director of knowledge management, and four years later, the World Bank was being benchmarked as one of the world leaders in knowledge management.

That's how I tell my story when I'm talking to a new audience. Through that story, I'm communicating a number of things about who I am:

- I am someone who has been a manager in a large organization, so I know the kind of stress that many people in the audience are going through.

- I am an analytical kind of person, not a wild and woolly artist who can't grasp the importance of the bottom line.

- I have felt some pain at the hands of a large organization and lived through the kind of experience that anyone might encounter and overcome.

- I have come to terms with the experience and can view the familiar antics of Dilbert-style management through the lens of laughter.

- I am unexpectedly frank about how things happen in organizations today.

- I am talking from the experience of having accomplished something significant in a difficult organizational context.

Overall, I am seeking to convey that I—a stranger—am someone who might be worth listening to. It does no harm that I am also drawing on a narrative archetype—the story of David and Goliath, in the form of a single individual facing a gigantic and apparently hostile organization and ultimately triumphing.

WHY YOU TELL YOUR STORY

The first reason to tell your story is to show people who you are—to stop being a stranger. Once upon a time, several eons ago, a stranger was a rare phenomenon. In a calmer, slower, more intimate time, people knew who you were. By reputation. They knew your family. They knew your upbringing. They knew your history. They knew what you had done. You had lived together. You had grown up in the same village. You were already known.

Now, in these turbulent, fragmented, rapidly morphing times, it's hard to know who anyone is. People don't have the background about one another. And they are often asked to trust others about whom they know very little.

Confronted with the stranger, people strive to put together the fragments of information they can find and weave them into some kind of coherent story. These fragments may come from announcements, newspapers, articles, handouts, biographical data, or even a brief encounter, but ultimately it's not the facts that are important. What everyone is groping for is understanding what the facts mean. What sort of person are they dealing with? Is this someone who can really be trusted with matters of importance?

Thus Kenneth Freeman, chairman and CEO of Quest Diagnostics, says about his early days as CEO:

> You have to establish your credibility. One thing I faced going in the door was people in the company saying, "Who is this 'glass guy' from Corning, coming to us with no lab experience? He has no health-care experience to speak of. He's not a 'laboratorian.'" At the time, we had 14,000 employees. I reached to the bottom to reach up, to establish my credibility first with the rank and file of the company.[2]

If you are a manager who has been appointed to take charge of a group, or an aspiring leader who is asking others to trust you, or merely someone about to give a talk to a new audience, you need to recognize the audience's dilemma. What expectation will they have about you? In today's low-trust corporate world, it's risky to assume that it will inevitably be positive. It's safer to be alert to the possibility, even probability, that the starting assumptions will be caution, skepticism, mistrust, or even distrust. In effect, you may need to take active and rapid steps to communicate who you are.

Reveal Who You Are Implicitly

How do you communicate who you are? People want to know what is driving you, what values you espouse, or what goals you have in life, what makes you tick. How will you act in a crisis? Will you level with people? Will you save yourself while stabbing others in the back? Are you someone who goes whichever way the wind blows? Or are you someone of character who stands up for what is good and true and right?

If you assert directly that you are an honest and trustworthy person, then the audience may begin to wonder: Why is this person saying such things? Since an honest and trustworthy person does not typically go around boasting of honesty and trustworthiness, the audience begins to suspect that there must be some reason for asserting this—and maybe you aren't honest or trustworthy at all.

Reciting your curriculum vitae won't help, because your uniqueness as an individual—your very identity—doesn't lie in the roles you have filled. It resides in the one-of-a-kind person that you have become as a result of the experiences that only you have had.

If the audience can understand the critical experiences that have formed you as an individual, they can begin not only to understand the unique individual that you have become but also to infer how you may act in the future. Giving them an account of one or more turning points in your existence can enable listeners to get inside your life, to go through what you have been through so that they can themselves experience what sort of a person you are. So you tell your story and let the listeners live your story as participants. They come to their own conclusions as to what sort of person you are. Because they have experienced you from the inside, their conclusions are likely to be more trusted than if they are asked to take them on faith.

Exploit the Fractal Nature of Identity Stories

Your character is generated not from a single incident, but from a whole lifetime of experiences. Even an uneventful lifetime might take many volumes to describe superficially, let alone in depth. So how could the account of a single incident possibly convey the richness of experience that has forged your character?

The answer lies in the fractal nature of identity stories. Just as the tiniest sample from your living body—blood, flesh, bone, saliva—can reveal the DNA of your whole biological person, so a brief, well-chosen story can shed light on your entire life history. A story you tell about an apparently trivial incident can expose the entire fabric of your character.[3]

Consider the following experience related by Michael Dell, founder and chairman of the $23 billion Dell Computer Corporation, about something he did when he was twelve years old:

> The father of my best friend was a pretty avid stamp collector, so now naturally my friend and I wanted to get into stamp collecting, too. To fund my interest in stamps, I got a job as a water boy in a Chinese restaurant two blocks from my house. I started reading stamp journals just for fun, and soon began noticing that prices were rising. Before long, my interest in stamps began to shift from the joy of collecting to the idea that there was something here that my mother, a stockbroker, would have termed "a commercial opportunity." ...
>
> I was about to embark upon one of my very first business ventures. First, I got a bunch of people in the neighborhood to consign their stamps to me. Then I advertised "Dell's Stamps" in Linn's Stamp Journal, the trade journal of the day. And then I typed, with one finger, a twelve-page catalog ... and mailed it out. Much to my surprise, I made $2000. And I learned an early, powerful lesson about the rewards of eliminating the middleman. I also learned that if you've got a good idea, it pays to do something about it.[4]

From this incident, you can infer a great deal about Michael Dell, the person. He is entrepreneurial, bold, aggressive, and direct—someone who sees life as a business opportunity. The story gets its significance from several dimensions:

- The bare facts of what he did at the age of twelve

- His current perspective on the importance of what he did back then and the meaning that he now sees in those events

- The trajectory from then to now, and its implications for where he may be heading in the future

Thus, you don't have to communicate the entire lifetime of experiences that have made you what you are to communicate identity. Your audience can determine who you are from a small sample of stories, even a single example.

DECIDE WHETHER YOUR LIFE HAS A PURPOSE

The question of whether your life story is consistent is related to another question: Does your life have a purpose? Is your life story thus far connected to some longer-term goal that has become and remains the principal focus of your energies?

Some people drift through life without any particular aim. They slip happily and comfortably into whatever role society assigns for them—wage earner, manager, spouse, citizen, whatever. They may make a useful contribution to society in these various roles and be relatively contented. Indeed, for millennia, most people had few, if any, other realistic options. In stable traditional societies, one's future was largely determined by the context in which one was born. In modern changing societies, many people still go along with the most obviously available options for the conduct of their lives.

Or they may identify a goal they are willing to commit themselves to accomplishing, and they devote their life energies to it above all others. The goal may be an ordinary one—simply being a good mother—or it may be grandiose—to reduce global poverty. It may be religious in nature—to be a God-fearing Christian—or it may be unashamedly secular—to amass great wealth. It may be moral in tone—to do good in the world—or frivolous—simply to have as much fun as possible. The commitment to the goal may remain lifelong, or it may shift from time to time, perhaps because the chosen goal no longer seems attainable or because some new goal now appears more attractive. The choice of a life goal thus inevitably remains in some sense provisional—a work in progress that may continue to evolve throughout life. Only when someone has died, and the life goal shows up in the obituary, can it be said that a lifelong choice was definitively made.

No moral judgment is being made here as to whether it is better or worse to have chosen a life goal. People who have made a definite choice of a life goal may appear to some as admirable but also obsessive and driven and difficult to live with, as Nick Hornby amusingly illustrates in his novel *How to Be Good*.[5] People who have made no choice of a life goal may appear to others as easy to get along with but also, at the extreme, indecisive, unfocused, and insubstantial.

Even if you've made up your mind where you're heading, you still have an important decision as to whether to communicate it. An explicit commitment to some overriding goal is typically a polarizing event. The communication of the goal may attract actual or potential supporters, but it may also alert potential skeptics, opponents, and competitors of your intentions, and it may enable them to take countervailing action to try to prevent or slow down the accomplishment of your goal.

For instance, in politics, an explicit articulation of your overriding goal to become president or prime minister can create antibodies: rivals and competitors may undertake explicit spoiling actions aimed at pigeonholing you as an overambitious upstart and preventing you from attaining your goal. In an organization, a specific commitment to head in a certain direction may be a liability for advancement in that organization if the top management decides to head in a different direction.

There are thus reasons pro and con for communicating where you're heading in life. Before deciding to do so, weigh the pluses and minuses of going public. In some circumstances, there may be no other way to attain your goal except by declaring it.

Take Nelson Mandela.

In 1964, Nelson Mandela was arrested by the government of South Africa and brought to court to face an apparent death sentence for treason. Mandela made a statement from the dock: "During my lifetime I have dedicated myself to the struggle of the African people. I have fought against white domination, and I have fought against black domination. I have cherished the ideal of a democratic and free society in which all persons live together in harmony and with equal opportunities. It is an ideal which I hope to live for and to achieve. But, if needs be, it is an ideal for which I am prepared to die."[6] He was sentenced to life imprisonment. During his prison years, he rejected several offers to be released if he would endorse the government's policy of apartheid. Upon his release from prison in 1990, he spoke not in anger but in the language of reconciliation: "Comrades and fellow

South Africans, I greet you all in the name of peace, democracy, and freedom for all."[7]

Mandela's unambiguous opposition to apartheid won him world-wide renown and eventually led to his being elected president of South Africa, a position he held from 1994 to 1999.

Since the communication of your life goal to others raises the stakes, it is not a step to be undertaken lightly. It effectively transforms a secret and privately held intent that can be changed without loss into a publicly declared promise likely to generate expectations from your audience that cannot easily be changed. By communicating your life goal, you are giving your word as to your intent. Henceforth people will judge you in part by whether you live up to the goal that you have articulated. If you don't, then your credibility will suffer, perhaps irrevocably. If you do live up to your goal, then you may win people's respect, even if they disagree with you, because they will know where you stand, where you come from, what's driving you.

Be Authentic

An effective leader's life story is authentic—something that comes from inner conviction. It is to be distinguished from the derivative life stories of those who attempt to trim their image to fit the current fashion. Such people treat themselves as a transaction in the making, allowing their value to be defined by others—an organization, a boss, a recruiter, a partner, an electorate—in other words, a commodity whose worth rises and falls according to the marketplace.

Such people may lubricate the machinery of the traditional management. But they will never be genuine leaders. Because they have no authentic life story, they will lack the traction needed to lead.[8]

There are many reasons that John Kerry, the Democratic candidate, lost the 2004 U.S. presidential election. One of the more important ones was his seeming inability to communicate who he is. His actions in Vietnam as a soldier and then afterward as a war protester, his votes against the First Gulf War and then for the war in Iraq but against the *funding for it—all these actions tended to pose questions in the minds of voters as to his real motivation—doubts the Republicans did their utmost to accentuate. Kerry seemed unable to come up with a succinct story that would communicate why he had conducted his life the way he had. Even ardent Democrats such as the editors of the New Yorker magazine found his efforts to explain himself "discouraging to behold."[9] The Republicans presented him as someone who went with whichever political wind happened to blowing at the time. The absence of any compelling countervailing story from Kerry himself made it easy for the Republicans to charge him with "flip-flopping on the issues." As a result, although he won the presidential debates, voters who disagreed with his opponent, President George W. Bush, on the issues and who felt that the country was heading in the wrong direction were still reluctant to vote for Kerry.*

According to psychologists, people typically begin to form a story about who they are in late adolescence, when they leave the comfort and protection of their family and confront head-on the question of what to do with their adult lives. Consciously and unconsciously, all of us begin working through the basic choices we are going to make.[10]

As we move into adulthood, we generally create and refine several main characters, since our lives are generally too complex to be handled by a single pattern. These actual or imagined personas become central protagonists within the self that interact—and sometimes conflict—in the making of identity. Hero or victim, leader or follower, wanderer or settler, warrior or nurturer, lover or loner, parent or celibate, employee or entrepreneur, creator or adopter, citizen or anarchist, believer or atheist, enthusiast or cynic: the potential characters we might become are infinite. The culture offers up role models that offer potential choices. Each of us ends up making a unique set of choices or nonchoices that reflect the course of action that we take or don't take, and embodies those choices in a personal story.

The resulting life story is usually a mix. Some patterns are consciously chosen as explicit goals: specific decisions as to a course of life. Other patterns may emerge over time: you look back and discover that you have made a series of decisions over a number of years that have pointed your life in a very different direction from what you believed you had explicitly chosen. Whether explicit or emergent, there is always a life story of some kind.

And it's this story that you as a leader need to tell.

HOW TO TELL YOUR STORY

The story that you tell as a leader to communicate who you are will not be the entire story of your existence, but it will be a representative selection from your authentic life story. It will be a story that communicates key choices that you have made in life. It will not be a story concocted for the occasion only, since that will quickly be exposed for what it is—a mere veneer over a different reality. As your actions become known, an unrepresentative selection will result in a backlash against you as an untruthful storyteller. Instead, your story will reflect your authentic self—the choices that you have made in life as a person, reflecting where you have come from, where you are now, and where you are going.

"Know thyself," say the philosophers, but it's easier said than done. For most of us, our hopes and fears tend to get in the way of realistic assessment of who we are. Usually the dissonance is mild and might be considered a foible. Where the dissonance between self-image and reality is so extreme as to cause difficulty functioning in the world, it may be necessary to seek therapy.

Your story will need to reflect a certain degree of coherence that has been attained in terms of reconciling the various competing personas in your life. Given that a personal story is always an ongoing work of construction and creation, the telling of your story can be a step toward tightening that coherence. In fact, the more you tell your story, the more likely you are to progress toward coherence. This of course is one of the underlying principles of psychotherapy: by creating a situation that requires personal storytelling, participants discover (or rather create) a degree of coherence that wasn't there before.

Howard Gardner contrasts the different fortunes of Margaret Thatcher, who became prime minister of the United Kingdom in 1979, and Newt Gingrich, who became Speaker of the U.S. House of Representatives in 1995:

> Thatcher strove as prime minister to show that Britain could recover its greatness through ingenuity and reliance on the private sector. The fact that she herself had succeeded through courage, cleverness, and hard work meant that she embodied the story she was telling and this contributed to her success. By contrast, Newt Gingrich, who rose to become Speaker of the House after the 1994 election, aimed at sparking a similar political revolution, but without the same consistency. He called for term limits—for others. He was for the private sector, but had been on the government payroll for most of his life. While promoting family values, he had several messy divorces, as well as an affair with an intern while he was attacking the Clinton presidency for the Monica Lewinsky affair. The gap between the story that he told and the story of his own life hampered the communication of his political message.[11]

It takes courage to tell a strong personal story, because the story implies certain values that you will hold to even if the world changes. Thus, you will need to be clear about what you believe and base your actions on those beliefs, time after time, even if this makes you unpopular.

Focus the Story on a Turning Point in Your Life

The turning points in life are a fruitful source of stories. These are moments of disruption when some incident gives us a glimpse of the regions of deeper feeling.

The following anecdote was related by Anita Roddick, chairman of The Body Shop. She was born in 1942 and raised in the southeast of England, near Brighton. Her Italian immigrant mother and American father ran a café where early on she was instilled with an intense work ethic. As she told it:

> Although I went to a Catholic school, my mother hated the local priest. When my father died, I remember sitting on the stairs in our house while my mother was furiously scrubbing the linoleum in the hallway. There was a knock on the front door and the priest was there to tell her that she was very lucky that my father was going to be given a Catholic

funeral. Mother just picked up the bucket of dirty water and threw it over him. I'll never forget that. Acts like that push you onto the edge of bravery. It is no wonder, having a mother and an upbringing like that, that I learned to challenge everything I was told—school, at church and in every other institution.[12]

Roddick turned a strong work ethic, an interest in social justice and respect for the environment, and a willingness to speak out into a thriving global business. Through telling a story apparently about her mother, she also communicated what sort of person she was. Rather than a direct discussion of her deepest feelings, she alluded to these feelings by implication. If the listeners follow and understand the story, they get a good sense of Roddick herself.

Why choose a turning point in your life? People always live on several levels. On the surface, we live a life that consists of the routine, predictable activities of the human animal: we wake up, we eat, we drink, we go to work, we get our job done, we relax and chatter about this and that, we get tired and go to sleep, perchance to dream, and get the tired mind and body ready for the next day.

But below this surface of routine, predictable activity, there exists a realm of deeper feelings—of the joy and exhilaration of being alive, of the desire for loving and being loved, of the pain of realizing that we may not realize all our deepest ambitions, of the dilemmas of balancing our own goals with those of others, of a looming sense of our own mortality. The nature and intensity of these feelings may vary from person to person, but the existence of this realm is not in question.

It is the former aspect—the superficial, routine side of life—that we typically present to others in the workaday world, even though it is in the latter domain of deeper feeling that our uniqueness as human beings is revealed. There are of course good, commonsense reasons for generally keeping these deeper feelings to ourselves—a desire for privacy, a lack of time to share these matters, a practical wish to avoid embarrassing our associates with the burden of our deepest feelings, or just simple ignorance of what our deepest feelings really are. Yet it is these deeper realms of feeling that provide the primary subject matter for stories that communicate who we are.

In communicating who we are, the balance to be attained is delicate. If we reveal too much of the deeper realms, we may be seen as wallowing in an unseemly public display of feelings that would be better kept under wraps. If we reveal too little, then we may remain a colorless cipher, living on the superficial level of the routine, the predictable, the conventional—a mere stereotype.

Characteristically, a suitable balance is best achieved not by direct confession of your deepest feelings but by a story that reflects a turning point in our life.

Tell a Story with a Positive Tone

For a leader, it is important for the story to show how he or she derived something positive from the experience. The message thus needs to be one of hope, that it is possible to accomplish something of importance, something of value that can carry the enterprise and the human spirit forward. The story may be about adversity and setbacks, but it will reflect what was learned from the experience (as in Anita Roddick's story) or how adversity was overcome.

Tell Your Story with Context

The story of who you are will implicitly reflect your fundamental views about the world and perhaps allude to how you developed these views.

It will follow the lines of a traditional story. It will talk about what happened to someone—the hero or heroine, usually you, the storyteller. There is a plot. The stories are typically told with feeling and context.

Identity stories are thus unlike the minimalist or springboard stories designed to spark action that I discussed in Chapter Three. The aim of the identity story is to put a human face on you as a person—the manager of the organization—and indicate that you have a heart.

Plot, setting, the sounds, the sights, and the feel of the place all help communicate what it is like being you. You want the audience to identify with you, even vicariously to be you, to be there facing the adversity you were facing so that they gain insight into what you are made of.

Use Humor to Brighten Your Story

The moment of disruption may also be a moment of comedy, when some unusual incongruity occurred, when nothing serious was at stake, but your action and reaction in response to it, a sympathetic pleasure in human idiosyncrasy, reveals what sort of a person you are. Thus, the telling of an experience of pain and difficulty can be lightened by a touch of humor. By referring to painful events in a humorous way, you demonstrate that you have mastered the experience, rather than that the experience has crushed you. Some examples:

- *John F. Kennedy:* In 1960, John Kennedy made fun of two apparent drawbacks to his candidacy as president—his inherited wealth and his Catholic religion—as a way of admitting his political liabilities and making light of them. On one occasion in the campaign, Kennedy held up what he said was a telegram from his "generous daddy" and read it aloud: "Jack, Don't spend one dime more than is necessary. I'll be damned if I am going to pay for a landslide."[13]

- *Amos Oz:* Israeli writer Amos Oz explains that as a child in Jerusalem, he hoped to grow up to be a book: "There was fear when I was a little boy. People would say, Enjoy every day, because not every child grows up to be a person. This was probably their way of telling me about the Holocaust or the fame of Jewish history. Not every child grows up. I know the Israelis become tiresome when they say that the whole world is against us, but back in the forties, that was pretty much the case. I wanted to become a book, not a man. The house was full of books written by dead men, and I thought a book may survive."[14]

Don't Overstate Your Good Qualities

Psychologists have shown that human beings tend to see their own lives in more positive terms than an objective appraisal would warrant.[15] These optimistic illusions can work well for us as long as they are not too extreme. When we believe that life is relatively good and we are in control of our fate, we tend to cope better with adversity and meet challenges with confidence and hope.[16]

It's important, however, not to let this overly positive image be communicated because it will sound like boasting. Hence, talk about adversity overcome. Don't glamorize too much. Be gracious toward all those who contributed to your success. Rather than talking about how you won a smashing victory and demolished the opposition, talk about how you were able to overcome great obstacles through the help of your colleagues.

WHERE YOU TELL YOUR STORY

People don't seek in a leader someone who is grappling with inner demons, who is angry and bitter at the inevitable injustices that life hands out.[17] Instead, they seek in a leader someone who has brought the opposing parts of life together into a harmonious whole, both for the prospective leader as a person and in terms of the new stories that may be generated for others. In fact, since no one achieves perfect coherence, any prospective leader will have unresolved tensions—with a spouse, a child, a parent, an employer, a business partner—that might be counterproductive if exposed to the light of day.

To communicate that you have achieved the requisite degree of integration, choose a part of your life story that links to the broader story of the audience. You communicate that you are someone who is likely to improve their lives in some way.

> In 1992, Bill Clinton presented himself as the embodiment of resilience—someone who could bounce back from apparent disaster. As the self-styled Comeback Kid, the Man from Hope, he was implicitly telling a story of hope about the United States. The stories about the candidate and the country were aligned, by design. Clinton successfully made the case that a vote for him would make the country come out stronger.

In 2000, George W. Bush played the role of the prodigal son. He had gone astray in earlier years, but through personal resolve and faith, he had reestablished moral clarity. Implicitly he was telling the same story to the country: after moral delinquencies of the Clinton presidency, Bush persuaded voters that a vote for him was a vote for bedrock beliefs and integrity.[18]

It's usually best to choose a story that not only reflects the way you overcame adversity but also points to its relevance to the audience in front of you. Present your story so as to suggest an analogy to the way you would handle the problems of today.

Make Sure the Audience Wants to Hear Your Story

One of the key tasks when telling your personal story is to make sure that your audience has the time and interest to listen to it. Avoid digressions, wasted words, and the epic tale. CEOs in particular need to resist the temptation to assemble the troops and force them to listen to epic tales from their youth.

Choose the occasion for telling your personal story carefully. Personal storytelling may be appropriate in moments like these:

- *First encounter:* When someone is nominated to a position, people are likely to be very interested in learning who the appointee is. This is an obvious opportunity to satisfy that interest with some concise and aptly chosen personal storytelling.

- *A difficult decision:* When a difficult decision is about to be made or has just been made, interest in or suspicion of the real reasons for it often runs high. Are the official reasons the reasons that drove the decision-making process? Or were there some other undisclosed factors that, behind the scenes, caused the chips to fall the way they did? Even if such factors don't exist, opponents or skeptics will be quick to supply them and distribute them through the rumor mill. Linking the decision to your personal life story and pointing out the consistency of the two can be one way of solidifying the authenticity of the decision you have made, as well as constraining the grapevine. Even where people do not agree with you, they will respect your integrity if your decision flows from the deeply held principles that your life story embodies.

- *Coaching and counseling:* When employees or associates come to you for advice when disaster strikes, direct advice can appear facile and unhelpful even when it is soundly based. In these settings, a personal story about how you handled an analogous crisis may be an effective method of getting the message across.

Understand the Audience's Story

The counterpart to being clear on the story of who you are is grasping the story of who the audience is. Just as you prepare for a presentation by figuring out your own life story, so you also invest effort in understanding the audience's interests, authority, and roles.

Thus, relevance is contextual. The more you know about the audience's story—what matters to them, what drives them, what they expect, what they fear, what makes them tick, what ticks them off—the more likely you are to be able to choose a story that is relevant to their needs. Ultimately it is the audience that decides whether you are relevant to them.

Make Sure the Audience Hears the Story You Tell

When you tell the story of who you are, the story must come from within, but its practical impact depends on what story the listener goes away with. You might be telling a story about how you overcame adversity to win a high school hockey competition with the objective of communicating your courage, your persistence, and your strength of character. But if your listeners are thinking, "What a boastful jerk!" then clearly your story is having the opposite effect of what you intend. It doesn't matter how brilliant your storytelling, the listeners are creating a different story from the one you are telling.

With your story, you endeavor to make a compelling aesthetic statement by integrating your remembered past, your perceived present, and your anticipated future. You don't discover your story from predetermined elements; you create yourself through telling your story.

The Transformational Leader Becomes the Organization

Communicating who you are is of vital importance in transformational leadership, because it transforms followers' self-concepts and links their identity with that of the organization. Transformational leaders forge this link by embodying the values of the change they are urging and emphasizing the intrinsic rewards of pursuing it. The leaders' clear sense of identity helps followers gain confidence and a sense of self-efficacy. It works by bonding followers and their self-concepts to the organizational identity, a concept to which I turn in Chapter Five.

A TEMPLATE FOR CREATING THE STORY OF WHO YOU ARE

This template is a set of steps to be used in crafting stories that communicate your identity and help your audience build trust in you:

1. The story of who you are is usually a prelude to some other communication—your main communication. Be clear on the purpose of this main communication—proposing a change, announcing a decision, or marketing or selling a product, for example.

2. Review the events of your journey through life, and select an event that was a turning point for you, say, when things did not turn out as you expected. Describe it briefly.

3. Is the turning point relevant by analogy to your main communication? If yes, continue on to step 4. If not, try to find a turning point that is relevant by analogy to your main communication. A story about how you fell sick at a restaurant might be an interesting, even gripping, story, but if it is not relevant to your main communication, it may be distracting and counterproductive.

4. When and where did it happen—for example, "In July 2003, in London, I was..."

5. Will the event in itself be of interest to your audience? If not, can the story be told so that it could become interesting to your audience?

6. Does the story reflect the values that you as a person espouse? If not, can it be adjusted so that it does reflect those values?

7. Does the story show by implication how you felt about the event?

8. If the story has a positive tone, that is, a happy ending, is there a risk that it will sound like boasting? If the story has a negative tone, that is, an unhappy ending, does it show what you got out of the experience?

9. At the conclusion, does the story link to your main communication—for example, "What this experience taught me was..."?

5

USE NARRATIVE
TO BUILD YOUR BRAND

The World of Social Media

"" Customers know everything about
your company.... That has
changed the rules of business
forever. **""**

Harvard Business Review[1]

If individuals can build trust in themselves by telling their stories, why
not organizations? In fact, storytelling has always been part of the arsenal
of branding and marketing departments. "One way of building internal
passion for brands," says Landor Associates, "is through the creation of
stories."[2] But which stories?

In the twentieth century, the main focus was on stories told by the
corporation. In recent years, as the credibility of corporate storytelling
steadily declined and the voice of the customer grew louder, the focus of
branding and marketing has shifted to catalyzing customers' stories.

Consider the following examples:

- In 2008, when United Airlines broke Dave Carroll's guitar, he made a
  singing YouTube video that told the story of the incident; more than
  8 million people have now viewed the video.[3]

- In 2008, when a mother took offense at a commercial for the pain reliever Motrin that implied, in her eyes, that mothers were wearing baby slings simply to be fashionable, she was able to launch a "Motrin Moms" protest movement that within two days became the most popular subject on Twitter.[4]

- In 2008, when Howard Schultz returned as CEO of Starbucks, he woke up one morning to find around a hundred e-mails in his inbox. It turned out that this was the result of a sensational story in the *Sun*, a London newspaper, about a problem that Schultz had never heard of. When his phone rang and a reporter asked him to comment, Schultz replied that he had no idea what it was. The reporter advised him to find out fast. Although the real-world issue in the story turned out to be insignificant, it had become an instant public relations crisis. Schultz recalls: "The lesson was that the world had changed. Something that happened in London had created a world-wide story that positioned Starbucks with venom and disrespect."[5]

These are just a couple of eye-opening illustrations of the revolution generated by sites like Twitter, Facebook, and YouTube. As a result, stories told by customers can instantly trump the marketing stories being told by organizations about their products and services. The scale and rapidity of the ensuing public relations crises are astonishing.[6]

At the same time, the positive opportunities for organizations to use the power of social media for telling the story of their products and services are equally dramatic:

- Procter & Gamble has used social media to reach otherwise unreachable customers when they helped create a community for teenage girls (beinggirl.com) that provides a friendly and helpful environment for them to converse and share stories, where the girls also learn about P&G's feminine care products.[7]

- Ford has used social marketing to launch a new car—the Fiesta—without traditional advertising by generating a massive

"Fiesta Movement," involving stories reflected in 6 million YouTube views, 740,000 views of Flickr photos, and 3.7 million Twitter impressions.[8]

Since 2005, when the first edition of this book was published, the dynamic of branding and marketing has been transformed. In 2005, the examples cited above could not have happened. Facebook and YouTube had just been created, and Twitter did not exist. Now in 2011, these three Web sites have hundreds of million of participants who can and do tell stories about the products and services that they use.

The ability to understand and use the power of story to defend against threats and take advantage of opportunities offered by social media has become a core organizational competence. Corporate storytelling in the twenty-first century is becoming less and less about the corporation telling stories and more and more about creating products and services that themselves catalyze customer stories of delight.

MARKETING IN THE TWENTIETH CENTURY

For much of the twentieth century, branding and marketing consisted mainly of crafting and communicating one-way messages to a mass audience. By mass-marketing the same product in roughly the same way to all consumers, companies could reach the largest potential market at the lowest cost. Moreover, they could interrupt whomever they wanted with any message they cared to transmit. And buyers were forced to watch it because there were only three television channels. And there was no easy way for customers to talk back.

Why the Model Changed

Four changes help explain why this model is less and less operative today.

One is the shift in the balance of power in the marketplace from sellers to buyers. By and large, the established twentieth-century firm was in control of the marketplace. But the situation changed as a few sellers turned into many sellers. Buyers acquired instant access to reliable information. As a result, unless customers are receiving a continuously added value from the firm, they can—and will—go elsewhere. This in itself is a game changer: the firm's goal shifts from merely satisfying customers to the more complex goal of delighting them.

A second change is the fragmentation of media. A few channels have exploded into multiple channels of television, the Web, and cell phones. Reaching a large audience becomes very expensive unless that audience wants to be reached. As a result, mass advertising has diminished cost-effectiveness. Targeting of advertising to those who are likely to be interested in the advertiser's products and services becomes a preoccupation.[9]

A third change is technological. Word of mouth has always been seen as important: the accepted maxim was that every unhappy customer told ten friends. Now the importance has been dramatically magnified. Social media make it wonderfully—and frighteningly—easy for anyone to communicate instantly with anyone else in the world about anything. Now a dissatisfied customer can talk back to millions of interested fellow customers. Employee stories about a firm are publicly available on sites like www.glassdoor.com. Customers can band together and use stories to rapidly form alliances that can work powerfully for or against an organization. Ignoring this groundswell of customer conversations and stories can be risky. For most firms, working with it will be more productive.

A fourth change is social. Customers are no longer docile pawns that can be manipulated at will with one-way messages sent by entrenched oligopolies. Customers are skeptical about the stories they are being told. "Advertising has no credibility with consumers, who are increasingly skeptical of its claims and whenever possible are inclined to reject its messages."[10] Now customers are able to exploit the power of the new technology to obtain information, address problems, and tell stories so as to get what they want. The twenty-first-century customer is different and more elusive than the customer of fifty years ago.

These changes require a revolution in marketing thinking. They raise issues not just about particular management practices, but with the very notion of how an organization should be run.

Three Kinds of Stories

Corporations tell three kinds of stories: the story of the firm itself, stories of the firm's products or services, and customers' own stories and their relationship to the firm.

Stories of the Firm Itself

The founder's story is the story of where the firm came from, how it grew, and what values it pursued along the way.

Some of the mystique of Apple Computer and Microsoft comes from the "geeks in a garage" stories of the early creation of those companies by Steve Jobs and Bill Gates, respectively. But care in the use of the founder's story is needed. The Steve Jobs story may have some resonance, as both Jobs himself and the firm of Apple still convey some of the boyish enthusiasm of a start-up. By contrast, "the geeks in a garage" story has little resonance with the current business colossus that is Microsoft.

Southwest Airlines is a story of people living life to the fullest, with humor and a sense of fun, being free to "roam about the country" because the airline makes it affordable to do so by providing cheap, reliable, entertaining flights to popular destinations. Its brand narrative is closely linked to the wit and character of its founder, Herb Kelleher.

And at Costco, cofounder and CEO Jim Sinegal regularly uses stories of how he has built the firm by a continuing commitment to provide high-quality, low-cost products to customers rather than raise margins, so as to convey the firm's corporate values and illustrate how those values are being brought to life throughout the company.

Milestone stories can also portray turning points in a firm's history and communicate the character of the firm. A famous example is Johnson & Johnson's handling of the poisonings from Tylenol bottles in the autumn of 1982 in Chicago. An apparent public relations disaster was turned into a triumph by the prompt action of management to pull all Tylenol bottles from the shelves at huge expense and replace them with new tamper-proof tops. Within a few years, Tylenol had become the most popular over-the-counter analgesic in the United States. The story, told and retold, can help communicate Johnson & Johnson's commitment to put the customer first, but only so long as the firm still adheres to those values.[11]

The Story of the Products or Services

The story of the products and services themselves as told by the corporation was a staple of twentieth-century advertising.

The most frequently cited success story for this approach is Coca-Cola. Through the use of an unusually shaped bottle, consistent deployment of a certain shade of the color red, and clever stories to communicate the notions that Coca-Cola's beverage is based on a secret formula kept in a locked vault and that it constitutes "the real thing," Coca-Cola created a brand worth tens of billions of dollars, despite the fact the underlying product—a brown carbonated beverage—is not outstanding, even in the firm's own blind tasting tests.[12]

In the twenty-first century, Coca-Cola found difficulty duplicating the success.[13]

In the spring of 2004, Coca-Cola decided to launch a brand of water called Dasani in the United Kingdom with a £7 million marketing push that told the story how Dasani comprised "pure water" having been cleansed by a "highly sophisticated purification process, based on NASA spacecraft technology."

The launch ran into some snags. First, it emerged that the water used in Dasani came from ordinary tap water, piped into its U.K. factory by Thames Water, leading to widespread public derision.

This was then compounded by news that the firm's "highly sophisticated purification process" was in fact the same reverse osmosis used in many modest domestic water purification units.

Then the story took an even worse turn: it emerged that the entire U.K. supply of Dasani was being pulled off the shelves because it had been contaminated with bromate, a cancer-causing chemical.

The Drinking Water Inspectorate confirmed that the water supplied to the factory by Thames Water was free of bromate. In other words, Dasani was less healthy than regular tap water, despite being sold at more than thirty times the price. As a result, the company shelved plans to launch a natural mineral water version of Dasani in Europe.

In the twentieth century, Coca-Cola might have gotten away with those stories and successfully launched the brand to a docile consumer base. In the twenty-first century, the stories were quickly identified as deceptive. Word spread rapidly, and the brand launch failed.

Today, in the atmosphere of cynicism and distrust toward advertising that prevails in the marketplace, it's difficult to make the firm's own story of its products and services convincing. Given the track record of firms telling half-truths or even straight-out untruths, customers discount most of what they hear directly from firms.

The anonymity of the corporation has had a lot to do with it:

> Most companies are adept at removing any sense of individuality or human connection from how they communicate. We commonly describe these companies as faceless. They are large inhuman blobs that do not listen or ask for our feedback, have incomprehensible policies, and use automated responses instead of real people to address our concerns. These faceless organizations are all around us. As consumers, we can spot them right away, and we universally dread our interactions with them.[14]

The Stories of the Customer

The third kind of stories are those of the customer. For example, an advertisement for Walgreens drugstores in a women's magazine, *Bazaar*, shows a photo of a young attractive woman smiling and carrying a shopping bag, apparently after leaving a Walgreens store. The photo is accompanied by a note in a handwritten font:

> I see fall as an opportunity to rethink my beauty routine and get back to basics. A trip to Walgreens always leaves me feeling refreshed and ready to face the season, rain or shine. This year, I'm focusing on the foundations for a fabulous look—great hair, amazing skin, beautiful lips, and irresistibly smooth legs.[15]

The advertisement simulates a real customer, although the ad makes no claim that the woman in the photograph ever had these thoughts and feelings. Walgreens hopes that the fictional story will plant the idea in readers' minds that a visit to one of their drugstores can be a wholesome journey of renewal. In the twentieth century, that may have worked. Today the problem for Walgreens is that the readers can also visit Web sites like www.yelp.com and obtain an instant picture of how real people actually experience a visit to a Walgreens drugstore.[16]

The story has more chance of having an impact if the audience can be induced to take an interest in the characters in it. As discussed in the excellent book, *Storytelling: Branding in Practice* by Klaus Fog and colleagues, this was accomplished in a series of television advertisements that introduced Renault's new car, the Clio, to the U.K. public. The series began in 1991 with a fictional scene set in the south of France:

> *An attractive young woman ("Nicole") is apparently on vacation with her father ("Papa"). Nicole is seen wearing a perky polka-dot dress and sneaking past her father, who is apparently asleep in the luxurious garden. She drives away in a Renault Clio to have a romantic rendezvous with her boyfriend. It is then revealed that Papa was merely pretending to be asleep: once she has left, he jumps up and goes to his own tryst with a lady friend. When they return, they cry respectively, "Nicole!" and "Papa!" The ad ends with the tag line: "Renault: A Certain Flair."*

The ad caught on and sequels were released over a seven-year period. The series helped position the Renault Clio as a car associated with France and a romantic and desirable way of life. The series became a prominent part of British pop culture. A 1996 survey showed that the actress who played Nicole in the series was recognized by more Britons than the British prime minister, John Major.

The series culminated with Nicole's marriage in 1998. The sponsors announced in advance that Nicole was getting married, but the identity of her husband was withheld until the showing of the actual commercial during a popular soap opera:

> *In the ad, Nicole abandons her planned marriage on the spur of the moment in the middle of the wedding ceremony and is shown running from the church to marry another man ("Bob"). This signaled Nicole's decision to abandon a traditional lifestyle (marriage and limo) and enjoy a free, modern life with Bob and her Renault Clio.*

The storytelling of the series was allusive and minimalist, with the only spoken words being "Nicole," "Papa," "Maman," "Bob," and "Yes!" The series was effective because the public became intrigued by the romantic fictional life of "Nicole," which in due course became associated with the Renault Clio.

The story of the customer can also succeed where it helps to establish a link between the brand's primary customers. In *How Brands Become Icons*, Douglas Holt argues that for any strong brand, there is a certain kind of person who loves the brand. If the seller can understand the story of these people and tell their story, it can resonate and help reinforce the brand.

> Thus Volkswagen has a track record of appealing to iconoclasts. When it presented itself as a company that made cars for iconoclasts in the 1960s and 1970s, it was hugely successful. In the 1980s and early 1990s, when it appeared to forget this part of its history and presented itself as a maker of cars for everybody, albeit higher-quality cars, it lost ground in the marketplace. In the late 1990s, when it suddenly remembered that its core clientele had been iconoclasts, it once again prospered.[17]

In a similar vein, Budweiser offers jokey television ads that suggest that these funny people kidding around and having a good time are the kind of people who drink Budweiser beer. The implication is that anyone could be as funny, and have as good a time, if only they drank Budweiser. The ads appear to be successful in promoting the brand, even though the underlying logic is not exactly rock-solid. Although in today's marketplace, the ads can make the sale, the question for the longer term is whether they are building enduring enthusiasm for the brand. At best, the continued strength of a brand based on such evanescent associations will depend on disseminating a never-ending supply of new stories in an effort to perpetuate the impression of Budweiser's distinctiveness.

Twentieth-Century Marketing: One-Way Communications

Twentieth-century marketers looked at the world through the lens of whatever they were selling, saying in effect: "We believe that our offerings will be useful to you and here's a story that will communicate why that is so." In this mode, marketers paid attention to and studied their customers, but they generally viewed them through the lens of the company's own goods and services, while ignoring the other problems that the customers might be facing.

The communications were one-way and made through official channels. The firm operated through a system of barriers, clearances, and controls that ensured that only the right messages were sent.

The thinking was linear. The firm created a brand idea, through selecting the right name, the right logo, and the right packaging and using the right stories in advertising to communicate its messages. The brand idea thus communicated led initially to awareness and ultimately to certain customer perceptions about it. These perceptions in turn led to customer behavior: the customer buys the firm's products or services, which generated satisfactory business performance.[18]

The core elements of marketing were the four Ps: product, price, promotion, and place. The mode of operation was manipulation. How can we adjust the four Ps so that the customers can be induced to buy more?

TWENTY-FIRST-CENTURY MARKETING: THE INTERACTIVE CUSTOMER STORY

The new world of social media not only demands greater honesty from organizations but also more openness and interaction. The sending of one-way messages is proving increasingly ineffective. It may create awareness, but it doesn't lead to a positive relationship with customers. And when customers sense manipulation, they become distrustful.

To cope with these developments, twenty-first-century marketing needs to look at the world from the point of view of the customer, with the attitude: "We seek to understand your problems and help solve them with our offerings." They need to understand the customer's story and continuously evolve their offerings to meet their customers' needs in order to surprise and delight them.

By immersing themselves in the customers' world, observing their behavior and listening to their stories, the firm learns how to meet even needs that customers themselves are unaware of. It seeks to anticipate the customers' needs even before they are aware of them. The world wasn't asking Apple to make cool-looking MP3 players or arrange an easy, cheap way to download music online. People didn't know they wanted iPods or easy music download services until Apple invented them. Going this route surprises the audience. "Apple did a bit of mind reading with respect to what their customers (or potential customers) would love, but didn't know could be available," writes Chip Conley in his book, *Peak: How Great Companies Get Their Mojo from Maslow*.[19]

Passion: The New Driver

Success in today's marketplace means having a skilled workforce that is passionately committed to delighting the customers of the organization and then catalyzing those customers to share their surprise and delight with other potential customers.

To the traditional four Ps of marketing—product, price, promotion, and place—is added the key driver of the twenty-first-century marketplace: the fifth P, passion. To elicit passion, companies must learn how to shed the lifeless armor of being faceless organizations and express authentic personalities that can elicit positive passion in their customers.

Apple is an example of an organization that has mastered this mode of operation:

> The most powerful aspects of the customers' experience with Apple are not confined to the logo, the name, the packaging or the advertising. Stories are generated by the products themselves—iMac, iPod, iPhone and iPad—and by the environment of the Apple stores that encourages customers to stay, explore, and interact with its products and by the ingenuity of its offerings and their simplicity of use. The helpfulness of their salespeople in person and online reinforces the impression, as do the enthusiastic stories that potential customers hear from other Apple users. The whole experience generates a seamless set of stories that spread virally and convey the central idea: cool people choose Apple products.[20]

Marketing now is thus less about crafting a set of messages that communicate the brand, as it is about creating products and services that themselves generate authentic stories by delighted customers, who share the stories with other customers.

Branding and marketing have become complex, interactive, and multidirectional. Firms being run in a traditional, command-and-control manner are no longer sufficiently agile to operate in this manner.

Defensive Interventions: Communicating by People with People

The traditional organizational arrangements, in which all communications from the firm with the outside world are made through official channels is unworkable in the world of social media. For one thing, it's too slow. Media crises can now spiral out of control in minutes. Going up the chain of command to get the formal response to problems being raised is too slow to be effective. Instead, individuals need to be following what is happening in the social media and be ready—and authorized—to respond on the fly.

For another thing, corporate communications often sound inauthentic. If a company representative intervenes in an ongoing conversation on a social media site in the traditional twentieth-century manner by restating company policies and guidelines, any issue that customers may have is likely to be aggravated. Frustrated customers will feel that they are not being listened to and sense that they are dealing with an unresponsive, inhuman machine. This is likely to lead to further concern or even anger, not only on the part of the customer who initially had the problem but also by all the other potential customers who are listening in.

For the intervention to be effective, it has to be a communication from one human being to another. As a matter of disclosure, the intervenors need to identify themselves as employees of the firm in question, so that their financial interest is explicit, but they need to communicate as themselves. They are speaking not as "the representative of the firm who happens to be Mary Brown," but rather as "Mary Brown who happens to be a representative of the firm." The difference is subtle but profound.

Because they are intervening as individuals, if they don't know the answer to a question, they say so. By listening to the stories being told, empathizing with the feelings being experienced, and telling the story of their own response to the issue, including their feelings, doubts, and uncertainties about what can be done about it, they humanize the face of the firm. If the problem can be resolved, they set about trying to find a solution and keep the customer informed of the progress of their efforts. If in the end the problem cannot be resolved, they do their best to explain why the firm is unable to act otherwise.

The firm's employees express their own personal views about the subjects under discussion, within limits explicitly or implicitly established by their employer. If it appears that they are simply parroting script dictated by the management, their communications will be perceived as inauthentic, and they will be counterproductive.

Proactive Interventions: Curating the Conversation

Customers give particular weight to the views of other customers. Amazon, the online bookstore, has been particularly effective in curating customer conversations.

> Visitors to Amazon's Web site often go directly to the customer reviews, and only later come back to look at what the publisher or the author said about the book. Amazon's role as a marketer has been to create an environment where the customers' stories are likely to be told. Amazon posts negative as well as positive reviews, knowing that its authenticity as a neutral convener of different viewpoints will be strengthened.

In a different context, Ford was able to seed customer conversations in launching a new model car.

> In launching the Ford Fiesta, the firm initiated a marketing campaign in the spring of 2009: Fiesta Movement. It distributed a hundred examples of European Fiestas to bloggers who used popular Internet sites to share stories of their experiences. Subsequently Ford brought the cars to public venues nationwide to offer 100,000 test drives over eight months. In Chicago, it offered a free shuttle service in Chicago from a site near the Union Station commuter rail terminal to Grant Park.

In March 2010, Ford worked with American Idol to promote the Ford Fiesta in North America. The final twelve contestants of the show were given an opportunity to create their own custom graphics on a Ford Fiesta. The personalized Fiestas were revealed on the show, and fans were given the chance to win one of the personalized cars.

In the campaign, Ford's focus is not on telling its own stories but rather creating opportunities and forums where customers can share their stories with other potential customers.

Procter & Gamble has used the approach to market feminine care products to girls:

In the Web site beinggirl.com, Procter & Gamble has created a space where girls can share their own experiences of the problems they face in growing up, while also learning about feminine care products. To be successful, the site has to preserve a delicate balance: if the site ever becomes dominated by messages aimed at selling products, its visitors are likely to vanish.

These examples of branding and marketing are quite different from the one-way messaging of twentieth-century advertising, in which a seller relentlessly sent advertising messages regardless of whether the listener wanted to hear them. The messages might have been a narrative or an abstract proposition, but the interaction of speaker and listener was absent. As a result, the listener was rarely engaged by the communication, and the results of these communications were increasingly ineffective.

Branding and marketing in the new world of social media is akin to authentic storytelling in that it is as much about story listening as it is about story "telling." Authentic storytelling is an interactive process, in which the response of the listener provides guidance to the teller as to how to proceed with the performance. A master storyteller practices deep listening even as the story is being told and adjusts the pace and the flow of the story to the response of the listeners. The interaction between teller and listeners tends to create a relationship as the two human beings share the experience of following a story.

Communicating the Brand Internally

Effective marketing starts with understanding the customer, then deciding the character of the firm, and reflecting that decision authentically in what the firm says and does. Authenticity means owning up to what you are and what you stand for. "If the company is posing, then the people who are the company will have to pose as well. If, on the other hand, the company is comfortable living up to what it is, then an enormous cramp in the corporate body goes away."[21]

When Bill George took over as CEO of Medtronic, he would meet with doctors who used the firm's products and attended operations. He discovered some gaps between what Medtronic said it was doing and what it actually did. George recalls:

> Not all of these early experiences were positive. I vividly recall an angioplasty case where the doctor was using a Medtronic balloon catheter to open up clogged arteries. The product literally fell apart in the doctor's hands as he was threading it through the patient's arteries....
> After the case, the sales rep told me he had seen this happen several times before. He had filed reports on the defects, but heard nothing back. We counted seven organizations his reports had to go through before it got to the people who designed the products in the first place. Something was terribly wrong here. In taking specific issues raised by our customers back to Medtronic's engineers, I found a high level of ignorance and even denial that the problems actually existed. Why? ... The engineers were not spending any time with customers and were insulated from customer problems.[22]

To George's credit, he didn't like what he was hearing, and he committed Medtronic to a ten-year program of making customer and patient focus central to the way the company operated.[23]

Communicating the Brand Narrative Within the Firm

Even delivering on an existing brand narrative usually requires a concerted creative effort throughout the organization. If an airline, for instance, decides that the most cost-effective way to deliver a "considerate" service is to speed up its check-in and security clearance procedures, it might strive for performance levels dramatically exceeding those of competitors—for example, a two-minute check-in and a five-minute security clearance. Persuading the whole organization to embrace and deliver on those goals will be more difficult than dreaming up the marketing message.[24]

Changing a brand in a major way is a heroic undertaking. As noted, when Bill George at Medtronic decided to refocus the firm on the customer, he committed it to a ten-year program of change—a realistic assessment of the time required.

As Doc Searls and David Weinberger write in *The Cluetrain Manifesto*:

> A company can certainly try to be what it's not. But the market conversation will expose the fakery.... Of course companies and products can change their identities (and even their natures) over time.... But such changes generally are gradual and often painful. If they are too rapid and too easy, the market conversation will be merciless in exposing the phoniness it sniffs.... If a company is genuinely confused about what it is, there's an easy way to find out: listen to what your market says you are. If it's not to your liking, think long and hard before assuming that the market is wrong. If you don't like what you're hearing, the market task is not to change the market's idea of who you are but actually to change who you are. And that can take a generation.[25]

How does one persuade the staff of an organization to align their words and actions with the brand narrative?

- If the brand narrative entails a major change, springboard stories will be needed to spark the change (Chapter Three), and a sustained period of innovation may be necessary (Chapter Eleven).

- In return for employees' committing to the brand values of the company, the leader should be looking for ways to draw on the collaboration of the staff, as discussed in Chapter Seven.

- In carrying out the change, the leader needs to take an interactive approach, as discussed in Chapter Twelve.

Base Your Brand Narrative on Your Values

Ultimately the story of who your company is depends on the values it has. It is to this issue that I turn in Chapter Six.

TEMPLATE FOR CRAFTING THE STORY OF THE CHARACTER OF THE FIRM

1. What is the specific aspect of the firm that you want to communicate with the story? Its client intimacy? Its operational excellence? Its innovation and creativity? Something else?

2. Think of an incident where this aspect was exhibited. Describe it briefly, including the date and place where it happened.

3. Is the incident truly typical of the way the firm always operates?

4. Who is the single protagonist in the story? Is the single protagonist typical of your specific audience? If not, can the story be told from the point of view of such a protagonist?

5. Is the story relevant to that audience?

6. Does the story fully embody the specific aspect of the firm that you are aiming to highlight?

7. Does the story make clear what would have happened without the specific aspect?

8. Has the story been stripped of any unnecessary detail? Are there any scenes with more than two characters?

9. Does the story have an authentically happy ending? Can it be told so that it does have such an ending?

10. Is the story distinctive of the firm? Does it differentiate the firm from its competitors?

11. Is the story linked to the brand narrative?

    - Can you show that the story is characteristic of the brand? Are there statistics, ratings, or awards, for example, to draw on?

    - Can you show why this story is characteristic of the organization? Is staffing or training relevant here, for example?

    - Can you show how the story is characteristic of the organization's processes, values, or something else?

TRANSMIT YOUR VALUES

Using Narrative to Instill Organizational Values

> "Acting on what matters is, ultimately, a political stance, one whereby we declare we are accountable for the world around us and are willing to pursue what we define as important, independent of whether it is in demand, or has market value.
>
> **Peter Block[1]**

Alisdair MacIntyre opens his classic book on ethics, *After Virtue*, with a startling assertion: our entire civilization has forgotten what ethical values really are.[2] The language still exists. References to ethical values are thrown about in everyday speech, company policy statements, and political campaigns. But the context that gave those fragments meaning is no longer available. "We possess indeed simulacra of morality," says MacIntyre, "we continue to use many of the key expressions. But we have—very largely, if not entirely—lost our comprehension, both theoretical and practical, of morality."

Douglas Smith, in *On Value and Values*, suggests that this has happened because society has lost sight of the importance of ethical *values* and instead pursued *value*: "Value arises in conversations about economics, finance, shopping, investment, business, and markets. People worry about getting value for money or shareholder value or market value. They use value to describe business or economic prospects. Value connotes a pointed estimation of current or anticipated worth never too distant from monetary equivalence. There is no value that is not a dollar value."[3]

Smith notes that the meaning of the plural *values* is something very different from the singular *value*: "Values are estimations not of worth but of worthwhileness. Unlike value, talk of values ignores money; it opines on timeless appraisals instead of transient ones. There is a deep backward- and forward-looking quality to values. If value is what makes us wealthy, values, we assume and regularly assert, are what make us human."[4]

DISTINGUISH THE DIFFERENT TYPES OF VALUES

When Smith argues that society has lost sight of values, he is talking of ethical values. However, even people or firms whose conduct doesn't appear to reflect ethical values have values of some kind. Four kinds of values are at play in organizations today:

- The values of the robber barons
- The values of the hardball strategists
- The values of the pragmatists
- Genuinely ethical values

The Values of the Robber Barons

At one end of the spectrum are organizations run by robber barons—firms whose only value is to crush the competition by whatever means. For robber barons, nothing is too precious to be set aside for the sake of winning—even legality. This might include Andrew Carnegie sending armed Pinkertons and gunboats into mill towns to fight the unions, or the predators at Enron creating phony partnerships to bolster the stock price. The robber barons have no values other than bare-faced greed. They practice a kind of storytelling—lying and cheating in breach of the law—that has a long and regrettable history.

The Values of the Hardball Strategists

Only half a step away from the robber barons are the hardball strategists celebrated by George Stalk Jr. and Rob Lachenauer in their *Harvard Business Review* article, "Five Killer Strategies for Trouncing the Competition." Stalk and Lachenauer provide a remarkably clear statement of hardball values.[5] Hardball strategists avoid illegality, but in all other respects they pursue a single-minded focus on winning.

According to Stalk and Lachenauer, in the dog-eat-dog world of business, hardball strategists disdain "squishy issues—leadership, corporate culture, customer care, knowledge management, talent management, employee empowerment and the like."[6] These strategists play rough and don't apologize for it. They stay just within the lines of legality, but venture closer to the boundary than others dare. Where feasible, they don't hesitate to bend the law to their advantage.

Hardball strategists take pride in being lean and mean. They are not willing to just hurt their rivals: they enjoy hurting them and watching them squirm. Hardball strategists may on occasion refrain from taking action that overtly hurts competitors, even if it is strictly speaking legal—not because it is wrong but rather because it might elicit the wrath of regulators or special interest groups and so get in the way of winning. In the end, for hardball strategists as for robber barons, winning is everything. It is not what is right that matters; it's what you can get away with.

For the hardball strategist, values are not something to be lived on a day-to-day basis but rather some kind of management gadget to be introduced like new accounting software or a new business process—the sort of thing to be continued if it adds to the bottom line or discarded if it doesn't. Hardball strategists are the heirs of Machiavelli: they live in an amoral world and, like the robber barons, have no worthwhile values to transmit.

According to Henry Mintzberg, hardball strategists represent a greater threat to society than robber barons do: "Criminality is the tip of the iceberg, easy enough to address in courts of law once exposed. The real problem is the legal corruption—the antisocial behavior below the surface of public awareness yet above the letter of the law. That is far more insidious, not only because it is more difficult to identify and correct but also because we are now so inundated by it."[7]

The Values of the Pragmatists

Then there are organizations that are pursuing instrumental values, that is, values that are a central part of the organization's business strategy. These organizations practice their values year in and year out. They live them on a day-to-day basis. Often the organization has been like this from the outset. Take, for example, the discount supermarket chain Costco Wholesale Corporation:

> Costco pays its workers more than Wal-Mart's minimum wage and gives them health insurance. It passes on cost savings to its customers, even when it has a chance to make windfall profits. That, coupled with a business strategy that includes a mix of higher-margin products, enables Costco to keep its labor costs lower than Wal-Mart's as a percentage of sales. The fact that the CEO, James Sinegal, the founder of the company, takes only a modest salary, and sticks to his course despite criticism from Wall Street suggests that he really does believe in the values of the firm as a way of life.[8]

The Costco values constitute central elements of its successful enterprise. They are instrumental to the success of the business model. Thus, if Sinegal—or his successors—were to stop valuing employees and start introducing the penny-pinching, downsizing, outsourcing, pension-threatening practices of some other companies, the business model itself would be undermined.[9]

Jim Collins and Jerry Porras in *Built to Last* argue that a key step in building a visionary company entails having a set of core values—enduring tenets that go beyond operating practices and are not compromised for financial gain or short-term expediency. According to Collins and Porras, the content of those tenets—which might include, in the case of Philip Morris, freedom of choice to smoke cigarettes—is less important than the fact of having any values at all. Their research indicates that being a hardball strategist isn't enough: instrumental values are a key element of long-term organizational survival.[10]

The range of issues on which it may be necessary for a successful corporation to have instrumental values has tended to grow over the past several decades. Thus, the movement known as corporate and social responsibility has been successful in getting some organizations to take a look at the implications of corporate responsibility. The public outcry led by Greenpeace at Shell's proposal to sink the Brent Spar oil rig in the deep waters of the North Sea when it was no longer needed led to major inroads into Shell's business in Europe and major changes in the way Shell subsequently approached environmental issues.[11]

Nike was arguably no different from a thousand other firms that market high-end consumer products through cost-efficient global supply chains, but the sweatshop labor practices of its contractors presented an attractive target to nongovernmental organizations (NGOs), which were able to generate significant adverse publicity. Nike went through a sequence of positions, going from initial defensiveness to legal compliance to embedding the issue in managerial processes, then integrating the issue into the company's strategy as an element of competitive advantage, and finally moving to a position of leadership in promoting broad industry participation in universal labor standards.[12]

NGO campaigns like these have led to increased reporting on nonfinancial issues.[13] Although it may not be clear whether good environmental and social practices always create value for shareholders, it is now evident that bad ones can destroy it.[14] Since the brand is often the most valuable asset on the balance sheet, firms are particularly vulnerable to bad news about their values. British Telecom, for instance, calculates that its social and environmental performance accounts for more than a quarter of its overall business and reputation, which is the second biggest factor driving change in its customer satisfaction rates.[15]

Genuinely Ethical Values

It is also possible to envisage a kind of organization that is driven by explicitly ethical values as a principal motivating force, values that go beyond what is necessary for the business strategy (such as winning in the marketplace, innovation, and customer focus). Ethical values imply viewing the staff of the organization not simply as a shifting population of individuals that haphazardly come and go as the result of unpredictable market forces that bear on the organization, but rather as a community of human beings to whose welfare they are reciprocally committed. They imply treating their stakeholders as ends in themselves, not merely as a means to make money.[16] They entail treating the environment not merely as something to be exploited for profit but as a heritage to be protected.[17] Being socially and environmentally responsible isn't simply a trick of predicting which issues are going to be politically significant; it involves acting on something that is lived year in and year out—something worthwhile in itself. Such companies could lay claim to having values that go beyond what is instrumental for winning in the marketplace—values that possess a genuine moral basis.

Are there examples of organizations pursuing genuinely ethical values? Some suggest that Southwest Airlines represents such a company. Its values are embedded in the organization—part of its fabric, its very strategy. The values are employee-centric and focus on providing value to customers while also having fun. Over several decades, chairman Herb Kelleher has won the trust and loyalty of his staff through consistently effective and caring behavior.[18]

Starbucks is another organization that has styled itself as socially responsible. It purchases and roasts coffee and sells coffees and other beverages in a network of some forty-five hundred retail stores around the world. From the outset, it has committed itself to providing a good work environment for a diverse workforce and to contributing positively to the community and the environment. It has extended health benefits to both staff members and their partners, and it provides financial aid to staff for extraordinary needs not covered by insurance, as well as stock options for staff who work more than twenty hours a week.[19]

Google set out to "do no evil," a principle that is more easily articulated than implemented. Should Google agree to censor its search capabilities to users in China? Should Google take advantage of the massive data that it possesses on the habits and inclinations of its users and use them as a marketing tool? Google continues to agonize about these issues.[20]

Southwest, Starbucks, and Google have their critics. Some would say that Southwest Airlines isn't consistently caring toward all its staff. NGOs have urged Starbucks to do more to contribute to a sustainable environment. Others argue that Google is losing its moral compass. But these three companies do appear to have an explicit commitment to doing the right thing and to be delivering in some areas on that commitment. They represent a contrast to many other companies where no explicit effort to pursue an ethical approach is evident.

What's the difference between ethical values and instrumental values? One simple litmus test for distinguishing whether an organization's values are moral or merely instrumental, that is, essentially amoral, is to observe the language in use in the organization, which can shed light on whether the organization views its own staff merely as means to its ends or also as ends in themselves. If, for instance, people employed by the organization are referred to as "human resources" rather than "people," or "staff," this can indicate that they are being viewed within the organization as elements to be measured, developed, mined, exploited, and ultimately disposed of, without any sense of reciprocity. Other indicative language includes describing laid-off staffers as "fat" that has been trimmed or "deadwood" that has been cut.

ETHICS IN ACTION

A genuinely ethical community has three basic components. The first is *trust*: the general expectation among members that their fellows will behave ethically toward them. The second is *loyalty*: acceptance of the obligation to refrain from breaching one another's trust and to fulfill the duties entailed by accepting that trust. The third is *solidarity:* caring for other people's interests and being ready to take action on behalf of others, even if it conflicts with personal interests.[21]

Can organizations stick to ethical values and still survive in the marketplace? One entrepreneur who set out on such a path was Anita Roddick, the founder of The Body Shop. She grew up in a large Italian immigrant family in a small town in blue-collar England, where she was inculcated with an intense work ethic and an irreverent, entrepreneurial spirit. Though she admitted to having opened her first Body Shop as a way to make ends meet, Roddick developed the company around her belief that it is more important than ever before for business to assume a moral leadership in society. Her concern for protecting the environment and indigenous people's cultures, and her vision of all of life as interconnected, for many years inspired the growth of the company. Roddick exhibited passionate activism in building community in her determination to make it as a woman and succeed in business.[22] Roddick died in 2007; time will tell how consistently the firm continues to pursue her philosophy.

Ben & Jerry's was another organization that many saw as following an ethical approach to business issues. But now that the firm has been taken over by Unilever, some, including the founders of the company, wonder whether it is still pursuing genuinely ethical values or whether it has been engulfed by the instrumental values of its parent company.[23]

Privately owned organizations like Tom's of Maine may find it easier than publicly held organizations to stick to ethical values.[24] In 1974 Tom Chappell and his wife, Kate, used a $5,000 loan to found Tom's of Maine, a company that makes products using only natural ingredients. By 1981 the company was registering $1.5 million in sales. Despite this success, Chappell was unhappy; he decided to recreate his company in a way that would encourage respect for the individual, the community, and the environment. Tom's of Maine became the leading producer of environment-friendly personal care products in the United States, and Chappell used his personal quest for meaning as the basis for a new management style that aspires to combine spiritual values with commercial success.[25]

Companies with an explicit commitment to implementing genuinely ethical values are rare today. Their very rarity corroborates the concerns mentioned at the outset of this chapter: it's possible that a whole generation has all but forgotten what having ethical values might entail.

To the hardball strategists of Wall Street, an organization consistently committed to implementing ethical values is acting stupidly and exhibits an insufficient commitment to enhancing shareholder value. Any publicly owned company that overtly pursues such a strategy risks being assessed as underperforming, and thus becoming a target for either removal of the management team or a takeover so that new leadership can be inserted to focus more sharply on maximizing shareholder return.[26]

Writing in the *Harvard Business Review*,[27] Roger Martin suggests that the era in which the purpose of every firm is to maximize shareholders' value is coming to a close. Martin notes that pursuing the maximization of shareholder value as a goal suffers from inherent internal contradictions. The harder the firm pushes to increase shareholder value, the more likely it will make moves that actually hurt the shareholders. Martin argues we are now entering an era of customer capitalism. In this new era, the purpose of a firm is to serve clients. If firms do that well, Martin argues, benefits for shareholders will follow.

Leaders thus need to think clearly about what kinds of values they are talking about before they start to use storytelling as a tool to transmit them. Declaring values that are not consistently acted on may be worse than not declaring any values at all.

Distinguish Personal from Corporate Values

People have their personal values and organizations have their corporate values. Sometimes they are the same, say, accountability or equality. Sometimes they are different, as with creativity or forgiveness. Sometimes personal and corporate values have a substantial overlap, and the overlap is mutually reinforcing. Sometimes there is not much overlap at all.

The discrepancy may arise because employees have not yet understood or accepted the values the corporation is pursuing. It may also arise because of a mismatch between the limited instrumental values that the corporation has adopted and the more extensive ethical values that often drive individuals. Whatever the cause, lack of overlap between corporate and individual values may generate dissonance. In the end, each person must find a personal relationship to the organizational values that are important to the company, whether those values are similar to or different from his or her own.[28]

Clarifying values, for instance in a workshop on the subject, can lead people to understand how they are personally connected with the organization's values—or not. This can help clear the air and enable individuals to decide what to do. Some individuals may, on becoming aware of the lack of overlap between personal and corporate values, decide to devote themselves to the company and its goals, adjusting their personal values to coincide with those of the company. Others may opt to move on. The dissonance between their personal and the corporate values may be such that they realize why they cannot stay with the company. They knew they were unhappy but didn't know the reason. Now it is clear to them. This can be a win for both the individual and the corporation, because the employees who are not aligned with the company's values leave, while the ones who stay may have a deeply felt connection to the company.

Some might decide—heroically—to try to work to change the company's values and urge the company to become more ethical in its practices. However, changing a company's values is a Herculean task with significant risk to the participants. At best, it will take many years and many allies to accomplish, including strong support from the top of the organization.[29]

Still others may recognize the lack of overlap between the corporate values and their own personal values, and decide to live with the difference. They don't tilt at windmills, but neither do they check their values at the door when they go to work. In its negative form, this stance may result in cynicism toward the corporation and its values (or lack thereof). In its positive form, it may result in individuals' embodying their own high ethical standards in the way that they conduct themselves at work. Indeed, some writers argue that the workplace should be a testing ground for the expression of ethical values. Personal example can encourage others to aspire higher.[30]

Distinguish Operational Values from Espoused Values

Whether instrumental or ethical, values are not just another management gadget. They are something to be lived, to be embodied in action.

It's easy to fall into the trap of espousing values that never become operational. *Espoused values* are ones that we think we should have. *Operational values* are the ones actually working in our lives. Sometimes there's a huge gap between the two. This is particularly true of organizations. Most value statements or lists of values that companies put together are dead on arrival and end up as wallpaper, just as Enron's "Statement of Values" failed to become the operational values of that failed corporation.[31]

Human beings are exquisitely sensitive to inconsistencies between what is said and what is done. Companies where executives purport to have certain values but don't consistently act on the values they profess end up with espoused values. The hypocrisy involved in espousing values that are not acted on generates significant distrust. The following example is typical:

> On his first day at work, a newly appointed CEO of a large international organization sent a letter to all staff announcing that he looked on them as family, although any external criticism of the organization would not be tolerated. The idea that staff would be treated as family was well received, while the remark about external criticism caused concern. Over the next several years, he systematically eliminated more than a thousand of the most senior and experienced managers and staff, particularly anyone who dared challenge his views, while he himself repeatedly bad-mouthed the staff of the organization to outside audiences. Not surprisingly, the values of "treating staff like family" and "abstaining from external criticism of the organization" never jelled as organizational values.

If companies want to embody certain values, then they have to begin by ascertaining what values are currently operational. Only then can they decide which values they want to change and how to go about it.

Changing values isn't quick or easy. As Karen Dietz, former executive director of the National Storytelling Network, told me, "Companies often say that innovation is a value, but in assessments of operational values, innovation ends up near the bottom of the list. So the gap between the espoused value and operational value is huge. If the company decides that innovation really is important, then they are looking at a multiyear effort to influence that value and get it embodied in the organization's operational values."

If Values Are Absent, Take Action to Reestablish Them

Sometimes a firm faces a values bankruptcy even though it remains solvent in financial terms. Such a case was the giant conglomerate Tyco, which was wracked by a spectacular corporate governance scandal. Systematic illegality and fraud at the very top of the organization had created a climate of uncertainty and a reputation that was toxic. Yet Tyco did not implode like Enron. Beneath the cloud of scandal, Tyco had solidly profitable manufacturing businesses providing a broad range of products, including duct tape, sprinkler systems, industrial valves, and security systems. It was a $35 billion company with 260,000 employees.

When the fraud was discovered, a new management team was installed, and part of their reform effort involved obvious structural measures: separating finance from operations, appointing a credible board of directors with real power, and conducting exhaustive audits. But the more difficult challenge was changing the hearts and minds of the people who worked there. How could they instill a new set of values? How could they establish the honesty and integrity that had been singularly lacking in the very recent past? Although the vast majority of the company's employees hadn't been involved in any wrongdoing, the scandals at the top of the firm had established an atmosphere where anything goes.

When new management took over, in addition to establishing new governance procedures, they set about trying to change the ethical climate and reestablish the firm's values.[32] They developed a guide whose intent was not simply to teach people to spout the right answers to obviously worded questions but rather to acknowledge that the issues are often nuanced and complex. How would you know if you're moving into territory where ethical judgment was required? How would you notice when things were beginning to smell bad?

The Tyco "Guide to Ethical Conduct" uses simple narrative vignettes to explain the meaning of abstractions like "fraud" or "inappropriate political activity."

Fraud looks like ...

- *Jordan's client takes him out for dinner after he makes a sales presentation at the client's company. Jordan then expenses the same US$65 dinner.*

- *Yin, a software training specialist, makes copies of software programs for use on her computer at home and gives copies to all her family and friends.*

- *Sophia, a comptroller, loans her employees money from the company, charges them interest and deposits their repayments into her personal bank account.*[33]

Tyco managers did more than distribute the guide. They also created six short videos dramatizing the situations, three of them set in an office and three in a factory. Employees gathered in several thousand Tyco locations not only to get their copies of the guide but also to see the videos and begin an ongoing dialogue about the content.

Making values explicit was a first preparatory step. Making the values operational comes through action.

Establish Values Through Action

Leaders establish values through action. Thus, the publication of Tyco's "Guide to Ethical Conduct" will have no impact at all unless it is backed up by the consistent action of the management.

For values to take hold, leaders have to live them on a sustained, consistent basis. The implication is, "Look, if I can do this, so can you." I experienced this myself as a manager in the World Bank:

In 1990, when I was appointed director of the World Bank's Southern Africa Department, I inherited an excellent staff, though attitudes to work-life balance were poor. Many staff members often worked in the office until midnight, in part because my predecessor had also worked late most nights. Part of the dynamic was that people had wanted him to see that they were there late. I had no desire to stay late at work, as I wanted to spend my evenings with my wife and my three-year-old daughter.

As a result, in my first meeting with the department managers and staff, I announced that I would be leaving every day around 5:30 P.M. and I encouraged all of them to do likewise. My subordinates looked at me in disbelief and suggested that this would not be possible: there were always last-minute demands and deadlines that prevented them from finishing the work in the regulation 9-to-5:30 period. But I was adamant: I would leave no later than 6:00 P.M. I would answer e-mail from home if necessary, but I wouldn't be physically in the office.

And so I began, day after day, leaving at around 5:30 P.M. At first, no one believed my story. Almost everyone continued to stay late, amid underground rumblings that I would soon be forced to work as late as my predecessor. But I continued to leave at least by 6:00 P.M. And staff could also see that I answered e-mail promptly from home, so that no substantive question remained unanswered. And if anyone wanted to discuss an issue face-to-face, I made myself available during the day for anyone who wanted to drop by.

After I'd spent several months on the job, as the story about my not working late in the office was confirmed by my actions, the number of people who stayed late fell significantly. It slowly dawned on people that I was not going to participate in the late shift in person, so there would be no one to observe their late-night dedication, and more and more of them went home at the regular time.

This also meant that they worked more effectively during the day, as extended lunches and lengthy coffee breaks gave way to a focus on getting the job done. With only eight hours available, people now used their time more wisely.

> *Yet a few hard-core late-nighters persisted, lamenting my unwillingness to join them. When they complained to me directly, I would tell them to "get a dog," "develop an interest in stamps," or "find a significant other"—anything to create an alternative source of interest in their lives beyond the office. Eventually everyone went home.*

Thus, merely telling the story of my values in itself had little effect. It was only when people saw that my actions coincided with the story that the value of proper work-life balance became established as a value of the department.

TRANSMITTING VALUES THROUGH NARRATIVE

Once values have been established, they can be transmitted by narrative. In this area, conventional management techniques are useless, if not counterproductive:

- Giving people instructions to be ethical or putting up posters with lists of values just doesn't register.

- Talking about sanctions for wrongdoing gets people's backs up.

- Issuing corporate value statements that require ethical behavior from employees and loyalty to the firm but offer no reciprocal commitment from the firm to the employees typically elicits cynicism.

In fact, transmitting values is one of the trickier management challenges. That's because it's easy to slip into moralizing and dictating behavior. We've all had the experience of a parent saying, "I know better than you, so do what I say." Most of us at some level resist moralizing and the command to comply. Moralizing is easy to discredit because as human beings, we are not perfect and our moralizing sets us up to be knocked down for our own imperfections.

Work can be dictated, but behavior only influenced. So how can leaders transmit values but not have them sound preachy or arrogant or parental? Telling a story embodying the values and letting the listeners themselves see the point can be effective. A light touch is desirable, without ramming home the point with an abstract label or a moral. For example, Jim Sinegal, cofounder, CEO, and president of Costco Wholesale, regularly uses stories to convey Costco's corporate values. He retold one of his favorites, the salmon story to Evelyn Clark, as she recounts in *Around the Corporate Campfire:*

> In 1996 we were selling between $150,000 and $200,000 worth of salmon fillets company-wide every week at $5.99 a pound. Then our buyers were able to get an improved product with belly fat, back fins, and collarbones removed, at a better price. As a result, we reduced our retail price to $5.29. So they improved the product and lowered the price.
>
> The buyers weren't finished with the improvements, though. Next our buyers negotiated for a product with the pin bone out and all of the skin removed, and it was at an even better price, which enabled us to lower our price to $4.99 a pound. Then, because we had continued to grow and had increased our sales volume, we were able to buy direct from Canadian and Chilean farms, which resulted in an even lower price of $4.79.
>
> Over a five-year period, a significantly enhanced product was lowered from $5.99 to $4.79. The final improvement was that the belly was removed, and the customers got the top fillet, and price further reduced to $3.99 a pound....
>
> We've used that story so much as a teaching tool that I've had other buyers in the company, such as a clothing buyer in Canada, come up to me and say, "Hey, I've got a salmon story to tell you." The story explains the essence of what we do."[34]

Sinegal tells and retells the salmon story because it exemplifies Costco's core values of delivering value to customers through high-quality products at low prices. It also demonstrates the results that can be achieved by staying focused on the organization's values.

Avoid Moralizing

Don't begin the story by naming the value. For example, starting with, "Let me tell you a story about courage," is likely to be ineffective. People will assume you are going to moralize and they will stop listening. Besides, it's also telegraphing the ending, which any good storyteller avoids since it removes any interest in the story.

Similarly, don't end by saying, "So you must do this too." Instead, the leader has the opportunity at the end of the story to say, "And this is what it means to me," or "And this is what I learned from that experience," or "These are the decisions I've made because of that."

Transmitting values through a narrative allows a leader to demonstrate a particular value and provide the meaning of that value, while at the same time allowing others to adopt their own interpretations of that value. It also allows the listeners the opportunity to reflect on their relationship with that value and understand more about it.

Thus, companies like 3M use stories to communicate the value they attach to innovation. The story of the invention of the sticky note has become legendary:

> It took five years from the time Dr. Spence Silver invented the peculiar substance—an adhesive that didn't stick very much—to the time a new-product development researcher named Art Fry came up with the concept that turned into the Post-It note. Recalling his frustration at trying to keep his place in his church choir hymnal, Fry realized that Silver's "failed" adhesive could make for a wonderfully reliable bookmark.[35]

What is less well known is that the innovation stories 3M tells put emphasis less on single serendipitous flashes of insight like this and more on a sustained effort involved in making innovation actually happen. Even after Fry's insight, it was still a struggle to get his idea accepted within 3M. Thus, the 3M story continues:

> There remained skeptics within 3M as attempts were made to launch this new product. Engineering and production people told Fry that Post-It notes would pose considerable processing and coating difficulties and would create much waste. Fry's response demonstrated the approach of the true innovator and saw the obstacles as an opportunity for 3M to excel.

Market research (always difficult with revolutionary new products) was another hurdle. Who would pay for a product that seemed to be competing with free scrap paper? Despite initial decisions to kill the program, Geoff Nicholson (a development manager for new products) persuaded the division vice president to come with him to Richmond, Virginia, and pound the streets to see if they could sell the product. They did, and Post-It notes went on to become 3M's most famous product.[36]

More recent stories at 3M have focused on career-long innovation. Such stories aim at helping 3M staff understand the importance of challenging and encouraging one another to look for innovative ways to meet customer needs and solve customer problems.

Use Parables to Illustrate the Conflict of Values

We can learn a great deal from the religious leaders who for thousands of years have transmitted values by way of parables, such as Jesus Christ's parable of the talents:

A man about to travel to a far country called his servants together, and put them in charge of his property. To one, he gave five thousand gold coins (the original word talents is still used metaphorically today), to another two thousand, and to another one thousand, to each according to his ability. Then he left on the journey.

The man who had received the five thousand gold coins traded with them and made an additional five thousand gold coins. Similarly the man who had received two thousand coins made another two thousand. But the man who had received only one thousand coins went and dug a hole in the earth, and hid the money.

After a long time the master of those servants came back and settled accounts with them. The man who had received five thousand gold coins came and brought another five thousand coins, saying, "Master, you gave me five thousand coins: look, I have earned another five thousand." His master said to him, "Well done, my good and faithful servant: you have been faithful over a few things. I will put you in charge of many things."

The man who had received two thousand gold coins came and said, "Master, you gave me two thousand coins: look, I have earned another two thousand beside those." His master said, "Well done, good and faithful servant; you have been faithful over a few things, I will put you in charge of many things."

Then he who had received the one thousand gold coins came and said, "Master, I knew that you are a hard man, reaping where you have not sown, and gathering where you have not scattered seed, and I was afraid. So I went and hid your gold coins in the earth. So here, I am giving back what is yours."

His master answered, "You wicked and lazy servant. You knew that I reap where I do not sow, and gather where I have not scattered seed: you ought therefore to have put my money with the money changers, and then at my coming I should have received my own money back with interest. Therefore take the thousand gold coins from him, and give it to the man who has ten thousand coins. For to every one that has something, more shall be given, and he shall have more than enough: but from him that has nothing, even the little shall be taken away from him. As for this useless servant, throw him outside into the darkness. There he will cry and gnash his teeth.'[37]

A parable begins with a narrative imagining—the understanding of a complex of objects, events, actors, and objectives as organized by a story. It then combines story with projection—one story is projected onto another.[38] The parable of talents might be projected onto various activities—the effort to be a better person, the investment of money, the education of children, or the launching of a change program in an organization.

A parable affords an infinite number of applications, as different readers or listeners use projection from the base story to imagine a new story in their own contexts. As a result, a parable tends to have great longevity: the parables of the Bible are still going strong, some two thousand years after they were created.

What makes the Bible's parables more memorable than Tyco's simple vignettes is the conflict of different values. Tyco's vignettes explicate a single value. The Bible's parables typically shed light on a conflict of values. How could a master praise his dishonest manager? How could a Samaritan be the hero of a story? What king would take to the streets to invite anyone he could find, good and bad alike, to come to his son's wedding? How could you take the money of the man who had only one thousand gold coins and give it to the man who already had ten thousand gold coins?

Thus, one of Jim Sinegal's stories is a parable that shows how Costco resolves the conflict between two competing values: serving the customer and making a profit. The story, as told to Evelyn Clark in *Around the Corporate Campfire*, is as follows:

> *We were selling Calvin Klein jeans for $29.99, and we were selling every pair we could get our hands on. One competitor matched our price, but they had only four or five pairs in each store, and we had 500 or 600 pairs on the shelf. We all of a sudden got our hands on several million pairs of Calvin Klein jeans and we bought them at a very good price. It meant that, within the constraints of our markup, which is limited to 14 percent on any item, we had to sell them for $22.99. That was $7 lower than we had been selling every single pair for.*
>
> *Of course, we concluded that we could have sold all of them (about four million pairs) for that higher price almost as quickly as we sold them at $22.99, but there was no question that we would mark them at $22.99 because that's our philosophy.*
>
> *I use that as an example because it would be so tempting for a buyer to go with the higher price for a very quick $28 million in additional profits, but ours didn't. That's an example of how we keep faith with the customer.[39]*

In telling such a parable, Sinegal risks Wall Street's wrath for not maximizing profit in the short run, and that is the point of the story. Sinegal stands by his values, having decided that this is the kind of company Costco is going to be. In doing so, he is following Friedrich Nietzsche's dictum: "Become who you are!"[40]

Tell the Values Story in a Minimalist Fashion

Although parables have an ancient lineage, they don't follow the principles of traditional storytelling laid down by Aristotle. These stories are typically very simple and one-dimensional, like European folk tales. There are few context-setting details, though the context that is established needs to seem relevant to the listeners.

Like springboard stories, the parables are told in a minimalist fashion—with no character development or attempt to set the scene. The lack of detail makes listeners imagine the details of the story and so involves them actively in the telling.

Tell a Timeless But Believable Story

Stories that transmit values are usually set in some kind of timeless past.

Unlike springboard stories, the parables tend to be imaginary narratives—they're not presented as true stories that purport to have actually happened at a particular time and place. Thus, we learn in the parable of the talents about "a man who went on a journey." Did the man ever exist? Did he ever go on the journey? It hardly matters. What counts are the values embedded in the story.

The facts of such tales can be hypothetical, but they must be believable:

> A colleague who worked for IBM recalled the story he heard about the CEO of IBM who was refused entry into the building because he had forgotten his security badge. The story was told as if it was the current CEO. Later on, he discovered that the CEO in question was Tom Watson in 1936. But as it happened, I heard exactly the same story several decades ago in the World Bank told about Robert McNamara. Which version of the story was true? It hardly matters. If it reflects current practice and belief in the organization, a story conveys the firm's values.

The parable may have either a positive tone as in the parable of the sower (some of whose seeds fell on poor ground but many on good ground where they prospered) or a negative tone as in the parable of the talents. The tone is less important in a parable than in a springboard story, since the aim is not to spark action but to solidify understanding of the values that are expected.

Find Values from Narratives or Narratives from Values

One way of exploring values is to work inductively and start with meaningful narratives and then figure out what the values may be.

People often have difficulty in answering direct questions as to what their values are or how they would rate a certain value on a scale of one to five. When formulated like this, values are abstractions. In reality, nobody walks around with a mental list of values in their mind, which they consult when deciding what to do. Values live in the actions that people engage in and the stories that they tell about those actions to try to make sense of them.

Here are some topics that can be used to prompt stories that reveal values:

- Occasions where you faced adversity
- Times when two values conflicted
- What you find most satisfying in working with your firm
- Something that showed you what your organization is really good at
- The worst thing that ever happened to you in your organization
- How a client or customer was badly treated but it eventually turned out well
- Your happiest day at work
- Something that your organization is good at but few people know about
- Something that showed you what you have to do to get ahead in your organization

Once you have told the story, then analyze it to see what values it reflects. For more, see the template at the end of this chapter.

Tell a Story About Someone You Admire

Asking people to tell stories about themselves is sometimes a little too intimate. One way of overcoming the discomfort is to ask them to share a story about someone who made a difference in their life:

- Someone they knew when they were growing up
- Someone in the organization who has meant a lot to them

- The person they admire most in your organization
- The person who is closest to them in the organization
- Someone who did better in the organization than anyone expected
- Someone who really taught them the ropes at the organization

Here is one such story, by Seth Kahan, author of *Getting Change Right*:

> This is a story that came to mind when you were talking about money and managing money. I didn't have a lot of experience with my family in managing money. But just after I got out of college, I wanted to start a business, and I needed to borrow $500. My parents wouldn't lend it to me. So I went to my Uncle Ben and explained what I was going to do with the money, and he lent me $500. And then the business foundered, and the money was gone. The business was gone, and I owed Uncle Ben this money.
>
> I didn't call him back. I just kind of severed the relationship. That's how I felt. After about six months of no payment, he called me. I remember he said: "You know, you just don't do this. This is not a way to treat someone who has trusted you. It's okay that you don't have the money. We can work out a way for you to get the money and pay it back over time. But it's not okay to break off the relationship like that." And that has stayed with me for my whole life, how one manages money, how one deals with people who have trusted you.

From this, the audience can begin to figure out that Seth Kahan is someone who:

- Establishes trust, since this is important to him in his relationships
- Works things out when they aren't going right
- Doesn't break off relationships just because things are difficult

When people tell stories about people they care about, they are revealing what they care about themselves.

Align Structure with Values

The transmission of values happens through both storytelling (capturing the hearts and minds of people and influencing behavior) and structure (establishing rules, regulations, and policies to support and reward innovation). When structure and values compete, structure always wins. It's therefore important to ensure that the organization's values and its formal arrangements are consistent.

Probably most important is the reward system. How much do advancement and compensation depend on bottom-line performance versus the other values? And what happens to top performers who don't live by those values? If promotions go to those who flout the espoused values, then staff get a clear message: the values are mere public relations pabulum and don't reflect the way things are done around here. At a minimum, the firm needs to make sure that the structure doesn't provide disincentives.

The question of providing positive incentives for implementing the company's values is trickier. Basically you want values to be inner driven, simply the way people live. You don't want people to be honest only if they are rewarded for it. But if an organization espouses an instrumental value like innovation and the compensation system rewards outstanding performance by operators who are not innovators, the arrangements will be perceived as a disincentive to innovate. Innovation is unlikely to flourish unless the compensation system is adjusted.[41]

Having Shared Values Enables People to Work Together

Shared values in an organization create trust. People have confidence that others will do what they say. Trust releases creative, uninhibited, innovative action toward other people. Members of the organization are more open toward others, readier to initiate interactions and enter into enduring relationships. People are released from the necessity of monitoring and controlling every move of others and constantly policing their behavior. Trust provides the basis for being able to work together with others, and it is to this issue that I turn in the next chapter.

A TEMPLATE FOR GENERATING VALUE NARRATIVES

1. What is the specific value that you would like to communicate: Provide quality service? Maintain our integrity? Honesty and public trust? Customer intimacy? Operational excellence? Innovation and creativity? Something else?

2. Think of another value that might be in tension with it. Profitability? Deadlines? Output targets?

3. Think of an incident where a conflict between two values arose. Describe it briefly.

4. Who is the single protagonist in the story?

5. Is the single protagonist typical of your specific audience? If not, can the story be told from the point of view of such a protagonist?

6. Does the story make clear the importance of your target value?

7. Has the story been stripped of any unnecessary detail?

8. Does the story link to the purpose to be achieved in telling it—communicating the specific value of your organization?

9. Can you show that the story is characteristic of the organization using, for example, statistics, ratings, awards, or something else?

10. Can you show why this story is characteristic of the organization? Is it about history, staffing, or training, for example?

11. Can you show how the story is characteristic of the organization's processes or values, for example?

GET OTHERS WORKING
TOGETHER

Using Narrative to Get Things Done
Collaboratively

> ❝ Stories are the language of communities. ❞
> **Garfield, Spring, and Cahill[1]**

When you start talking about teamwork in a traditional organization, don't be surprised if you hear a groan. That's because most people have been subjected to large quantities of fake collaboration. Yet working together is essential to organizational effectiveness. So let's go back to basics and review the four major ways in which human beings work together.

Work groups are the traditional subunits in an organization: departments or divisions. They entail people working on the same subject and sometimes in the same space. Each person has a defined responsibility, and each reports to a common supervisor. In many of these organizational subunits, people work alone at jobs that are independent. The work group is the most common form of arrangement, and it exists wherever you find organizations.

Teams are organizational groupings of people who are interdependent, share common goals, coordinate their activities to accomplish these goals, and share responsibility for the performance of the collectivity. There are many different varieties of teams—including ad hoc task forces, project management teams, functional operating teams, cross-functional teams, self-managed teams, and self-defining teams.[2] Many work groups are called teams but are teams in name only; they lack some or all of the attributes of a real team, namely, common goal, interdependence, and shared responsibility for performance.

In recent years, the concept of *community* has emerged in organizations. In its original sense, *community* meant a group of people in a specific geographical area who lived, worked, played, worshiped, and died together, sometimes over many generations. The word has now been extended to groupings of people who don't live or work in the same place but who share common interests, practices, and values. Thus scientific communities include scientists who may be scattered around the world, but who pursue research on the same subject, write to each other, attend the same conferences, and publish in the same journals. With the emergence of knowledge management, communities of practice have materialized as an essential component of getting knowledge shared across functional boundaries both within and beyond organizations. Technology—e-mail, the Web, videoconferencing—has dramatically expanded the possibilities of low-cost global communication, and hence facilitated the extraordinarily rapid growth of geographically dispersed communities and teams.

Communities are often confused with *networks*. Networks, however, are collections of people who maintain contact with each other because of a mutually perceived benefit of staying in touch for purposes that may or may not be explicit. Examples include the alumni of a business school or a consulting firm. Most of the groups that interact by way of discussion groups on the Web are networks rather than communities, because there is no web of affect-laden relationships or commitment to shared values. Table 7.1 summarizes the various forms of working relationships.

TABLE 7.1   Taxonomy of the Ways People Work Together: Work Groups, Teams, Communities, and Networks

	Work Group	Team	Community	Network
Objective	Each individual has specific responsibilities within an overall group objective.	A team has a specific operational objective.	A community has a domain of information or knowledge or activities of common interests.	Network members want to stay in touch with each other.
Time frame	Individuals have their own time frame, depending on their responsibilities.	A team disbands when the objective is met.	A community disbands when members no longer perceive any value in its continuing to exist.	A network disbands when it stops being useful to members.
Authority	The group's objectives are decided by the group supervisor.	A team's objective is decided by someone in authority.	A community's goals are decided by the members and permitted by whoever is in authority.	A network's goals are self-determined, usually without any authorization.
Membership	The supervisor selects the members of the group.	The members are selected by someone in authority (team leadership or management).	A community is self-selected.	A network is self-selected.

continued

TABLE 7.1 Continued

	Work Group	Team	Community	Network
Driving force	Assigned responsibilities.	Commitment to get the job done right.	Passion for the focus of the community.	Usefulness of members for each other.
Raison d'être	Getting the job done.	Getting the job done.	Sharing information, knowledge, or activities.	Making and maintaining connections with others.
Commonalities	Shared supervisor, shared work space, shared fate.	Shared goal.	Shared values and knowledge.	Complementarity of the members.
Success and failure	May be explicit or implicit.	Usually explicit.	Usually implicit.	Implicit.
Risks	Individuals don't collaborate effectively and potential synergies are lost.	No clear goal; micromanagement by the organization.	Lack of passion, resources, or leadership; management interference.	Different interests; lack of time.
Examples	Traditional work units.	Project management teams, task forces, standing committees.	Communities of practice, communities of interest.	Alumni of a business school or consulting firm, listserv of people interested in the same project.

While work groups, teams, and communities are conceptually distinct, in practice the modalities also tend to overlap. Thus a work group or a network may also become a community. For instance, in *Communities of Practice*, Etienne Wenger gives a particularly vivid description of a group of medical claims processors who were formally structured as a work group in an insurance company, who didn't particularly enjoy their work, but who nevertheless were functioning as a community of practice.[3] The patterns are not mutually exclusive: many people have jobs in a work group but also participate in various teams, communities, or networks in the same organization.

HIGH-PERFORMANCE TEAMS

With the emergence of communities as an important organizational arrangement, writers have been at pains to point out that communities differ from teams.[4] Whereas a team typically has a time-bound, predefined operational objective, with commitments to produce some product or service, a community often has no such time-bound objective. The essence of a community is the members' personal investment in an area of shared interest. Whereas a team is focused on accomplishing a task, a community is generally focused on learning more about the subject of common interest. Whereas members of a team are connected by interdependent tasks and values, members of a community in an organizational setting are usually connected by interdependent knowledge and values. Membership in a community tends to be voluntary, whereas membership in a team tends to be a matter of appointment by the organization.

Emphasis on the differences between communities and teams has tended to hide an important truth: high-performance teams resemble communities. Relatively few communities are teams, because their typical goals relate to enhancing understanding rather than doing something. But all high-performance teams have the characteristics of communities. High-performance teams are exceptional. In addition to having the basics in place—clear goal, appropriate leadership and membership, and adequate resources and support—high-performance teams exhibit characteristics of community as well:

- High-performance teams actively shape the expectations of those who use their output—and then exceed the resulting expectations.[5]

- High-performance teams rapidly adjust their performance to the shifting needs of the situation. They innovate on the fly, seizing opportunities and turning setbacks into good fortune.[6]

- High-performance teams grow steadily stronger. Over time, members come to know one another's strengths and weaknesses and become highly skilled in coordinating their activities, anticipating each other's next moves, and initiating appropriate responses as those moves are occurring.[7]

- The members of a high-performance team grow individually. Mutual concern for each other's personal growth enables high-performance teams to develop interchangeable skills and hence greater flexibility.[8]

- Fueled by interpersonal commitments, the purposes of high-performance teams become nobler, team performance goals more urgent, and team approach more powerful.[9]

- High-performance teams carry out their work with shared passion. The notion that "if one of us fails, we all fail" pervades the team.[10]

The experience of being a member of a high-performance team is deeply meaningful. As Peter Senge has written, "When you ask people about what it is like being part of a great team, what is most striking is the meaningfulness of the experience. People talk about being part of something larger than themselves, of being connected, of being generative. It becomes quite clear that for many, their experiences as part of truly great teams stand out as singular periods of life lived to the fullest. Some spend the rest of their lives looking for ways to recapture that spirit."[11] Thus even when the job is over and the team has disbanded, the members tend to have reunions to reminisce and relive the experience.

High-performance teams differ markedly from merely competent teams. Competent teams get the job done, generally without hostility or alienation. Yet the sense of excitement that might have brought them to the job in the first place isn't there. Being on the team is just a job.[12] As Katzenbach and Smith say in *The Wisdom of Teams,* "What sets apart high-performance teams... is the degree of commitment, particularly how deeply committed the members are to one another. Such commitments go well beyond civility and teamwork. Each genuinely helps the others to achieve both personal and professional goals. Furthermore, such commitments extend beyond company activities and even beyond the life of the team itself."[13] To put this another way, high-performance teams have the characteristics of effective communities: a web of affect-laden relationships; a commitment to shared values, norms, and meanings; a shared history and identity; and a relatively high level of responsiveness to members and to the world.[14]

Managers Can't Force High-Performance Teams or Communities

Managers have important roles in establishing the basic operating arrangements for both teams and communities. In the case of teams, managers need to establish direction, membership, resources, recognition, and accountability.[15] In the case of communities, they need to provide recognition, support, resources, and integration of the outputs of communities into the work of the organization.[16] Managers can implement these basics with conventional management techniques by taking the necessary hierarchical decisions.

But hierarchical approaches cannot generate either high-performance teams or communities. As Richard Hackman writes in *Leading Teams* "There is no way to 'make' a team perform well. Teams create their own realities and control their own destinies to a far greater extent, and far sooner in their lives, than we generally recognized."[17]

And the same can be said of communities, as Wenger, McDermott, and Snyder note in *Cultivating Communities of Practice:* "You cannot cultivate communities of practice in the same way you develop traditional organizational structures."[18]

It's not merely that the standard management techniques are ineffective in the area of high-performance teams and communities. They can be actively harmful. Attempts to formalize or blueprint processes typically kill the passion of high-performance teams or communities,. The result is that high-performance teams slide back into mere competence, and communities simply evaporate.

The techniques of directing, controlling, and deciding that are used in traditional management to optimize and standardize repetitive processes are ill suited to inspiring and energizing high-performance teams or communities. That's because these techniques aren't "designed for aliveness."[19]

Collaboration Rests on Shared Values

If collaboration is so important for organizational performance, why isn't it a more prominent aspect of organizational life? Why do so many company mountain-climbing expeditions or white-water rafting trips leave people less likely to collaborate than before they began? Why is it so hard to get from "me" to "we"?

It's partly the rah-rah cheerleading that isn't backed by substance. Often the basics aren't in place to enable teamwork to happen. Sometimes management practices and incentive systems are geared to the traditional work unit and individual responsibility and accountability, so that processes systematically undermine well-intentioned team-building exercises.

These are partial causes of the bad odor surrounding the whole notion of collaboration. But the root cause lies deeper: collaboration rests on values. And in traditional management, the espoused values of collaboration and the operational values at work often exist on opposite sides of a deep gulf.

Even Richard Hackman, a champion of teams, describes an experience that is common to many of us who have worked in an organization:

A few years [ago], the president of the university where I worked had asked me to serve on a committee to identify candidates for a dean-ship that had become vacant. According to the first of the three criteria for team success or team effectiveness [that is, getting the job done; the other two are growing as a team and growing as individuals], our committee was a success. The president liked the candidate we rec-ommended and appointed him as dean. By the time that happened, however, I had already made my vow. Never again, no matter what, would I do anything that required me to work with the other members of that search committee.[20]

When we're in this sort of situation, we see that the other members of the group have different values, and this leaves us with the feeling that future collaboration would be horrible to contemplate. Where people don't share the same values, a work group may be the most effective modality of working together in the short run. But if time is available, it may be possible to get everyone to take a step back and examine their underlying values to see whether common values can be discovered or generated, as discussed in Chapter Six.

Narrative Catalyzes High-Performance Teams and Communities

Narrative establishes common meanings and transmits the values char-acteristic of high-performance teams and communities. It enables the members of high-performance teams or communities to see the world differently, to experience that internal "aha!" that revitalizes them and reframes how they connect with each other and the world.

The leader who has mastered the narrative tool kit helps high-performance teams or communities establish compelling objectives and actively shape the expectations of those who use the group's output. And in turn, members of high-performance teams or communities understand the evolving narrative of the situation in which they find themselves, so that they can adjust the team's performance to the rapidly shifting needs of the actual situation. And because members of a high-performance team or community know each other's stories, they can predict what each of their fellows will do and be on the spot with the next required piece of the project.

Narrative stimulates high-performance teams and communities to participate with passion, creating the pervasive feeling that the failure of any individual member is a failure for all. Narrative gives teams and communities the spark that will help them lift their game to a new level and work together with shared passion.

The rest of this chapter discusses how to use narrative to make this happen.

WORKING TOGETHER

The last few decades have seen a massive shift toward working together, for many reasons:

- *The work requires it.* Working together with others is necessary to achieve increased speed to market, faster product development, better customer service, lower costs, and the opening of new markets. No individual has the expertise necessary to get everything done. Collaboration has become a critical competency for achieving and sustaining high performance.[21]

- *People want it.* After several hundred years of emphasis on the development of the individual, the pendulum has begun to shift back toward an interest in being together. Growing numbers of people are interested in moving from a world of "me" to a world of "we."[22]

- Technology has made it possible. Radical changes in the ability to stay in touch with others, by e-mail, the Web, and cell phones, have resulted in a global explosion of connectivity. Technology makes it possible for people to be spatially dispersed and still connected together.[23]

The rapid growth of the numbers of teams, communities, and networks is likely to continue:

- *Geographically dispersed teams* can now be scattered around the world and communicate fully with each other. As global supply chains proliferate, it's increasingly common to see goods designed on one continent, manufactured on another, and sold on a third. Ever-faster cycle times require closer and more agile collaboration.

- *Communities of practice* are recognized as essential for knowledge sharing in an organization. All organizations eventually discover that sharing knowledge happens systematically only when informal networks or communities of practice are in place.[24]

- *Mergers and acquisitions* tend to fail as a result of the clash of cultures. Often a merger brings together groups that have been fighting each other as competitors, maybe for generations. The management then expects the members of these groups to work together. These situations make it urgent to figure out how to get people working together rapidly and naturally.[25]

- *Supply chain management* is moving toward federated planning. The traditional approach in which the organization being supplied is seen as the commander of all the organizations that provide products or services, with the result that communications flow in a single direction and suggestions from suppliers are not put on the table, is giving way to an approach in which supply chain partners collaborate to address the trade-offs and break constraints across the extended enterprise. Suppliers become genuine partners.[26]

EXAMPLES OF FOUR PATTERNS OF WORKING TOGETHER

Work Group

Many so-called teams are not genuine teams but work groups mislabeled as teams. For example, from 1990 to 1994, as director of the Southern Africa Department of the World Bank, I participated in a group called the regional management team. Its members were the vice president of the Africa Region, the five other country directors, a technical director, and several senior advisers. The group was called a team, but it functioned as a work group, not a team. Each director had a defined responsibility and reported to the same vice president. Although the directors maintained amiable relations with each other, they had little need for active collaboration or interdepartmental coordination to get their work done. The main things the directors had in common were that they had similar work tasks and reported to the same supervisor.

Team

By contrast, the unit that I headed up in the World Bank from 1996 to 2000 was called a work group but it was also a genuine team. The unit's task was to spearhead the knowledge management initiative in the World Bank. Its stretch objective—established in early 1997 amid widespread skepticism as to its feasibility—was to have the World Bank benchmarked as a world leader in knowledge management by the year 2000. The unit's five members and its resources were clearly designated by the World Bank management. The unit had practically no decision-making power across the organization, so it worked by using its advice and influence. Although each member had defined responsibilities, the work itself depended on the ebb and flow of a rapidly shifting organizational scene and involved gathering intelligence on opportunities, identifying threats to the accomplishment of our objective, and establishing spheres of influence where that could help. Accomplishing the mission required a high degree of interaction among the unit's members, who got to know each other's strengths and weaknesses extremely well. I left the unit—and the World Bank—in December 2000 when the stretch objective had been accomplished. Since then, the team has continued to have reunions.[27]

Community

Between July 2001 and 2008, I was a member of a small community of people—located mainly in Washington, D.C., though some came from as far away as Erie, Pennsylvania—who were interested in and practicing the emerging discipline of organizational narrative. The origin of the group was a conference on this subject in April 2001, after which participants felt the need to continue the discussion.[28] Over this period, the community met once a month, usually in the same place, and had an annual conference in April each year in collaboration with Smithsonian Associates. Some members had been with the community since the outset. Others joined and became active. Others who used to be active have moved away and were no longer active, although they remained in e-mail contact. The community was self-organizing: its leadership responsibilities were shared by those who volunteer to facilitate meetings, organize events, build the Web site, and contribute know-how and information. Its members are heterogeneous, but they shared common values and interests related to organizational storytelling. They had different views on many issues, but the discussion was healthy and constructive. In 2008, the group lost access to its meeting place. An alternative meeting place was found, but somehow it wasn't the same. Gradually the group lost energy and ceased to meet on a regular basis. There is an annual reunion every spring with a storytelling conference, but the group no longer meets monthly.

Network

Among the huge number of networks now active on the Web is the Workingstories discussion group—a collection of several hundred people around the world who share an interest in organizational storytelling. They use the network to stay informed about events, books, or articles of common interest and occasionally discuss issues. The participants have never met face-to-face as a group, although many subsets of individuals have met. Those who join make no mutual engagement to do anything in particular except stay in touch by way of the list. Although some members of the list would like the group to become a community, it currently lacks the necessary web of interpersonal relationships to attain that status, and so it remains a network.[29]

ORGANIC ANALOGIES

Hierarchy is still the dominant concept of organizational discourse today, so it's tricky to use analogies aimed at freeing an organization from hierarchical thinking about high-performance teams

163

and communities. The hidden implications of some analogies can unwittingly reintroduce the hierarchy through the back door.

For instance, Wenger, McDermott, and Snyder write movingly about "cultivating communities,"[30] and in a sense, this is real progress. The idea of cultivating a garden is certainly more relevant to eliciting high-performance teams and communities than the simple cause-and-effect notions of command-and-control. Cultivation recognizes that high-performance teams and communities are organic entities that flourish or wither based on the conditions for growth they encounter. And it is true that a plant does its own growing: it's not a good idea to pull a plant out of the ground to check whether it has good roots. All these aspects of the cultivation analogy are apt.

But other implications are less appropriate. Those who talk of "cultivating communities" may inadvertently imply that communities are being gardened like vegetables—unthinking, mute, unconscious, operating according to some predetermined genetic program. By contrast, communities and high-performance teams are active, thinking, dynamic, living entities that have views of their own and don't always take well to being cultivated.

Similar issues exist with talk of "choreographing the dance" of communities.[31] Once again, while the analogy has positive associations—the free-flowing motions of dance are certainly more relevant to the impromptu and spontaneous creativity of high-performance teams and communities than the mechanistic notions of command-and-control. But here also, "choreographing" carries with it implicit notions of hierarchy. The quintessential choreographer was Marius Petipa of the Russian Imperial Ballet, who had the talent and expertise to lay out in advance the precise steps and body movements that every ballet dancer who dances ballets like *The Nutcracker* or *Swan Lake* is required to follow. By contrast, the work of high-performance teams or communities might be likened to a dance, but it isn't choreographed. Much of it is spontaneous, impromptu, and unprogrammable. It's precisely these unchoreographed characteristics that enable high-performance teams and communities to exceed expectations. A more relevant analogy is jazz or basketball, not the choreography of classical ballet.

CATALYZING HIGH-PERFORMANCE TEAMS AND COMMUNITIES

High-performance teams and communities emerge—and continue to exist—only so long as the members want them to. These groups generate and sustain themselves. Outsiders can't do it for them. Only insiders can understand the intricate web of interpersonal relationships at the heart of a high-performance team or community—who the real players are and what relationships they have to the community issues. And in complex fields, it's often only insiders who can appreciate the substantive issues that make up the subject matter of the community, the challenges the field faces, and the latent potential in emerging ideas and techniques.[32]

So ultimately the viability of a high-performance team or community is going to depend on its members. But they must have a minimum degree of understanding of the nature of the entity that they are creating.

Where this understanding is lacking, one of the first steps is to communicate the idea of what's involved to the potential members. Potential members of high-performance teams or communities can visit vibrant teams or communities and create for themselves the story of what a dynamic team or community looks and feels like and how it carries on its business. If that isn't possible, then leaders can tell the story of one or more vibrant teams or communities—how they came into being, what they do, how they function, and what benefits ensue to members.

This is where springboard stories can be brought into play to win hearts and minds to the new way of doing things, as discussed in Chapter Three. Typically the stories will be examples of cases where a team or community—preferably within the organization—was able to achieve extraordinary performance. The Pakistan highways story in Chapter Three is an illustration.

Better yet, bring in members of vibrant teams or communities to tell the story of their community. This can directly communicate the passion that members of a living group exhibit, making the effort seem more feasible to the prospective members of the new group.

It may also be necessary to persuade the hierarchy to allow the high-performance teams or communities to exist. Creating such groups usually implies changes in the power structure of an organization. It often offers new answers to questions such as these: Who has the right to make decisions about how work is carried out? Who is responsible for performance? Where are resources allocated? How are monetary rewards allocated, and who has access to learning and career opportunities? Changes in these areas are likely to threaten the prerogatives of powerful individuals and groups in the organization, some of whom may overtly or covertly resist changing the existing ways of working.[33]

Use Narratives to Set Objectives for the Group

The objectives of high-performance teams and effective communities need to be clear, compelling, and flexible. If objectives are too complete, they are likely to stifle initiative. If objectives aren't clear enough, the team may get lost. Effective objectives have specificity but also have some fuzz around the edges.[34] They indicate what is to be achieved, but generally leave open how it is to be accomplished.

But how do you achieve clarity with incompleteness? Stories can convey the idea of what's involved without being prescriptive:

- *Stories about the past* can give examples or analogies of what is required—for example, describing a team that used an unexpected methodology to achieve its results faster than anyone expected, or a community that was able to provide a rapid answer to a complex operational question just in time, or a team that was able to redefine its goal so as to achieve extraordinary performance.

- *A future story* describing how the eventual client will use the product or service being generated by the team is usually more motivating than a set of abstract performance targets. The form of such user stories is discussed in Chapter Ten.[35]

- *The combination of an example from the past and a future story* about what the end state will look like when the group has succeeded, plus guidance on the attributes of the output, can enable the group to understand the journey on which it is setting out while leaving it freedom to innovate about how to get there in the most effective manner.

Shape the Client's Expectations Through Narrative

The output of a great team or community exceeds the client's expectations. Where the client is the group itself, the group surprises itself. Surpassing the client's expectations happens not only because the group performs very well but also because it has an interactive relationship with its clients and actively shapes their expectations and then exceeds them.[36]

Narrative is the way groups communicate to clients what to expect without pinning down the group in detail as to how to go about the work. For instance, in November 1995, when Lou Gerstner as head of IBM was setting out to persuade the computer industry and his clients that they needed open standards, he presented two alternative narratives of the way the industry might evolve:

> *Think about the networked world that we see before us ... every digital device connected to every other digital device in the world, all supporting seamless, easy access. How are we ever going to get around the problem of incompatible hardware and software systems?*
>
> *I think we have two choices.*
>
> *We can ask customers to set aside their freedom of choice and preferences in hardware, operating systems, applications and user interfaces ... junk their trillions of dollars of investment in information technology ... and all of us—everyone, everywhere—move to one architecture provided by, priced by and controlled by one company.*
>
> *Or ...*
>
> *We can embrace open industry standards.*
>
> *Open means that software from one vendor can operate on or with hardware and software from any vendor—not just one guy's. We need to work with standards organizations. We need to openly agree on APIs [application programming interface], interfaces, tools and protocols—on anything the customer sees and touches in the journey to get something done.*

Compliance with standards does not mean that we won't compete aggressively or that we can't distinguish our products. We will. But we'll compete on the basis of innovative implementation of industry-standard technologies and architectures, on performance, features, design, service and support.

Besides, in the long run, closed, proprietary architectures—that's a losing strategy. I bet you thought you'd never hear that from IBM. But having had a near-death experience, we know what we're talking about.

Every time I meet with customers, I say the same thing. I urge them to demand compliance with open industry standards in the products they buy. And you know what? They're beginning to listen. They understand the need for the industry to move to this level.[37]

Narrative can also be used when the group's client has misguided expectations or requirements, for example, when the manager to whom a team reports sets a direction for the team that is wrongheaded, or when the management sets conditions for the performance of a community that members can see are at odds with the very purpose of the community.

Writers on traditional management advise people to do what the manager says, because "those who own an enterprise, or act on behalf of the owners have the right to specify collective directions and aspirations."[38] Nevertheless, teams have more constructive options to deal with such situations, beyond simply doing whatever they are told.

Use Narrative to Adjust the Mandate

With access to the manager or client, the group may be able to tell the story of another team where a similar direction led to an unsatisfactory result, as well as a narrative of a different approach that led to a better result. If no such narratives are available, the team may be able to construct a future story that fleshes out the consequences for the team and the organization—if the wrongheaded course is persisted in.

Use Narrative to Uncover the Deeper Reason for Managerial Misdirection

In many organizational situations, the team may lack the hierarchical status that is needed to have such narratives taken seriously. In such circumstances, one avenue may be to explore the deeper reasons that the client or supervisor is adopting a wrongheaded approach. Seemingly irrational behavior usually has a reason—a story—behind it, and if the group can discover this story, it may be able to find a new way to respond to the deeper reason driving the manager.

> Thus, some years ago when I was appointed to head a task force in the World Bank to streamline the organization's procedures, the senior vice president gave me clear instructions at the outset as to which process changes were possible and which were not. One difficulty was that one of the principal substantive problems in the existing procedures lay outside the boundaries specified in these instructions. I could see that if this restriction was maintained, the report of the task force would be stillborn.
>
> At the outset, the senior vice president was adamant against any expansion of the task force's mandate. However, in the course of continued interactions with him, I realized that his opposition to expanding the mandate had two sources. First, he was in the grip of a story that the board of directors would oppose any change beyond the boundary he had indicated, and second, current processes included certain elements that helped him carry out his own review function. Once I had discovered these reasons, I set about finding out why the board of directors would oppose the change and discovered that they wouldn't: the board members in fact would welcome change. So I was able to put together a proposal to both solve the underlying problem and show the senior vice president why the proposal would continue to meet his own review needs and be embraced by the board of directors. He accepted my story and became enthusiastic about expanding the team's mandate—retroactively.

Have a Respected Messenger Tell the Story

Sometimes the group cannot find the reason for the management opposition. It may simply be that one is rarely a hero in one's own organization. In such circumstances, the team may be able to bring in a respected outsider who has the standing and stature to tell the story in an effective way.

> In 1999, the senior management of the World Bank had become uneasy about the large number of communities of practice that were untidily

occupying the landscape of the organization and asked for a cleanup. An external panel of world-class experts was called in to examine the situation and essentially told the management that communities of practice are an inherently untidy phenomenon: the experience of other organizations indicated that any drastic cleanup of the communities would likely result in killing them. The management was willing to listen to a story from an outsider that it had been reluctant to accept from staff inside the organization.

GETTING THE GROUP TO WORK TOGETHER

Leaders should exploit every opportunity to bring people together and get them to see their common goals and shared values. In fact, every chance encounter is an opportunity to build alliances and nurture shared values and purpose. An informal lunch, a chance meeting in the corridor, a business trip together—all represent opportunities to build a sense of communal purpose and discover an interest in pursuing a common goal through sharing stories.

In late 1996 in the World Bank, the president, Jim Wolfensohn, announced an institutional commitment to knowledge management. I was immediately appointed program director for knowledge management, but no arrangements were in place to implement the approach. Thus, I was faced with a dilemma as to how to mobilize and channel support for the initiative when I had no formal mandate to do anything in particular. Eventually I hit on the idea of calling a weekly meeting at the same time and the same place for "the friends of knowledge management." Anyone in the organization was free to attend, and the agenda was open: the sessions generally involved the exchange of stories, gossip, rumors, ideas, and possible plans about the unfolding initiative. Some people came and kept coming. Others came and decided that this was not for them. Over time, the membership of the meeting stabilized. When in July 1997 the management finally put in place arrangements to oversee the knowledge management initiative, this group of "friends of knowledge management" became the knowledge management board that was officially charged with oversight of the initiative.

Use Story to Jump-Start High-Performance Teams or Communities

Bringing members of teams and communities together is critical at the launch of the group when work patterns are about to be established. For groups that have existed for long periods, bringing together the members from time to time may also be necessary as energy flags and trust fades.

To attract people from diverse backgrounds and cultures and get them working together, it helps if they discover what aspirations, goals, needs, and dreams they have in common. People inevitably differ in some respects in what they value. If they can find what values they have in common, it's easier for them to work together. People learn about others' values most effectively through listening to each other's stories.[39]

Storytelling is contagious. If one member of a team or community tells a story full of passionate caring, that tends to spark others who share the same passion to tell a story reflecting their own experience with it. This process of contagious storytelling occurs naturally in social settings. This is one reason that coffee breaks and meals are often seen as the most productive aspects of retreats or conferences. In formal sessions, storytelling typically isn't permitted, so its benefits are rarely felt there. However, if a space is created for storytelling in the formal sessions, and a powerful story begins the discussion, then there is no reason that the same process of collective storytelling cannot be generated. At the end of this chapter, I include a template of procedures for accelerating collective storytelling and hence catalyzing passion.

Bring Participants Face-to-Face to Tell Their Stories

Healthy groups get better over time, in part because members get to know one another's stories. They learn where the other group members are coming from and what their strengths and tendencies are likely to be, and so each can anticipate what the others will deliver and adjust their own performance accordingly. This process happens easily and naturally when people meet face-to-face.[40]

Virtual teams and communities are pervasive in forward-looking organizations, especially for knowledge work and for work that involves people on the road much of the time. In such arrangements, members of teams or communities interact electronically by e-mail, the Web, telephone, and videoconference. I described one such community in Chapter Three—the Pakistan highway example.

Virtual teams and communities have a number of advantages over groups that meet only physically. They can be larger, more diverse, and collectively more knowledgeable than those that depend on face-to-face communications, because their members can be scattered around the world and still stay in touch. As a result, widely dispersed expertise can be brought to bear on complex issues quickly and efficiently.[41]

Nevertheless, periodic face-to-face meetings with members of the group are necessary for the group to become and remain a dynamic living entity. If members of a community have never met, the group tends to remain somewhat blurred, with no one really feeling comfortable as to who is in the group. As a result, willingness to pitch in for group activities is difficult to elicit. Of course, it depends on the complexity of the task at hand as to what is the most suitable mode of interaction: simple updates on project status or requests for information can be conveniently transmitted by virtual means. But when it comes to solving complex problems or figuring out what the group should be doing or creating new designs and concepts, it may be more efficient to meet. The following experience reported to me by Ohio consultant Valdis Krebs is not uncommon:[42]

I spent more than a year working on a software development effort with folks in another city. We tried to do everything by e-mail, phone, and WebEx. It was possible to make some progress, but we also experienced many misunderstandings and restarts and do-overs and flare-ups. So we said, "Heck, Let's meet." We did, and it was amazing how much we accomplished in two days. People who appeared to have difficulty communicating via the Net all of a sudden were clear and precise and open to feedback and understood each other perfectly—what an amazing transformation! This project would have taken many fewer hours *if more of them had been spent face-to-face. A $650 plane ticket is cheap compared to a programmer at $125/hour. After our face-to-face meeting, we all came to the conclusion: "Just like a picture is worth a thousand words, a day face-to-face is worth a thousand e-mails!"*

One reason that people need to meet face-to-face is that asking for advice is an implicit admission of ignorance. In low-trust organizations, public admissions of ignorance may lead to career setbacks or worse. Hence, before people will be willing to show ignorance and ask for advice, they need to have a sense of who's listening when they expose their ignorance. Once people have met, exchanged stories, and established the minimum level of trust, they can disperse around the world and exchange views openly.

Encourage the Group to Develop and Tell Its Own Story

Human beings see meaning in being part of a larger story. So to create high-performance teams or communities, it is important to link individuals to the story of the group and link the story of the group to the larger organizational story.

In much of life, we are uncertain what story our life fits into, and hence our experience is somewhat murky. Deep meaning is generated by narratives that show how our actions relate to broader objectives. When we see that our work is part of a larger activity whose goal is worthwhile, then our own smaller activity also seems more valuable. When group members themselves formulate the story, they see that they are making a contribution. Their own story becomes interwoven with the larger story of the group.[43]

This phenomenon can be catalyzed by encouraging the team or community to develop and tell its story. The following actions can help group members see themselves as part of the larger story and link their own individual identities with the story of the group:

- *Give the group a name.* Even an unimaginative name may be better than none. If the group is allowed to determine its own name and is given the opportunity to exercise its imagination a little, that can help instill a sense of ownership among group members.

- *Allow the group to create its own work space.* This will let members feel some ownership with the space. It might be a physical space—a kind of clubhouse where members can hang out informally. It might also be a virtual space—a Web site—where team members have something to say about the layout and how the content is presented. If these spaces—physical or virtual—are totally controlled by the hierarchy to ensure a consistent corporate "look and feel," the chance that the group will feel ownership is lower than if they have a voice in the matter. Some minimum standards are needed, since users may find it difficult to navigate among sites with extremely heterogeneous layouts. Nevertheless, if corporate consistency is taken too far, it will stifle group spirit and kill passion.

- *Adopt some common objects to foster teamwork.* Some groups have a common uniform—sports teams, airline crews, branches of the military—but this may be impractical or inappropriate for most other teams. However, other physical objects may help strengthen the group identity—hats, T-shirts, satchels, whatever—and generate a proprietary sense of playfulness that contributes to identity.

- *Consider encouraging the group to socialize together or participate in sporting events together.* Shared social activity can create opportunities for sharing stories and so help build group identity. Unfortunately, work hours may already be so long that active encouragement of socializing after work can appear as intrusive into private lives and upsetting work-life balance. In each case, the context should be examined to determine what makes sense.

- *Create occasions for a successful team or vibrant community to tell its story to other teams and communities.* External storytelling is an important way for the group to strengthen its sense of identity and let other teams or communities learn of the success.

174

- *Keep a successful team together.* Many organizations pay little attention to keeping successful teams together, even though powerful evidence indicates that—except in R&D teams, where infusions of new blood may be needed—good teams get better over time.[44] The members of a team that has been together for an extended period not only get to know each other well, they develop the story of the team. Having an opportunity to tell that story and celebrate their success can strengthen their ownership of the group and hence nurture the passion that leads to more success in the future.

In all of these steps, be careful to ensure that strengthening the identity of the team isn't a substitute for meaningful work. If the task isn't worth caring about or if organizational incentives aren't aligned with group performance, then these gestures will be seen as sugarcoating a bad situation and will be counterproductive.[45]

Get Extraordinary Results from Ordinary People

Management theorists put a lot of emphasis on getting the membership of the team right. For example, Jim Collins in *From Good to Great* cites getting the right people on the leadership team as the first step in building a great organization. Similarly Richard Hackman in *Leading Teams* stresses that getting the right team membership is among the most important ways that managers can help strong teams develop.[46]

In practice, however, there are limited degrees of freedom in selecting people. Often you inherit the group assembled by your predecessors or the management. Initially you live in a WYSIWYG world—what you see is what you get. Practical considerations prevent a leader from always having first-round draft choices for every position. There is competition for the best people, who in any event may have other plans.

What to do with the set of imperfect individuals you have to work with as members of the group? The conventional management approach is to figure out what needs to be done, decide on a division of work, make an allocation among existing team members (perhaps even allowing them to choose assignments), and then get on with the job. This often gets reasonable results: people usually pitch in and do the best they can with the job they are assigned even if it's not what really inspires them. But such assignments often leave them waiting until work finishes each day or until the team's work finally gets done, so they can get back to what they really enjoy doing.

If you want extraordinary performance from a group, you need a more interactive approach to draw on the members' resources of emotion and caring. By finding out the story of the individual members—who they are, what drives them, where they have come from—you can adjust the work of the group so that their assignments can reflect their deeper feelings. Any complex task offers more than one route to success. If you can find a route that draws on the passions of team members, then what looks like an ordinary team can become extraordinary.[47]

> In 1997, almost a year after my five-member knowledge team began working together at the World Bank, I discovered that one of my staff was a professional storyteller. At once I encouraged him to see how we could use this in the work. Eventually his expertise and contacts contributed powerfully to our capability to persuade the organization to change.
>
> Another staff member was skilled at team building, training, and groupware. In due course, she became an expert in organizing knowledge fairs. Holding a knowledge fair was not part of our game plan, and when she suggested it, it seemed to me an unlikely possibility for the overly solemn World Bank. But she was passionate about it, and she made it succeed. Thus, these two areas—storytelling and knowledge fairs—became central features of the successful World Bank program, in part because the team members were able to weave their own stories into the work, and their work became their passion. Members of this group still look back on this period as an extraordinary time in their lives.

One can also create the space to let people express their individuality and have some fun.

> Southwest Airlines has done this brilliantly by encouraging individual team members to weave their own story into the company's story of a

fun airline. I was on a Southwest flight recently, and the flight steward introduced himself as follows: "Hello. This is Bingo, and I'll be your flight steward on today's flight from Baltimore to Orlando. Some of you might be wondering why I'm called Bingo. Simple! You see that's the name my parents gave me. Why? Well, I was the fifth child in my family. My parents desperately wanted to have a boy and their first four children were girls. So when I showed up after four girls, it was quite natural for them to shout, "Bingo!" So that's what my name is."

That simple but unforgettable explanation makes the flight steward's story part of Southwest's story and becomes part of my story about Southwest Airlines.

Contribute to Group Learning Through the Exchange of Stories

The learning of high-performance teams or communities is very different from conventional approaches to coaching, which typically involve identifying problems and getting agreement on what to do about them. Here the thrust is on inspiring improved performance—in a situation where no one may know what better performance would look like.

Participants must not only look at objective measures of how the work is proceeding but also listen carefully to each other's stories—finding out what they think is going on—while at the same time formulating their own story about what has happened so far and what could happen next. The objective is to see how the stories mesh so as to determine which story offers the most promising way forward.[48]

Learning can take place before, during, and after the work of the group:

- Before the work begins, the group can invite others who have undertaken similar efforts to come together to share stories and so devise the best approach for undertaking the new task. This is sometimes called a "peer assist."[49]

- While the work is ongoing, pausing at milestones and other key incidents to discuss what has gone well and what could be improved can clarify the group's story so far and lay the basis for future learning. This is sometimes called an "after-action review."[50]

- When the work is over, a more thorough review can enable the group to piece together the story of what happened and why and secure lessons learned for the benefit of future groups. This is sometimes called a "retrospect."[51]

The effectiveness of such measures can be seen from a comparative Harvard Business School study of teams of surgeons as they introduced a new technique of minimally invasive cardiac surgery. All teams came from highly respected institutions and received the same training, but there were major differences in results. Some teams were able to halve their operating time, while others failed to improve at all. In *Complications*, Atul Gawande describes the differences between the best and worst teams as follows:

> Richard Bohmer, the one physician among the Harvard researchers, made several visits to observe one of the quickest-learning teams and one of the slowest, and he was startled by the contrast.
>
> The surgeon on the fast-learning team was actually quite inexperienced compared with the one on the slow-learning team—he was only a couple of years out of training. But he made sure to pick team members with whom he had worked well before and to keep them together through the first fifteen cases before allowing any new members. He had the team go through a dry run before the first case, then deliberately scheduled six operations in the first week, so little would be forgotten in between. He convened the team before each case to discuss it in detail and afterward to debrief. He made sure results were tracked carefully. And as a person, Bohmer noted, the surgeon was not the stereotypical Napoleon with a knife. Unbidden, he told Bohmer, "The surgeon needs to be willing to allow himself to become a partner [with the rest of the team] so he can accept input."
>
> At the other hospital, the surgeon chose his operating team almost randomly and did not keep it together. In his first seven cases, the team had different members every time, which is to say that it was no team at all. And he had no prebriefings, no debriefings, no tracking of ongoing results.[52]

Whereas the poorly performing team was the cocksure type who is "sometimes wrong but never in doubt," the team that did well benefited from a leader who was willing to admit the possibility of doing better and who encouraged the team to learn. The study dramatically illustrates one of the great strengths of working together effectively. Collaboration establishes the basis for learning from experience and sharing knowledge. And it is to this issue that I turn in the next chapter.

TEMPLATE FOR NURTURING COLLABORATION

One way to help get people working together is to spark a series of stories among the group that enables the group to see that they have common problems, common goals, and a common perspective on how to address the. This is a story aimed at beginning a story chain to boost collaboration.

A key is for the initial story to be one that moves the audience, who begin to think: *This is interesting. I want to hear more stories like that. And I would like to share my story about the same subject.*

1. Have someone tell a moving story about something that happened to the group: for example, a turning point in the group's story, a time when the group ran into a difficult problem, a time when things went terrifically well for the group, or a time when the group faced a real challenge.

2. Who was the single protagonist of the story?

3. Is the single protagonist typical of your specific audience? If not, can the story be told from the point of view of such a protagonist?

4. When and where did it happen?

5. Has the story been stripped of any unnecessary detail?

6. What happened after the incident? Did things get better or worse?

7. How did the protagonist feel about the incident?

8. What was the significance of what happened for the group?

9. After the story has been told, ask if anyone else has had a similar experience.

8

SHARE KNOWLEDGE

Using Narrative to Transmit Knowledge and Understanding

> ❝ We value stories because they are like reports of research projects, only easier to understand, remember, and use.
>
> **Gary Klein[1]**

Contrary to conventional wisdom, much of what we know is composed of stories. We have a certain amount of *abstract understanding* of the world—theories, principles, processes, and heuristics useful for dealing with recurring, repetitive tasks: thus, airplane pilots follow checklists to make sure they don't forget a crucial step on takeoff. We also have a certain amount of *tacit understanding*, which we acquire through experience and may be able to articulate explicitly: thus, we may be able to ride a bicycle or perform a complicated surgical operation even if we cannot explain exactly what we do.[2] But a substantial part of our expertise also lies in *narratives* that describe how unusual situations have been handled in the past. Cognitive scientists have discovered that we turn experiences—both our own and those of others—into stories to help us remember them and communicate effectively.[3]

The phenomenon of sharing knowledge through stories is astonishingly pervasive and mundane. Take this example from Julian Orr's *Talking About Machines* about the repair of Xerox copiers. It's about a routine service call of a technician, who insists on hearing directly from the users who actually had the problem with the machine so that he gets the most accurate possible description. He knows that second-hand or third-hand descriptions can distort things, so he finds the users, and they tell him their story:

First user: I was having the problem with the feeder. Uh, I didn't bring my originals with me, but I was telling Richie [the manager] that they were flat, new originals, never had staples in 'em or anything. 'I would feed 'em through [opens machine cover] and one would get caught right in here.

Second user: That's where mine got caught.

First user: And then I would have two layin' on the glass.

Technician: Two on the glass? . . . Thanks. That's big input.

Second user: She was having problems with double-sided the other day.

Technician: Two-sided original? . . .

First user: Yeah. It would make it through. It would go through on the first side, but then on the second time it would catch right in here. On top . . .

Technician: As soon as you hear that extra noise, where it's clunkety-clunk, clunkety-clunk, as it's turning over . . .

Users: Uh-huh. Yeah . . . .

Technician: Okay, thanks. You told us a lot.[4]

When the repair technician hears the users' story, he knows immediately what it means: there's too much play in the reversing roll—the roll that turns the paper over to copy the other side in double-sided copying. He confirms the diagnosis by wiggling the roll. After doing other routine maintenance, he can see which parts he needs to complete the repairs.

His experience has provided him with a set of narratives from which he can diagnose the problem and find the solution. These narratives may concern surface features, such as sights and sounds or touch, or thematic features such as goals, plans, or types of surprises. In this case, it's a sound: when the paper catches, there is the distinctive sound—"clunkety-clunk, clunkety-clunk"—and a touch—the wiggle in the reversing roll. Through the users' story, the technician is able to get a fix on the symptoms of the malfunctioning machine, thereby enabling him to diagnose the cause of the problem and repair it.

In this case, the users' story fits into a set of stories that the technician has heard many times, and so the problem is easy for him to solve. From his accumulated experience, he knows at once what to do. Over time, the particular stories that the technician has come across blend into a common repository of expertise, so that he may not be able to recall the times he has seen this particular pattern before. He sizes up the situation, recognizes a familiar pattern, and knows immediately how to proceed, without any explicit reasoning by analogy. Through such pattern recognition, the technician lessens the burden of coping with new events.[5]

Other repair problems may be trickier. For instance, recall the story in Chapter One about the copier with the E053 error message, which might mean either a problem in the 24-volt interlock power supply or a shorted dicorotron. In that case, the E053 story may not by itself solve the technician's problem, but it sets the technician on a path that may lead to a solution without wasting time on the wrong diagnosis.

An extensive source of knowledge-sharing stories is *Car Talk,* the weekly U.S. National Public Radio show (it is also available on the Web at www.cartalk.com). On the show, people ring in with car problems that they're having. The two hosts, brothers Tom and Ray Magliozzi, open the discussion with some jokey questions about the listener's name or the place where they live ("Is that Amy with a 'y' or 'i-e'?") and in the process, we learn something of the caller's context. Then the hosts move on to the problem that the caller has with the car. The discussion is along the lines of: "So your '69 Toyota is making what kind of a noise? . . . Is it tch-tch-tch or is it tcho-tcho-tcho? ... Oh, I see.... And your boyfriend worked on the car? Aha! Now we're getting to the heart of the matter!" The hosts have deep knowledge of cars, as well as of people. The discussion is freewheeling and funny, but focused on solving the problem at hand. The hosts match the story of each caller with stories from their own experience, and in the process they come up with the most likely explanation of what's bothering the callers and their cars. Like most other environments where knowledge is being exchanged, the discussion is edgy, curious, insightful, and lively.[6]

Exchanges of knowledge-sharing stories occur to everyone countless times every day. In the stories, we are sometimes teaching ourselves what we know and think. Sometimes we are telling them to others. The stories, when heard, can become part of their lived experience. Through the acquisition of this new experience, existing thoughts and beliefs can evolve. This is how we learn, and this is why the transmission of knowledge is largely made up of storytelling.[7]

When we encapsulate our experience in a story, we include some details from the actual experience, sometimes embellishing it with potentially fictional details, and leaving out much of the experience altogether. This process is called *leveling and sharpening*. We do this so that the story doesn't take as long as the original experience took to live, and so that we can give a coherent account of the experience to our listeners. Each time we tell a story, we level and sharpen it in different ways to meet the current context. As the story changes, so our memory of the underlying events changes.[8]

Easy to overlook, the knowledge-sharing story is the workhorse of narrative—unashamedly unentertaining but eternally useful.

TELLING THE KNOWLEDGE-SHARING STORY

Stories focus on anomalies—events that go counter to expectations. When everything goes as you expect—the sun comes up, spring follows winter, the airplane works flawlessly—there's no story. The regular recurring events of our existence are simply the way things are. They are unremarkable. To have the basis for a story, we need something unusual, something different, something out of the ordinary, something strange.

It has been so since time immemorial. The distant puff of smoke might mean a forest fire. The faint roar of a lion might mean an attack on the village. Tiny deviations from the norm attract our attention so we can take preventive action before it's too late. Paying attention to apparent anomalies is one of the reasons that we have survived as a species.

Most of the anomalies that we notice are potential bad news of one kind or another. The stories cited at the start of this chapter were about photocopiers that had broken down or cars that needed repairing. It is when a problem arises that there is something to tell a story about.

Weak signals are the fertile area for knowledge-sharing stories. We can learn a great deal from stories about near misses—for example, two airplanes that almost collided in midair or the terrorist who almost slipped through security. In such cases, there's still time to learn. If we understand the root cause, we may be able to avoid the mistake in future. If we don't pay attention to these weak signals, we may encounter a real disaster—the plane crashes or the bomb explodes—and then it's too late to learn. We may no longer be alive. All that can be done is for the survivors to send in detectives to try to figure out what went wrong and how to prevent it in future.

If we pay attention to minor anomalies, we may be able to prevent them from escalating into large disasters. Peter Senge illustrates the exponential growth of problems with the following fable (paraphrased here):

One morning a farmer observed that a lily pad had sprung up on his pond. The following day there were two lily pads, and on the third day there were four. Since they did not seem to be doing any harm he took no action. However, the number of lily pads continued to double every day until the pond was completely covered on the thirtieth day. He didn't notice 'til the twenty-eighth day, and on the twenty-ninth day, he sees the pond is half covered. He thinks about what to do, but it's too late. The pond is totally covered the next day.[9]

185

According to the report of the 9/11 Commission, the United States suffered various small-scale terrorist attacks by al-Qaeda prior to 9/11 so that the attack on that day should have been "a shock but not a surprise." Here are some of the early warnings:

- In February 1993, a group led by Ramzi Yousef tried to bring down the World Trade Center with a truck bomb.

- In November 1995, a car bomb exploded outside the office of the U.S. program manager for the Saudi National Guard in Riyadh, killing five Americans and two others.

- In June 1996, a truck bomb demolished the Khobar Towers apartment complex in Dhahran, Saudi Arabia, killing nineteen U.S. servicemen and wounding hundreds.

- In August 1998, al-Qaeda carried out near-simultaneous truck bomb attacks on the U.S. embassies in Nairobi, Kenya, and Dar es Salaam, Tanzania. The attacks killed 224 people, including 12 Americans, and wounded thousands more.

- In October 2000, an al-Qaeda team in Aden, Yemen, used a motorboat to blow a hole in the side of a destroyer, the U.S.S. *Cole,* killing seventeen American sailors.

The 9/11 attacks on the World Trade Center and the Pentagon were far more elaborate, precise, and destructive than any of these earlier assaults. But by September 2001, the executive branch of the U.S. government, the Congress, the news media, and the American public had received warning that Islamist terrorists meant to kill Americans in large numbers.[10]

Positive Stories Can Work

It is frequently said that people learn more from failures than from successes. It's also true that people do learn from stories with a positive tone. For instance, Gary Klein tells the following story in *Sources of Power:*[11]

> In 1996, a physician called Norman Berlinger had to deliver a baby that was diagnosed in the womb as having a large cystic hygroma on the

side of his neck. The sonogram suggested that the hygroma had grown inside the neck, wrapping around the trachea, with the implication that the infant would die shortly after delivery because his air passage was blocked. Berlinger's strategy was to pierce the trachea and insert a breathing tube into it.

Upon delivery, the infant gave a cry, suggesting a clear breathing passage. But then the passage sealed up. The infant could not even grunt. Berlinger remembered an earlier situation, when he had been called in to operate on a young man who had run his snowmobile into a strand of barbed wire strung above the ground to discourage trespassers. The wire had jumbled the victim's neck tissue into sausage-like chunks. On that occasion, when Berlinger arrived, he found that the emergency technician had already inserted a breathing tube, and Berlinger had wondered how this was done. The technician later explained that he stuck the tube where he saw bubbles. Bubbles meant air coming out.

So in the delivery room, Berlinger looked into the mouth of the infant for bubbles. All he saw was a mass of yellow cysts, completely obscuring the air passage. No bubbles. Berlinger placed his palm on the infant's chest and pressed down, to force the last bit of air out of the infant's lungs. Berlinger saw a few tiny bubbles of saliva between some of the cysts and maneuvered the tube into that area. The laryngoscope has a miniature light on its tip, and Berlinger was able to guide it past the vocal cords, into the trachea. The infant quickly changed color from blue to a reassuring pink. The procedure had worked.

Just as Berlinger learned from the positive story about looking for the bubbles, human beings have always learned from positive stories. They learned from the positive story that rubbing two sticks together would cause fire. They also learned from the story of the Wright brothers in 1904 that a heavier-than-air machine could fly. In the 1950s, they learned that cheap photographic copying on plain paper was possible. In the 1990s, they learned from stories about the Web that cheap global communication was a reality.

These were all positive anomalies at the time they occurred. Today they are no longer anomalies. Making a fire or flying a plane or making a photocopy or communicating through the Web have become so commonplace that they are no longer fit subjects for stories unless some additional element is present.

The point is not that we don't learn from positive stories; rather, it is that at any time, negative anomalies far outnumber positive ones. Hence we learn more often from failures than from successes. Positive teaching stories are few compared to negative ones. But what they can teach is immensely valuable.

Knowledge-Sharing Stories Aren't Inherently Interesting

An unusual feature of knowledge-sharing stories is that they don't necessarily follow the principles of the well-made story as Aristotle described several thousand years ago in his *Poetics*. The well-made story has a beginning, a middle, and an ending; it has characters and a plot that combines a reversal and a recognition. The storyteller visualizes the action and feels with the characters so that listeners immerse themselves in the world of the story.

Knowledge-sharing stories tend to be about issues and difficulties and how they were dealt with and why the course of action solved the problem. They don't necessarily have a protagonist, that is, a hero or heroine, or even a recognizable plot, let alone a turning point and a recognition.

Think back to the story that began this chapter: the malfunctioning Xerox copier. Or look at the story in Chapter One about the copier with an E053 error code. These are stories in the broad sense of events linked in some kind of causal sequence, but they don't follow the traditional pattern of a well-made story. As a result, they aren't inherently interesting because the human implications aren't made explicit.

To make the sequence of events interesting, you need to graft something scary or exciting onto it, say by adding a hero who undertakes a journey—as is done in business school case studies with varying degrees of success. Klein's *Sources of Power* gives a brilliantly successful example. Like the E053 story, it features a generally reliable piece of equipment that occasionally gives misleading information. But this time, the story *is* interesting:

A nurse in a neonatal intensive care unit has been providing primary care for a baby in the isolette next to the baby described here. She has noticed this baby having subtle color changes over a period of several hours.... Then in a matter of seconds, the baby turns blue-black ... his heart rate drops but then levels out and holds steady at eighty beats per minute.

She knows immediately that he has suffered a pneumopericardium. Air has filled the sac that surrounds the heart and turned it into a balloon.... The heart is essentially paralyzed. She knows he will die within minutes if the air around his heart is not released. She knows this because she has seen it happen once before, to a baby who was her patient. That baby had died.

Meanwhile, the baby's primary nurse is yelling for X-ray, and a doctor to come and puncture the baby's chest wall. She figures that the baby's lung has collapsed, a common event for babies who are on ventilators, and, besides, the heart monitor continues to show a steady eighty beats per minute. The nurse who first spotted the problem tries to correct her—"It's the heart; there's no heartbeat"—while the team around her continues to point to the heart monitor. She pushes their hands away from the baby and screams for quiet as she listens through the stethoscope for a heartbeat. There is none, and she begins doing compressions on the baby's chest. The chief neonatologist appears, and she turns to him, slaps a syringe in his hand, and says, "It's a pneumopericardium. I know it. Stick the heart." The X-ray technician calls from across the room that she is right: the baby's pericardium is filled with air. The physician releases the air, and the baby's life is saved.

Afterward, the team talks about why the monitor had fooled them. They realize that the monitor is designed to record electrical events, and it continued to pick up the electrical impulses generated by the heart. The monitor can record the electrical impulse but cannot show whether the heart is actually beating to circulate blood through the body.[12]

By embedding the equipment story in a human context and turning it into a traditional well-told story, the narrator makes it not only interesting but moving. In Klein's telling, the raw knowledge-sharing story about misleading information from a piece of equipment has been transformed into a gripping story about the human dynamics of dealing with a life-and-death situation in a hospital. The audience sees the story through the eyes of a heroine who not only knows what to do but also has the courage to contradict the nurse who is giving the primary care for the baby in question and issue a blunt ultimatum to the higher-status neonatologist. And it helps that the story has a happy ending. The focus is on the baby who was saved, not on the baby who died. As a result, the story has a positive tone. We learn not only about the functioning of the misleading equipment but also about what it takes for a nurse to apply that understanding in the real-life tensions of an intensive care unit in a hospital.

By including details that bring the story within the listeners' frame of reference, the teller helps listeners imagine themselves in the story. If the situation is one the listeners have already faced in the past or may face in the future, it becomes personally relevant—and the more personally relevant the story becomes, the more likely it is to be indexed in memory, and the more likely they are to draw from it in future situations. The story about the pneumopericardium is thus easier for a nurse to remember than any list of pneumopericardium symptoms.

Note also that considerable storytelling skill has gone into producing this succinct but gripping story. Klein trains his people for months before they are able to spot potential stories and retell them effectively.[13] If you simply gather stories in the field, you will tend to get stories like the Xerox repair stories: bland, useful, and uninteresting—except to those whose lives and livelihood may depend on the content.

For Knowledge Stories, Include an Explanation

While a knowledge-sharing story often lacks the elements of a well-told story, it also has something that the traditional story lacks—*an explanation*. Human knowledge, including scientific knowledge, consists primarily of explanations—generic stories that explain the causal relations between a set of phenomena. Facts can be looked up, and predictions alone are merely useful for testing alternative explanations. Explanations provide understanding that allows us to comprehend the past and grasp how the future will unfold.[14]

Without an explanation, a story about something that has happened is mere information. Thus, the users' story of the malfunctioning copier that opened this chapter was in itself mere information because the users didn't know what was causing the symptoms. The story becomes knowledge once the technician completes the diagnosis and adds the explanation: the reversing roll needs to be repaired.

To build an explanation, define the beginning state, the end state, and the causal factors, and then assemble an action sequence that ties the elements together. Test the sequence for *coherence* (Do the steps follow from each other?), *applicability* (Does it account for the end state?), and *completeness* (Does it pick up everything important?). If it passes these tests, it becomes the explanation of what happened. If the beginning state is a frequently occurring one, it may also become a mental model on which to base future actions.[15]

In this way, explanations can come to represent lenses through which we view the world. Every time we make plans or take action, our choices are based on a mental model or story in the back of our head that leads us to believe that the action being taken will lead to the desired result. Having the correct explanation for phenomena is the key to accurate knowledge and wise action.[16]

Tell the Knowledge-Sharing Story with Context

Knowledge-sharing stories typically are told with considerable contextual detail. Detail enables listeners to conduct case-based reasoning, that is, determine whether it is appropriate to reason from one case to another in a new context.[17]

In this respect, the knowledge-sharing story is the opposite of the springboard story discussed in Chapter Three. Whereas the knowledge-sharing story is focused on enabling the recall of the story on future occasions, the springboard story is aimed more at generating a new story in the minds of the listeners about what they might do in their own setting. If you tell the springboard story with a lot of detailed context about the surrounding sights and sounds, you use up the listeners' precious mental space, thus reducing the likelihood that they will imagine new stories in their own contexts. The springboard story itself is a catalyst. Enabling the listeners to remember it is secondary to the primary goal of sparking a new story and consequent action. The springboard story is mere scaffolding that can be set aside once the listeners' stories have been generated. By contrast, remembering the story itself is the raison d'être of the knowledge-sharing story.

Draw on Narrative Fragments

Although we continually draw on past experience, many situations have no exact counterpart. When Klein studied the work of firefighters, there was never an entire fire that a commander saw as an exact copy of a previous one. Years of experience were blended together in their minds. Some aspect of the incident, not the entire fire, would ring a bell—for example, the firefighter notices billboards high on the roof of a building on fire and remembers a case where billboards came crashing down, and so he moves the crowds of spectators back in case these billboards fall.[18]

But the fragment of experience that is relevant to the case at hand is usually just the starting point for the solution, not the solution itself. For instance, in the story about the surgeon who looked for bubbles to find an infant's breathing passage, the solution derived from a story about an adult, not a newborn infant. It was about an accident, not a birth. It was about someone else's actions, not his own. In the original story, the bubbles were present of their own accord, while in the case at hand, the surgeon had to invent his own method of generating air bubbles. When someone extracts the fragment from the original story and adapts it to a different situation, new knowledge is created.[19]

Use Stories to Make Sense of Events

Stories about the past enable us to make sense of the past and so move into the future. Thus, juries in legal trials find it difficult to hold all the evidence in their minds at the same time. Instead, they tend to organize the evidence into a story, which then makes the task of recalling and understanding further evidence easier. Jurors compare the stories presented by the prosecutor and the defense attorney and accept the claim that more closely matches the story that they themselves have constructed.[20]

People who have had a hard day's work doing different tasks often gather in a coffee shop or a bar to swap stories of their different adventures, just as mothers in a park may gather on the benches to swap stories of their efforts to get their children to go to sleep. In the social vetting process of telling and listening to and commenting on the stories, the stories may get further refined, sometimes becoming "tricks of the trade."[21]

Listening to these stories isn't merely entertainment: it leads to the acquisition of vicarious experience by those participating. The limitation of sharing stories in an informal setting is that those who don't hear the story can't learn from it. This limitation was overcome by the Xerox Corporation in its Eureka program, in which photocopier technicians were given two-way radios so that they could be in constant contact to share experiences; the most useful of the stories were vetted and made available on the Web to the entire workforce of twenty-five thousand technicians.[22]

Expand Experience Through Storytelling

Experts typically make decisions by recognizing patterns from cues, as when a photocopier technician recognizes that the reversing roll needs repairing, or a nurse recognizes that a newborn baby is suffering from a pneumopericardium, or the hosts of *Car Talk* recognize a familiar problem with a '69 Toyota.

Experts tend to see the pattern almost instantly, test it for applicability, and apply it if it fits. If it doesn't fit, they try a different pattern to see whether that fits. It's usually only if there is no obvious pattern that an expert stops to carry out a rational comparison of alternatives. Rational analysis is more commonly applied by novices who lack experience or by groups that want to develop a shared understanding of the approach to be followed.[23]

An expert's ability to understand the past depends partly on recognizing common patterns and partly on the ability to run mental simulations. The photocopier makes a certain noise when it jams, and so this is what must have happened. The newborn infant is turning a certain color and showing no heartbeat, so that is what must have happened.

The ability to run such mental simulations in new situations is what distinguishes experts from journeymen. Journeymen have mastered some routines, and their actions are smooth: they show many of the characteristics of expertise. But if pushed outside the standard patterns, they have difficulty improvising. They lack a sense of the dynamics of the situation. They have trouble explaining how the current state of affairs came about and how it will play out.[24]

The more we can expand our array of experience, the more we are able to develop an understanding of the dynamic of what's involved. This is how journeymen move up to the level of genuine expert. The acquisition of experience can be accomplished directly or virtually by listening to the stories of earlier experiences.[25]

Use Groups to Accelerate Storytelling

Within a well-functioning community of practice, the interchange of experience is often rapid. The stories are likely to exist in a state of continuous flux, with fragments and allusions, as people contribute bits, often talking together. For example:

> In 1999, I attended a session of one community of practice in the World Bank concerning public enterprise reform. The group had invited one of its clients from India to make a presentation about their experience in public enterprise reform. This in itself was remarkable for the World Bank at the time; it would have been unthinkable just a few years before. Until the knowledge-sharing initiative, World Bank staff had tended to see themselves as experts—people who told their clients what to do—rather than as participants in a mutual learning experience. But here the community was explicitly trying to learn from the client's experience. The other striking feature of the discussion was the repeated

interruptions and questions from the audience. "Did you try this?" "Did you examine that?" "Did you notice this impact?" Rapid-fire questions bombarded the presenters. To a nonspecialist the discussion would be very esoteric. But even a nonspecialist could feel the excitement in the air. These were people who were passionate about their subject. The session had no formal outcome, but those who were there ended up with a richer understanding of what worked—and what didn't work—in public enterprise reform.[26]

Make Sure to Capture the Stories Shared

When knowledge-sharing stories occur in mere fragments, barely intelligible to outsiders, capturing them can be a major challenge. Most of the expert participants at the discussion may get it, but the organizational value may be lost unless the learnings are gathered for later transmittal.

People who listen to stories have the problem of not hearing in the first place and then of forgetting what they heard. It's an old Talmudic saying that we see things not as they are but rather as we are.[27] That is, we observe the world through a set of mental filters that focus our attention on the things that we have come to see as important. We overlook new elements because they do not fit our existing mental frames. Even if we do observe what is in front of us, memory is treacherous.[28]

If this isn't the first telling of the story, there's also the risk that it may have evolved significantly through leveling and sharpening. Each time the story is told, the teller adjusts it in subtle ways to meet the current context. Over time, through multiple tellings, the story can change significantly. As the story changes, so memory of the events changes.[29]

It is therefore important to take steps to improve both the registering of the initial story and its later recall. At knowledge-sharing sessions, things typically happen very fast. A person taking notes can't be fully following the discussion. A person fully following the discussion doesn't have time to take notes. Where feasible, routine audiorecording of sessions should be considered, provided that the recording itself does not get in the way of interchange.

In addition, other steps can be taken to enhance story capture:

- *Using narratives to summarize:* Where complex issues are discussed over an extended period, for instance, at an off-site workshop, the amount of material can be daunting. Getting the group to craft a story of the event before leaving can result in participants' leaving the session with a shared narrative that weaves together many disparate insights. This can lay the foundation for improved future collaboration.

- *Transcribing:* Where sessions result in significant learning, recordings can be transcribed and then lightly edited to remove inconsistencies and nonsequiturs.

- *Hyperlinking:* The transcribed text can be hyperlinked to reports and references so that a slender document can become a web with rich content.

- *Corroborating and verifying:* The person responsible for capturing should also explore the need for corroboration so that mistakes or misunderstandings are not disseminated.

An aspect of knowledge capture of particular importance to organizations is what to do about experienced staff who leave the organization and walk out the door with highly valuable know-how in their heads that may be crucial to the future work of the organization. This chapter's template lays out steps that can be taken to use storytelling to capture this know-how before it is lost.[30]

CREATING CONTEXT FOR
THE KNOWLEDGE-SHARING STORY

Most knowledge management programs expend great energy on improving the supply of knowledge, while leaving demand to take care of itself. Unfortunately, the demand side is often the more serious problem. Thus, what enables the transfer of knowledge in the photocopying story at the start of this chapter is the desire of the technician to hear the users' story. He insists on hearing it directly from the users to avoid distortion. Similarly the surgeon dealing with the newborn infant in danger of dying from a blocked windpipe learned the trick of looking for air bubbles by asking the paramedic how he managed to get the tube in. In those cases, the people who possessed the relevant knowledge had no trouble telling the story once asked—but someone had to ask.

In fact, knowledge is useful only to those willing and able to learn, as Martine Haas discovered in her research on the impact of access to knowledge on the performance of teams in an international organization:

> *Results showed that teams operating in a context that encouraged learning and innovation did improve their performance as compared to teams that didn't have access to knowledge. But when teams were operating in environments where the result of their work was predetermined, with little flexibility allowed to the team to adapt and innovate, performance didn't improve along with improved access to knowledge. In this constrained setting, access to knowledge just slowed the team down. Without a desire to learn, improved access to knowledge was a liability, not an asset.*[31]

Stalk Sensitive Knowledge Through a Story

Knowledge sharing normally happens within communities or teams that already have the basis of trust. Where this basis isn't present, eliciting knowledge stories can be difficult, particularly for stories that involve pejorative details.

If the knowledge isn't particularly significant to the acquirer, the task is easier. If I have a shorter route for getting from one location to another, you might be willing to listen to me. But if the knowledge has deep meaning for you, such as how you should exercise your profession or how you should raise your children, you may not be so willing to accept something new that implies jettisoning the elements that are part of your existing identity.

How can you encourage people to explore new knowledge? One approach developed by Dave Snowden is to use a story as a stalking horse.[32] He tells a story about one thing as a way of communicating potentially threatening knowledge about something else. Thus, when Snowden goes into an organization to coach managers on innovation, the dilemma that he faces is often the managers' lack of self-understanding of their counterproductive management practices.

One of the things he does is to invite the participants in advance of the session to read Dava Sobel's book *Longitude*:[33]

> This is the story of the search to solve one of the thorniest scientific problems of the eighteenth century, how to determine longitude. Thousands of lives had been lost at sea over the centuries owing to the inability to determine an east-west position. To solve the problem, a prize was offered that amounted to a fortune in today's currency.
>
> While some of the most brilliant scientists of the day sought to find a solution through astronomy, self-taught English clockmaker John Harrison devoted much of his life to finding a solution by making an accurate clock. Harrison imagined a mechanical solution—a clock that would keep precise time at sea. By measuring the angle of the sun at noon and comparing it with that of a fixed point like Greenwich, one could calculate one's longitude. Most scientists of the day discounted the idea of a clock because there were too many variables at sea. They were certain that changes in temperature, air pressure, humidity, and gravity would inevitably render a clock inaccurate.
>
> After years of work, Harrison developed a series of clocks that would work aboard a ship at sea and keep time to within the tolerances required to maintain enough accuracy to figure longitude. But once he had found the solution, Harrison had to battle with the Board of Longitude and its commissioners to get it accepted and so win the prize.
>
> He underwent a long series of unfair trials and demonstrations. Ultimately he received recognition, after years of dealing with incompetence, stupidity, arrogance, and closed-minded blindness, and was awarded the Copley Medal in recognition of his work by the British Royal Astronomical Society, an award that was later bestowed on persons such as Benjamin Franklin, Captain James Cook, and Albert Einstein. Harrison's clock was proven accurate in 1762, but it was not until 1773 that he received the prize money.

When Snowden arrives at the session with the managers, he asks the audience to give instances when they have treated their own staff the way that Harrison was treated by the scientific establishment, and he easily receives a large number of instances. If by contrast he had asked the participants to give occasions when they treated their own staff in a callous, pig-headed, stupid manner, he would find that participants would be offended by the question.

Tease Out the Knowledge-Sharing Story

Because knowledge-sharing narratives tend to be about issues and difficulties, they typically have a negative tone. In any organization, much of the challenge in sharing knowledge lies in creating settings that enable staff to talk about what has gone wrong. This can be a significant problem where overall trust levels within the organization are low.

The best solution, of course, is to deal with the root cause and address the problem of distrust. Raising the level of trust in an entire organization is a long-term undertaking. Nevertheless, even in low-trust environments, organizations can generate communities of practitioners who trust each other, even if they don't trust the organization as a whole, as outlined in Chapter Seven.

Regardless of the level of trust, it's impossible to say all we know, if only because we know what we know only when we need to know it. When asked to say what we know in general, it's natural to feel at a loss; when asked about a specific situation, by contrast, we find that our knowledge becomes available for transfer. Some methods are more successful than others in eliciting knowledge-sharing stories.

The most obvious approach is to generate a free-form discussion in an informal setting, as discussed in the Template for Nurturing Community at the end of Chapter Seven. Get together everyone who has something to contribute in a relaxed setting and spark an interchange about how and why things happened the way they did, and what the difficulties were and how they got fixed. Make sure you have enough time, the right kind of physical space, the right participants, and appropriate facilitation skills on hand.

An alternative method is by way of observation—a kind of anthropological method. Go and live with the community, and observe it in action to see how it functions and gather the stories that the members tell each other. If you are careful to blend into the scene and spend enough time there, you may get to know how that community functions. You can then construct stories that approximate the stories that people in that community use. You get inside the idea of what's going on.

Then there is role playing. Given that knowledge-sharing stories are often about mistakes, there's likely to be a lot of ego at stake. There may be negative repercussions within the organization for exposing mistakes. So when people tell stories about their mistakes, they're often so busy presenting their public identity as competent individuals who don't make unintelligent errors that they may not get around to revealing what actually happened. Role playing allows participants to adopt a throwaway identity (for example, play-acting how an organizational team would normally handle a particular problem) that can free them to present the truth of what actually happens.

A what-if discussion can also be useful. What if we'd done this? Or what if we hadn't done that? This frees up everyone to tell stories not about what actually happened with all the emotional attachments associated with having made mistakes, but about what might have happened. The stories can be open because no one is risking self-image. Although the topic is something that didn't actually happen, talking about it can shed light on what did happen, as well as on how things could be different in the future. In the process, participants reveal what they really know.[34]

You can also make progress by asking experts how novices might get confused if they were undertaking the task. If novices were by some chance pressed into service during an emergency, would they see this in the same way that the experts did? What mistakes would they make? Why would they make them? This approach can elicit useful understanding of what experts know that novices might not.[35]

Finally, thinking and doing can be combined in a kind of cycle. We try something, and it doesn't quite work right. We think about it and then imagine how it could have been different. We try that out and see what happens. It seems to be working better. So we try it out again, and we see what happens. Our concrete experience leads to reflection on what worked and the construction of a story leading to further active experimentation. It's the combination of storytelling and active experimentation that leads to insight.

SPECIAL KINDS OF KNOWLEDGE-SHARING STORIES

Although stories often help people make sense of the world, three common kinds of stories are generally unhelpful:[36]

- *Scapegoat stories: "It's all your fault!"* Scapegoat stories assign all the blame to others and turn them into villains. Inevitably it's not true: they aren't all to blame. But both tellers and hearers are likely to think, "They are stubborn: we are principled," or "They are weak: we are appropriately flexible." In an organizational setting, this frequently occurs when the finger-pointing starts after a disaster. When such stories emerge, it's often time to rethink your own role in creating the situation.

- *Victim stories: "It's all our fault!"* In this version, tellers and hearers assign all blame to themselves. In an organizational setting, this tends to occur after a string of failures and the organization loses confidence in its own ability to perform in the future. When such stories emerge, discussing the organization's strengths can be helpful.

- *Stories of helplessness: "There's nothing we can do!"* Very few situations really leave nothing for the participants to do, whether the situation is personal or organizational. Even people facing imminent death can take steps to make sense of life. And those who tell stories of helplessness are generally not facing imminent death. Such stories are typically a pretext for inaction. When you encounter them (or find yourself telling them), you need to start thinking realistically about what can be done.[37]

Official Versus Underground Know-How

The idea that much knowledge resides in stories has not yet received universal acceptance, as shown by the experience of Gary Klein and four associates in trying to prepare a document that would record what had been learned at a conference:

> The presenters had all submitted abstracts of their talks, but the documents were tedious to read. The organizer wanted a more useful record of the proceedings. So Klein and his associates agreed to participate in each of five concurrent tracks at the conference and prepare an account of what was said. As it turned out, each time a presenter showed a slide about a major idea, everyone in the room would start writing furiously, while Klein and his associates would just sit back. Every time a presenter told a story, Klein and his associates would be writing furiously while the audience would just sit back. By the end of two days, Klein and his associates had assembled a wonderful set of stories, brimming with insights.
>
> Klein comments: "We know that all the official viewgraphs listing the five key steps to do this or the seven ways to do that are fairly useless. You can exchange these slides from one session to the next, and no one would notice. These slides are filled with useful tidbits like, 'Keep the lines of communication open,' and 'Don't wait too long when problems are building up.' Presumably these bits of wisdom are going to help those who keep trying to close lines of communication and who insist on waiting too long whenever a problem is detected."
>
> Klein gathered together the stories that he and his associates had heard and put them into a thirty-page conference "proceedings." The conference organizer was delighted with the product and wanted to expand it into a book. But the project fell apart when the document was sent to the presenters for clearance. The presenters were shocked that the official record didn't focus on their abstract conclusions; they didn't want to be remembered as people who "just swapped stories and anecdotes." Klein's efforts to prove that the presenters' slogans

were of little value compared to insights of the stories were to no avail, and the conference "proceedings" could not be released.[38]

Most useful knowledge thus lies not in the bland generalities that are bandied about so often in organizations and at conferences but rather in the interstices of the narratives and anecdotes that show how problems actually get solved in a real-life context.

This is particularly the case with the unofficial underground knowledge of an organization—the rumors, gossip, and heterodox ideas that flow along the grapevine. Some of this underground storytelling is negative and undermines the management and the organization. Some of it is potentially valuable—sometimes, as I outline in Chapter Eleven, even more valuable than the officially accepted knowledge of an organization.[39] Whether good or bad, the underground flow of stories is central to the health of an organization, and the question of what a leader can do about it is the subject to which I now turn.

AN APPROACH FOR SAVING THE KNOWLEDGE OF DEPARTING STAFF

Many organizations face the risk of loss of knowledge with the retirement of seasoned staff. Although there is no way to capture or codify such knowledge completely, steps can be taken to palliate any institutional damage from these departures:

- Assign junior staff to work with and be mentored by the most valuable senior staff. This is usually the best way to ensure knowledge transfer, although it requires careful advance planning and may involve significant resources.

- Encourage retirees to remain members of networks after retirement, offering the incentive of obtaining work as consultants.

- When prospective retirees have specific and rare expertise that is of high value to the organization, arrange interviews with them before departure:

  - If possible, arrange one or more interviews well before the expected departure date.

  - Prior to the interview, make an assessment of what knowledge is of particular interest and value to the organization and outline the interview. Leave the door open to serendipity. Allow the interviewee to add anything she or he deems fit.

  - Have one or more experienced interviewers who are intimately familiar the topic conduct the interview.

  - Make an audiotape of the interview. Transcribe the tape, and have the interviewee review and edit the transcript for accuracy.

  - Hyperlink the interview transcript to written reports, data, issues, projects, or items specifically mentioned in the interview.

  - Include the expert's phone number and e-mail address and a brief biography in the transcript.[40]

9

TAME THE GRAPEVINE

Using Narrative to Neutralize Gossip and Rumor

 Wisdom cries out in the streets, but no man regards it.

William Shakespeare[1]

When knowledge management was being introduced under my leadership at the World Bank in the late 1990s, I was convinced that the program was soundly based. Unless the World Bank, as a development institution, learned to share its knowledge, it was doomed to irrelevance.

Jim Wolfensohn, president of the World Bank, agreed; in October 1996 he'd announced his strong commitment to implementing a knowledge-sharing program. We were going to become "the knowledge bank." Colleagues who shared the vision were full of energy and enthusiasm. What I hadn't realized was that for the next couple of years, as we were implementing the vision, a significant number of people would stay on the sidelines, surreptitiously second-guessing and undermining everything we were trying to accomplish.

Open conflict would have been one thing. I could have confronted it, presented the solid reasons for implementing the change program, gotten decisions made, and moved on. But surreptitious resistance was something else. Everything looked calm. People appeared to be supporting the program. But below the surface, the rumor mill was going full tilt. It took the form of gossip, snide remarks, imagined bad news, and attempted character assassinations of the proponents of change. Some sections of upper management were even actively circulating the canard that I was "trying to launch Star Wars." It was difficult even to learn about, let alone deal with, this groundswell. And as the designated leader of the change, I was the target for much of the flow.

The gossip and rumors were prompted not by any rational analysis of the costs, benefits, and risks of getting the World Bank to share its knowledge but rather by a lack of understanding as to what was involved in the new strategic direction, disagreement over how quickly to implement it, and anxiety as to whose careers, budgets, or turf might benefit or suffer. The underground criticism made it difficult to get the cooperation needed for the enterprise-wide program that we were undertaking.

What to do? At the time, I had no idea. I could see that denying the rumors and gossip would give them credibility. Asking how they got started would ensure their spread. Ignoring them altogether risked allowing them to grow out of control. So not knowing what to do, I went about the business of implementing the knowledge-sharing program, answering any explicit criticisms, but largely ignoring the rumors and gossip and hoping they would in time go away. I was eventually vindicated in the sense that knowledge sharing did finally succeed.[2] But the rumors and gossip were a significant distraction, a handicap to moving forward rapidly with implementation of the program.

Since then, I've discovered that the torrent of gossip and criticism that pours from the rumor mill is the normal organizational response to any effort to launch basic change. Whether you're the head of the organization desiring to take it in a new direction or an insurgent aiming to persuade the leadership of the organization to change, you will always find a significant number of people who don't agree. Maybe they have a personal or professional interest in the status quo. Maybe they disagree with the reasons for change. Maybe they would like to take the organization in a different direction. Perhaps they are just wary of any change. So although you have mobilized an energized army of champions to lead the change and patiently explained the basis for it, some holdouts will always hug the sidelines, surreptitiously using the grapevine to undermine and even sabotage the transition.

I further discovered that the grapevine is at its most dangerous after the decision to proceed with the change program has been made. As Rosabeth Moss Kanter points out, this is when the initial excitement of a new vision has worn off, the practical difficulties of implementation are being resolved, and the full benefits of the change are still not fully realized.[3] I could have moved much more quickly and efficiently had I understood how stories define an organization's culture. Once I grasped the power of narrative, I could see how narrative tools could help me deal with and even tame the grapevine.

THE STORIES THAT FORM THE CORPORATE CULTURE

Corporate culture, says Edgar Schein, is "a pattern of basic assumptions that the group learned as it solved its problems of external adaptation and internal integration, that has worked well enough to be considered valid and, therefore, to be taught to new members as the correct way to perceive, think, and feel in relation to those problems."[4]

Any group that has been together for a significant time tends to develop a shared view of the way the surrounding world works, of the methods for problem solving that have been be effective in that world, and of the appropriate ways of acting in that world in the future. When this shared view of the world has been in place long enough and is reflected in the actions of the members of the organization, it tends to be taken for granted. It comes to constitute the unspoken know-how or culture of that organization.[5]

Knowing how to speak and act in an organization is what makes its members different from recruits or outsiders. But the know-how involved in a culture is not merely about having access to facts. It also includes a capacity to speak and act accordance with the expectations and norms that are in play there.[6] Being part of a corporate culture thus involves much more than an observer's intellectual understanding of what constitutes acceptable and unacceptable ways of speaking and acting in that organization at that time. A true member is able—without thinking or referring to explicit criteria—to speak and act in the expected way.

What makes certain speech or behavior acceptable or appropriate in any particular organization? While successful learning from prior experience is one source, other aspects of an organization's culture are decidedly less rational. Personal or institutional histories, turf wars, career gaming, custom, or mere thoughtlessness often play a part. These aspects are communicated in narratives that constrain behavior, even creating path dependency. Larry Prusak discusses one example from IBM, when he was executive director of the Institute for Knowledge Management:

> I was on a number of committees, acquisition committees at IBM, and very often in these discussions, someone would say: "We tried that and it didn't work." Now, what they said was true. We had tried it and it hadn't worked. And that didn't mean that it would never work. But the story they were telling and the way they were telling it bounded the behavior. It constrained behavior. It was as though they were saying, "The Bishop wills it" or "God wills it."
>
> IBM tried three times to buy a telecom firm, and each time it was a disaster. Does that mean necessarily that the fourth time it will also be a disaster? Not at all. There is no logic behind it. But the story is powerful and it becomes embedded in legends and myths. There are opportunity costs since people's careers were killed because they did this. The associations of the story become so powerful that it constrains behavior, often to the detriment of what could be done. The story itself becomes a powerful factor."[7]

Understood But Unwritten

Organizations usually have a remarkable degree of consensus as to what behavior is acceptable and what isn't, even though the relevant norms are rarely, if ever, written down or codified.

How does it happen? Ethnologists have shown that culture is transmitted not in formal doctrines or official processes but mainly through stories—anecdotes, jokes, epigrams, or proverbs.[8] These pithy utterances are unapologetically ad hoc. They often recount prior successes or failures.

"Somebody did this one time in this organization and got fired!" There's emotional power there. People think, *I'd better not do that or I'll be fired!* Or: *Somebody did this and got promoted.* Then people think, *Well, maybe I should do that! That's the way to get promoted.*[9]

The utterances reflect not something that has to be argued for, but rather life as it is lived there—a commonsense apprehension of the way things are. The stories pass on obvious realities, which any wide-awake person who took the time to look would grasp.[10] Some examples:

- *Procter & Gamble:* "What P&G knows more than anything else is TV. No brand manager at P&G ever got fired for recommending a 30-second TV spot."[11]

- IBM: "You can't open an office in Kuala Lumpur."[12]

- *World Bank:* "Why would we spend resources on sharing knowledge? We're a bank. The World Bank. Got it?"

Talk in this maddeningly knowing tone occurs continuously all over the organization—before, during, and after department meetings; in cafeterias, at breakfasts, lunches, receptions, and dinner parties; in corridors and around the office coffee machine or watercooler; by e-mail and in telephone conversations—in effect, wherever the members of an organization get together and start talking. The subject matter of the narratives may include who is getting along with whom, or not, and why, or who is considering what move to make, or who or what is being viewed favorably or unfavorably by the top, or how the organization is reacting to external developments—in effect, anything that might shed light on what is going on in the organization and what may happen next. The stories may at times be mere idle talk and at other times be launched with a specific agenda—measuring who's up and who's down, exploring what others know, testing opinion, identifying possible alliances or detecting possible conspiracies, advancing a cause or undermining a competitor's career.

The stories that are told and retold in an organization are learning experiences for the participants, whether positive or negative. They are among the principal means by which people are integrated—for better or worse—into the culture.

Stories Create a Social Bond

The stories that are told and retold in an organization communicate not only the story itself but also the values of the organization—that is, what one must say in order to be heard in that organization. The storytelling that occurs in an organization involves the actions not only of the people the story is about but also of the person telling the story and the audience consenting to listen to the story. It is through these actions that the relationships of the people are played out. What is transmitted through these narratives is the set of pragmatic rules that constitute a kind of social bond. If the social bond is violated, the transgressor may be ejected from the organization. Here's one example:

> From 2005 to 2010, Mark Hurd was highly successful as chairman, chief executive officer, and president of Hewlett-Packard, the largest information technology company in the world by revenue. On August 6, 2010, Hurd resigned these positions, following the discovery of inappropriate conduct in relation to a claim of sexual harassment made by a former reality TV actress, Jodie Fisher. A probe conducted by HP's board concluded that Hurd had not violated the company's sexual harassment policy but he had infringed the firm's standards of business conduct, in relation to expense claims that did not reveal Hurd's relationship with Fisher. The amounts of money involved in the expense claims were small in comparison to Hurd's compensation, but the board insisted on his resignation. Hurd said he "realized there were instances in which I did not live up to the standards and principles of trust, respect and integrity that I have espoused at HP."[13]

Overall, the telling of stories encourages compliance. The narratives may refer to the past, about who did what to whom, but they are also contemporaneous with the act of reciting them, in the sense that the values implicit in the story—the appropriateness of the behavior—are being strengthened or questioned by the storyteller, as in this example from a computer programmer in the United Kingdom: "Try telling your manager sometime that you want to redesign a piece of code because 'It's aesthetically displeasing' or because 'The design sucks.' He'll laugh you out of the office and quite possibly the company. Never mind that you were right or that your redesign would drastically improve maintainability and probably speed things up."[14]

The Stories Are Endlessly Repeated

A characteristic feature of organizational culture is the repetition of the same stories. Stories become mere fragments that need not be retold in full but perhaps only have a label, like "Lehman Brothers!" or "BP!" It's as if in this repetition, people are reminding themselves: "Never forget!"

Although each telling of a particular narrative may seem to an external observer like the same story, the story continues to evolve as each new storyteller recounts the events slightly differently. In this way, the news of the organization is passed on humor, anxiety, praise, or despair. With each new telling, the story's impact spreads.

Stories Differ in Different Parts of the Organization

Stories are used for different purposes at different levels of the organization. At the top of the organization, there is always a core group of people who call the shots.[15] The stories this group tells typically reflect the complacencies of power. They generally feel no need to question themselves or their assumptions. Stories told by and about the group reflect the preoccupation with own needs and priorities.[16]

In small start-ups, for example, the core group often consists of the founders, an angel-mentor or two, and a confidant. By contrast, a large and complex organization such as General Electric or Procter & Gamble can have hundreds of interlocking core groups, each active in its own division, department, or region. They vie with one another for the attention of the ultimate core group: the people in the CEO's kitchen cabinet. This group generally (but not always) includes the people at the top of the hierarchy.

But it may also include people who—because they are respected, popular, successful, or manipulative, or because they control access to some critical bottleneck—have gained the loyalty and attention of others throughout the organization.[17]

At lower levels of the organization, there is typically a tangle of informal networks—groupings, coalitions, alliances, and friendships, with the participants linked by background, expertise, region, personal interest, common ambition, or whatever. Here the stories that are told and retold can provide a vehicle for those who are trying to advance their various causes and interests—or to undermine a competing group. They may also constitute a resource for those who regard themselves as subordinated, oppressed, or dispossessed, offering a means of self-expression and solidarity, not too different from the traditional griping of troops in a military unit who exchange experience and information: the general tone here is one of satire, ridicule, and disrespect for those in control and their ideals.[18]

This is what the computer programmers in a U.K. company who felt themselves at odds with the management of the time said:

> Managers don't want good code. They want code that you can squat and shit as quickly as possible because the only metric they look at is the deadline. It may not smell good. It may self-destruct in a few months. It will certainly keep your team in "fireman mode" for the rest of the time they're at the company, but by God it made the deadline and that's all that counts.[19]

The stories that are told and retold in organizations lend themselves to a variety of functions: they transmit information, also prescribe what ought to be done, question what should be happening, evaluate what is going on, express solidarity, or satirize whatever is regarded as ridiculous. The stories may nevertheless reflect a unified viewpoint. Some common refrains:[20]

- "How did that jerk get promoted?"
- "Why did the stock price go through the floor?"
- "Where has our pension gone?"

Narratives told within the organization also tend to flow outward and communicate the persona of the organization to clients and partners—for instance:

> While most airlines strive for a culture that exudes seriousness as ensuring safety, Southwest Airlines has deliberately cultivated narratives that express an atmosphere of fun: its staff persistently make light-hearted and humorous comments that communicate friendliness.

Stories Reflect the Organization's Health

Different types of stories can be classified according to the willingness to communicate them to others and the level of agreement on their content. *Overt and agreed stories* are openly communicated throughout the organization and also willingly communicated to outsiders in the form of publications and newspaper articles. *Covert and agreed stories* are not revealed to outsiders because they contain sensitive information or business secrets. *Overt and contested stories* emerge in disputes between management and labor, or when there are accusations of wrongdoing. *Covert and contested stories* may be told either among the core groups running the organization or among unsatisfied staff and build the basis for conflict. Contested stories at lower levels of the organization cannot be controlled by management.[21]

Management literature and managers typically dwell on the stories that are overt and agreed. Other chapters of this book deal with how to effect changes in the overt story, mainly with springboard stories (Chapter Four), future stories (Chapter Ten), or inspiring innovation (Chapter Eleven). Even a healthy organization, however, is likely to have some difference between the stories that occur covertly and the official organizational stories that are overt and agreed. Such differences are particularly likely when organizations are trying to cope with a rapidly morphing environment.

The advent of transformational change will cause divergence between the official story and the stories that emerge in the underground of the organization. This is because the transformation will inevitably threaten some existing power structures.

In some objective sense, the transformation may be a win-win situation for everyone. But in any transformation, there will be perceived losers as well as winners, as some careers will be expected to flourish more than others, and some types of expertise will become more important than others. These shifts inevitably cause both hope and anxiety among the participants and become the source of covert stories that will challenge the official story that everyone is a winner.

Until the transformation plays out, risks and opportunities will loom for participants. The fears and hopes of the participants will emerge in rumors, gossip, and innuendo about the pending change and those responsible for it.

> Back in 1996, when I was pushing for the World Bank to adopt knowledge management as a strategic thrust, I was making the case for change to anyone who was willing to listen to me. In the period before the president of the World Bank endorsed the strategy at the annual meeting in October, I was still in the role of an insurgent. Some years later, I discovered that at the time, the senior managers were referring among themselves to knowledge management as "the Denning problem." Instead of seeing knowledge management as a strategic opportunity for the organization they had turned it into a surreptitious competition concerning careers.[22]

Even when no significant transformation has occurred, the career "losers" may be embittered by the struggle and may seek to exact revenge. "The ideal," says Robert Baron, a psychologist who has studied workplace reprisals, "is to ruin the other person without him knowing what happened, without him knowing if anything happened."[23]

In an unhealthy organization, dissonance between the covert stories and the official organizational stories will be significant. Management may say that the company has great products or services, is innovative, and has a prosperous future. Staff may not disagree openly with this interpretation but among themselves share their own views of how the company is run, as in Case and Piñeiro's study of a computer programming community:

> Just to make matters worse, a lot of managers believe that if they give their programming teams Rational Rose or Visual C++ or whatever, that those tools will magically make the code the team is producing well designed. Well, if you give a monkey a computer, he's still a monkey and you won't get anything out of him at the end of the day except a bunch of monkey shit.[24]

An organization in difficulty will also have a vast underground river of negative storytelling at odds with the official stories being put out by its management. These stories may be invisible to outsiders and even to the management itself. The rest of this chapter discusses the range of feasible alternatives—what is possible and what isn't—as well as usable tools to deal with it.

Management Cannot Control the Flow of Stories

While the top managers may have formal power over much of what happens in the organization in terms of structure, strategies, plans, programs, budgets, schedules, salaries, hiring, firing, promotions, and the like, one thing they don't control is the ongoing and relentless process of organizational storytelling. They may, of course, use their hierarchical power to compel the staff to listen to their stories. But they can't control how much attention the members of the organization will pay to their stories or how the staff will retell those stories among themselves. The managers' stories may be retold by the staff with approval and support in those organizations where managers and staff are largely in accord, or with derision and contempt in those organizations where there are divisive tensions between managers and staff—for example:

> I like to write beautiful code ... as I imagine most real programmers do ... us geeks that live, breathe, and dream in code ... but in real life, there usually is not enough time or resources given to manage to write really well planned out code.[25]

In organizations with significant disagreements between managers and staff, the managers are often barely aware of the stories being told and retold among the staff, particularly stories critical of the organization and its managers. Given the actual or perceived sanctions flowing from any discovery by the managers of the telling of such stories, managers can usually discover their existence only indirectly, and even then only partially. Direct requests to the staff to retell the stories to the managers are likely to yield only anodyne versions. The use of ostensibly independent researchers may elicit more of the stories, if assurances of confidentiality are believed. Even with a significant effort, managers thus usually have a very incomplete understanding of the stories being told in their organization.

The Need to Tame the Grapevine

Managerial unconcern about the stories being told by staff may reflect a view that what you don't know can't hurt you—mere gossip, rumor, the usual whining and griping—nothing to worry about! There is, however, a significant risk that any substantial divergences between the overt official strategies and plans of the organization and the covert negative stories being told and retold by the staff will constitute a significant impediment to the work of the organization, particularly where any major change in behavior is under way. It is also likely that the covert negative stories will eventually flow out of the organization and have a corrosive effect on interactions with customers, partners, and analysts. It is therefore important for leaders to identify such divergences as early as possible so as to understand what is occurring and do something about it.

The ongoing flow of storytelling cannot be stopped by managerial fiat any more than a river will stop flowing or the tide will stop rising as a result of a king's instruction. But leaders do have narrative options for dealing with the underground flow. In effect, they can fight story with story.

TAMING THE GRAPEVINE

Since corporate culture is embodied in the ongoing narratives that are told and retold in any organization, one way of altering the situation is to inject a new story into the flow in an effort to change its nature and direction. One fights rumor or gossip not with arguments or decisions but with counter-stories.

Use Satire to Kill a Rumor

To scotch a rumor or a piece of alleged bad news, you may be able to use gentle satire to mock what's being said or its author, or even yourself. Success on any of these fronts can undermine the impact.

Humor can draw attention to the absurdity of rumors and invite the reader to conclude: *This is unreasonable! It couldn't be true! How ridiculous for me to have taken this seriously!*

The particular form of humor involved is satire. Most jokes are not satires: rather they play on the existing views and prejudices of the audience and leave the listeners' perspectives untouched. A satire aims at subverting the listeners' beliefs, perhaps permanently.

Although stories to tame the grapevine are usually remarkably brief, they are tricky to construct but immensely powerful when successful. Such stories typically seize on some hidden or unexpected aspect of the bad news and point out the incongruity.

Bill Clinton: Campaigning Against an Unreasonable Attack

An interesting example from U.S. politics comes from the early stages of the 1992 U.S. presidential campaign: President George H. W. Bush was relentlessly attacking Hillary Clinton as unsuitable to be First Lady after she had admitted that she hadn't spent her adult life baking cookies. White House sponsorship of the attacks ended when the Clinton campaign responded by saying, "George Bush isn't running for President—apparently he's campaigning to become First Lady."

Bill Clinton: Whitewater

President Clinton spent much of his presidency under investigation for a real estate matter in Arkansas known as Whitewater. Eventually, after years of investigation and many millions of dollars spent, no wrong-doing by Clinton was discovered. However, during his presidency, the Washington journalists had made Whitewater a household word. During the ordeal, Clinton used self-deprecatory humor at a dinner for journalists: "I am delighted to be here tonight. And if you believe that, I have some land in northwest Arkansas I'd like to sell you."

But having taken his self-administered medicine, Clinton then clearly savored the opportunity to deliver a broadside at those who had spent the last few months poring over his financial records: "I don't want to alarm any of you, but it's three days before April 15, and most of you have spent more time with my taxes than your own." And then in gently taunting, singsong voice, he said, "Many happy returns!"[26]

It can also be effective to ridicule the authors of bad news as a class or group. Talking about one's opponents as a class rather than as individuals is what dissident staff do to their bosses: they talk about "the system" and "them" rather than about "Mr. Jones" and "Ms. Smith."[27] Such criticism is difficult to defend against because it's hard to pinpoint what exactly is being criticized. However, the good news is that leaders can adopt the same tactic and satirize their detractors as a class and in the process avoid sounding personal.

Bill Clinton Gets a Tax Cut

Former President Bill Clinton did this brilliantly in his address to the Democratic Convention on July 27, 2004, when he satirized "Republicans" rather than George W. Bush personally: "At home, the president and the Republican Congress have made equally fateful choices, which they also deeply believe in. For the first time when America was in a war footing in our whole history, they gave two huge tax cuts, nearly half of which went to the top 1 percent of us. Now, I'm in that group for the first time in my life. And you might remember that when I was in office, on occasion, the Republicans were kind of mean to me. But as soon as I got out and made money, I became part of the most important group in the world to them. It was amazing. I never thought I'd be so well cared for by the president and the Republicans in Congress. I almost sent them a thank you note for my tax cuts until I realized that the rest of you were paying the bill for it.[28]

Managers can do the same thing to cynics and skeptics by ridiculing the general position they represent.

Don't Be Mean-Spirited

It's important to use satire appropriately and sparingly. Mean-spirited ridicule can generate a well-deserved backlash. Finely tuned and appropriately timed satire is a blend of love and truth. It is not merely putting someone down in an isolated comic event. It is directed at all and everyone, including even the storyteller. But satire has a point, which makes it effective. It is important to be sure that you are making a valid point through your satire without causing cruel laughter or blame.

Consider Karl Kraus's satire of psychoanalysis:

Psychoanalysis is that mental illness of which it regards itself as therapy.[29]

This definition works because it addresses a field of serious study but makes a point about the ambiguity of what can be known. It is gentle and self-effacing.

In the following ad, however, the humor is too aggressive to be effective:

One fur hat: two spoilt bitches. Don't let fur creep back into fashion.[30]

Here, the verbal attack on the target of the satire—the woman wearing the fur hat—is excessive. The risk is that the satire will rebound on the satirists.

Use Self-Deprecatory Humor

One reason that humor is a dangerous tool is that satire is about the exposure of truth—and the truth can wound. Self-deprecatory humor is one of the safer forms of satire, because you are the target. Laughing at yourself shows that you've mastered the issue; it hasn't mastered you. Better yet, deprecating yourself gives you a right to deprecate others.

The Case of JetBlue

Thus, in August 2010, when flight attendant Steven Slater grabbed a couple of beers and slid down the emergency chute of a JetBlue plane, he became an instant folk hero, with several hundred thousand followers on Facebook. As David Zax noted in *Fast Company*, "JetBlue itself is in an increasingly tricky position. If one of their employees became a folk hero for quitting, then didn't that make them something of, well, a folk villain?"[31]

So how did JetBlue respond? For two days, not at all. Then, on the third day, JetBlue issued the following single post on its company blog, *Blue Tales*:

> It wouldn't be fair for us to point out absurdities in other corners of the industry without acknowledging when it's about us. Well, this week's news certainly falls into that category. Perhaps you heard a little story about one of our flight attendants? While we can't discuss the details of what is an ongoing investigation, plenty of others have already formed opinions on the matter. Like, the entire Internet. (The reason we're not commenting is that we respect the privacy of the individual. People can speak on their own behalf; we won't do it for them.)
>
> While this episode may feed your inner Office Space, we just want to take this space to recognize our 2,300 fantastic, awesome and professional Inflight Crewmembers for delivering the JetBlue Experience you've come to expect of us.

David Zax noted: "It's a wily little post, expertly done—mixing cheeky self-deprecation, ostensible privacy concerns, an apt and funny YouTube link (to the Office Space movie), and only the tiniest dose of PR pablum." Thereafter, the tide of opinion shifted more positively toward JetBlue. Its message was: if we can laugh at this, then it can't be very serious.[32]

Who Can Be a Storyteller?

Here's an example of self-deprecatory humor from my own work. My challenge as a speaker is to quickly overturn the widespread presumption of my audiences that they are not, and cannot become, good storytellers. I seek to achieve this by making gentle fun of my own taciturn character:

> *Who can be a storyteller? I cite in evidence—my wife! She says: "Here you are: Steve. Australian! Monosyllabic! Never tell me stories! Never tell me jokes! But here you are, going around the world, making a living out of being a storyteller! If you can do it, anybody can." And of course that's the point: Everybody does. We're all storytellers.*

It makes fun of me, but it also makes fun of the audience. The implication is: "Hey! Wake up! If even a taciturn person like me can do this, then so can you!"

Don't Ridicule a Rumor or Bad News That Is True

The trick is to work with, not against, the flow of the vast underground river of informal communication that exists in every organization. Of course, you can't ridicule a rumor into oblivion if it's true or at least reasonable. If that's the case, your only real option is to admit the rumor, put it in perspective, fix it if you can, and move on.

"They're Launching Another Reorganization!"

Given the universal propensity of embattled corporate managements to launch a major reorganization when they don't know what to do, a rumor of a reorganization is hard to satirize because it is inherently so plausible. It's exactly the kind of thing that a weak management does when in trouble. So it's tough to satirize the bad news itself as implausible. The fact is, it's very plausible!

And if the rumor is anonymous, one cannot satirize the author of the bad news.

What can you do? In some situations, you may be able to satirize yourself: "What a knucklehead I was to try all those previous reorganizations that bombed!"

That might work to a certain extent—if you're in charge. But someone other than the CEO can't kill the rumor by satirizing the CEO; it might even strengthen the rumor. When it comes to killing the rumor, the satire has to come from the top.

"We're Going to Be Taken Over!"

Assuming that the rumor isn't true, one possibility may be to satirize the feasibility of the idea itself. If, for instance, the company rumored to be behind the takeover lacks the capability to make a satisfactory offer, then one might be able to satirize the rumor in terms like these: "How could we be taken over by a company whose financial condition is even more critical than our own!"

Remove the Cause of Negative Rumors and Criticism

When you're thinking about what to do about gossip, rumors, and criticism, keep in mind the possibility that your own behavior may be contributing to the talk. If it is, you may be able to change the talk by changing the behavior.

Suppose you find yourself being ridiculed for being insincere or less than fully frank with your staff. You might want to check out why this is happening. For example, "When one manager videotaped himself talking about different topics, he realized that his voice tone and lack of eye contact caused his audience to think he was insincere. With practice, he was able to relax and send the messages he intended to send."[33]

Top managers are often unaware of how intimidating they can be. Given the perceived likelihood of sanctions for speaking out of turn, it is unsafe to assume that inviting people to share their thoughts will be enough to elicit open conversation. On the contrary, it may generate a storm of underground criticism. Active efforts to open channels of communication can help:

> A large bank's IT manager encouraged initiative by having staff suggest their own solutions to business problems. At first, people were silent for fear of seeming stupid before a highly educated boss. Realizing

this, he schooled himself to listen thoughtfully, with a serious, inquiring demeanor, even when he knew their ideas were flawed. When they felt taken seriously, his staff became willing to tackle larger projects knowing he would support them. Eventually most people started suggesting, refining, and implementing their own ideas. Dealing with them as equals, both verbally and nonverbally, helped him reinforce the attitudes and behaviors of initiative-taking.[34]

Taming the Organization-Wide Grapevine

Once a decision is made at the top to proceed with a change, it can be risky for members of an organization to oppose the change openly, as top management may see this as putting their authority in question. So opposition tends to go underground. The skeptics and the cynics feed the grapevine with gossip and rumors, waiting for the moment when some adverse circumstance or setback enables them to bring their opposition to the surface.

Psychologists have found that people often wait for years to get even with others who had themselves probably forgotten the offense, plotting until they have an opportunity to torpedo their enemy's career.[35] The shadow side of an organization remains in place as long as the organization is alive. The workforce remains a battleground of competing stories, each struggling for supremacy in the fight for the organization's soul.

BEYOND THE GRAPEVINE

If you see widespread and open opposition to the officially announced change, then you're dealing with more than the grapevine, an underground guerrilla movement of skeptics and cynics. You're dealing with a large-scale rebellion, and you have a different and larger task on your hands. You are facing a pitched battle.

Such pitched battles generally involve three main groups:

- The enthusiastic champions who willingly lead the charge for change—generally on the order of 20 percent of the population.

- The resisters who launch the counterattack—again, probably no more than 20 percent of the population.

- The fence-sitters and laggards who wait and watch to see which way the organizational wind is blowing—usually the majority, around 60 percent.

The following steps can be helpful:

- Use positive stories to win the set battles.

- Assemble the rational case for change.

- Use ridicule to fight the rumor mill.

- Help your supporters tell your story.

- Bring in big guns to help in set battles.

- Put in place structural measures to reinforce your story.

Positive Stories

Winning the big battles will depend less on skirmishes with enemies and more on inspiring the top of the organization and your army of champions to carry the message of change throughout the organization. The principal storytelling instruments for this task are springboard stories (Chapter Three), future stories including business models and scenarios (Chapter Ten), and stories to inspire innovation (Chapter Eleven).

The Rational Case for Change

The rational case for change isn't going to win the day for you, but it can lose the day for you if you don't have it. You need to have answers to relevant questions. You have to be able to respond to critical arguments with supporting facts and analyses that show that your change makes sense in conventional terms of costs, benefits, risk, and time lines.

Ridicule

At the same time, you shouldn't neglect the rumor mill, which will be going full tilt, at a more aggravated level than appears in the open debate about change. The arguments that are too extreme and derogatory and scandalous to make in open discussion will be whispered in private and transmitted along the grapevine. You fight story with story and satirize the critics—they are so ridiculous that they can't be right.

Counterstories for Your Supporters

Once you have prepared your weapons of persuasion, make it easy for your supporters to find out what is being said and make sure they have the positive stories and the defenses against the negative stories. This is developed to a high degree in U.S. presidential campaigns, with almost instant e-mailing to supporters of the defense to be used against attacks.

In an organization, it can be done by making available PowerPoint presentations on the organization's intranet, which make it easy for your supporters to tell your story.

The Big Guns

After years of skirmishing with skeptics and critics, you may not be a hero in your own company. If you bring in people with big reputations, even world experts when you can get them, to review what's going on, they can help defeat determined attacks.

Structural Countermeasures

You are unlikely to win the war without structural help. You need to put in place structural measures that will eventually compel compliance, such as budgets, incentive systems, and measurements of progress. These measures won't win the war by themselves. They won't inspire the champions, and they won't win over the passionate resisters, but they can do something else that's important: they can prod the majority of fence-sitters and laggards to get with the program. And they can make it costly for opponents to keep resisting.

THE DRIVING FORCE BEHIND THE GRAPEVINE

What drives the grapevine is uncertainty about the future. People are desperate for news, and more informed news, that will shed light on the future. Similarly, management efforts directed toward neutralizing bad news and rumors in the grapevine are essentially about reducing uncertainty about the organization's future. But the organization can also be more proactive in clarifying the future through narrative. And it is to this challenge that I turn in Chapter Ten.

TEMPLATE FOR STORIES TO TAME THE GRAPEVINE

When constructing a story aimed at taming the grapevine, take the following principles into account:

1. Before trying to satirize a rumor or bad news, make sure that it is untrue or unreasonable. If the rumor or bad news is true, admit it, remove the cause of it if you can, put it in perspective, and move on.

2. If you know the author of the rumor, explore whether it is possible and appropriate to satirize that person.

3. Assess the inherent plausibility of the rumor or bad news to determine whether it can be satirized as lacking inherent credibility.

4. Explore whether your own relationship to the content of the rumor or bad news can be exploited to show its inherent improbability; self-deprecatory humor is often the most effective tactic.

5. To avoid a potential backlash, make sure that any satire you attempt is not mean-spirited.

10

CREATE AND SHARE YOUR VISION

Using Narrative to Lead People into the Future

> ❝ All human action occurs in time, drawing
> on a past which cannot be undone and
> facing a future which cannot be known. ❞
>
> **J. M. Barbalet[1]**

We have no difficulty telling ourselves stories about the future. In fact, scientific studies show that the human brain is constantly engaged in this activity.[2] Every moment of our lives, we instinctively create action plans and programs for the future—anticipating the moment at hand, the next minutes, the emerging hours, the following days, the ongoing weeks and anticipated years to come.[3]

The process is familiar to us all. As we make our way through the day, we run through potential simulations. For instance, as I write, I am also thinking: *If I continue writing this chapter, I will be delayed in getting out my newsletter. If I help my daughter with her homework, I won't be able to read the book that I was planning to read. If I undertake that engagement in Germany, this will extend the message of storytelling to new territory, but I will be unable to attend Richard's party. Unless I make a booking now for that ski holiday, the flight may be full. If I open that bottle of Chateau*

Montrose today, I won't be able to taste it at maturity. And so on. The simulations are sets of potential actions and their consequences. They are time paths into the future.

For most of the human race's existence, these future imaginings took place within a fairly stable context. Tomorrow was seen as an inevitable continuation of today, which in turn was not very different from yesterday. People knew and kept their places, geographically as well as socially. Tradition was largely undisturbed by innovation. Overall change proceeded at a pace that was barely perceptible. Each generation was a replica of its predecessor. The central element of wisdom was seen as permanence.

WHY WE TELL FUTURE STORIES

More recently, audacious scientific and technological innovation, instant global communication, expanded travel, increased international trade, intensified competition, shifting social roles, cultural mixing, biological transformation, and environmental shifts have made rapid change a pervasive phenomenon of life.

The world has come to believe that although the future is still unpredictable, it is in many ways in our hands. Rather than seeing ourselves as helpless pawns in the hands of fate, our societies perceive themselves as driven by human agency.[4] Whereas the future used to be, like the weather, something you discussed but couldn't do anything about, now we dream about it, worry over it, save for it, invest in it, plan for it, game it, and, in the process to a certain degree, make it happen. Goal setting and strategic planning have become institutionalized as a central function of the management of organizations.[5]

Leadership is now seen as explicitly connected with the future. As Kouzes and Posner say, leaders "share the characteristic of being forward-looking, of being concerned not just about today's problems, but also about tomorrow's possibilities. They're able to envision the future, to gaze across the horizon of time and imagine the greater opportunities to come. They see something out ahead, vague as it might appear from a distance, and they imagine that extraordinary feats are possible and that the ordinary could be transformed into something noble." They go on to say, "All enterprises or projects, big or small, begin in the mind's eye; they begin with imagination and with the belief that what's merely an image can one day be made real."[6]

The Rarity of Compelling Future Stories

The telling of stories about the future has thus come to be seen as a central task of leadership. Indeed, according to Noel Tichy in *The Leadership Engine*, "Winning leaders create and use future stories to help people break away from the familiar present and venture boldly ahead to create a better future. They not only describe the future in terms that are personal and compelling, but they help others understand why and what they must do to get there. Without being able to do that, would-be leaders never get the sustained effort required to move toward their goal."[7]

Nevertheless, although future storytelling is said to be a key task of leadership, the compelling future stories that leaders are supposed to tell are harder to find than one might expect. Certainly there are many examples of compelling stories that leaders tell, but they are generally stories about the past.[8]

And where the stories are about the future, they usually aren't compelling. Look at this example of an allegedly successful mission statement quoted in Steven Covey's *Seven Habits of Highly Successful People*:

> Our mission is to empower people and organizations to significantly increase their performance capability in order to achieve worthwhile purposes through understanding and living principle-centered leadership.[9]

This statement was drafted by a company's management team at a retreat high up in the mountains, surrounded by the magnificence of nature. According to Covey, the ambiance of the retreat was empathetic, courageous, synergistic, creative, exciting, even exhilarating. Perhaps to the participants, the mission statement they drafted may recall that ambiance, but to those who weren't there, the mission statement is a blur. Just imagine the reaction of staffers of that company who weren't at the high-altitude, high-energy mountain gathering as they read this statement. Whatever it was the management team was getting high on, it hasn't been communicated in the draft that emerged from the gathering.

It's not that Covey gives a particularly bad example of a mission statement. In fact, it's a fairly typical instance of the genre. Mission statements or strategic plans are rarely if ever compelling documents. And it's not through want of effort. Arguably more ineffective time is spent in strategic planning exercises than in any other area of corporate activities.[10]

Or look at the most celebrated example of future storytelling in business history—the use of scenarios in the early 1970s to alert Shell to the implications of a steep rise in the price of oil. Pierre Wack and his planning team developed a set of future scenarios that included the possibility of an oil price hike. After presenting them to Shell's managing directors in September 1972, Wack was given a mission of presenting them to Shell managers and governments around the world. The result? Many Shell managers walked out of the presentation angry. "Just give me a number," many of them said. Since the scenarios offered no single number to plug into their calculations, they chose the business-as-usual number, which required what Wack called "three miracles" for its realization: major new oil finds, change of heart in the Organization of Petroleum Exporting Countries, and no unexpected events to affect oil production capabilities. And governments disregarded Wack's scenario of an oil price hike as unrealistic.

Despite the mythology that has grown up around Wack's scenarios, little changed in Shell before the crisis in September 1973. Even after the crisis had happened and the price of oil had soared, Shell's operating managers were still slow to change their behavior. They could see what had already happened in terms of the rise in the price of oil. Intellectually they could understand the forces at play, which meant that the trends would continue. But still they stuck to old habits. Admittedly Shell ended up acting more agilely than the other oil companies, largely as a result of Wack's scenarios, which enabled some of Shell's managers to recognize events for what they were. But even so, the process was agonizingly slow, and it took some parts of the organization, such as maritime shipping, years before they got it. Presenting the scenarios to managers was, according to Wack, like "water on a stone." To affect behavior in a useful way, Wack saw that the task was not to argue with the managers or lay out the facts: he had to change the way people viewed the world.[11]

So what's going on here? On one hand, it's said that the role of a true leader is to tell compelling stories about the future. On the other hand, the genre offers precious few examples. Why is this?

The Inherent Difficulty in Telling Future Stories

The reality is that telling a compelling story about the future is very difficult. No matter how thoughtfully you look ahead, the future is uncertain and inherently unknowable. Any story that appears to give it certainty and predictability will automatically be suspect. Even a future story that appears believable when first told is likely to become unbelievable quite rapidly, as events unfold that show the future will not take place as envisaged in the story. The more detail the story includes, the greater the likelihood there is of error—and hence loss of credibility.

The inherent unpredictability of the future is reinforced by a set of three related psychological phenomena that make people unwilling to believe in any future story, particularly one that implies they will have to change. First is anchoring—as humans, we naturally remain anchored to our past. We are also programmed to have an aversion to loss: people are typically more concerned about the risk of loss than they are excited by the prospect of gain. And a similar bias, the endowment effect, gives us a strong desire to hang on to what we own; the very fact of owning something makes it seem more valuable.[12]

So it's not just that the likelihood that the imagined story will occur is low. The truth is that people usually don't want to believe a future story that involves significant disruption. So what's a leader to do?

HOW TO TELL A COMPELLING FUTURE STORY

By definition, future stories aren't true stories. Since the future hasn't happened yet, it's impossible to say anything totally reliable about it, particularly where human beings are involved. The first step in augmenting the credibility of a future story is to explore whether the length of the causal chain between the situation today and the imagined future can be reduced. The longer the chain of causation, the greater the chance is that one or more of the links will break, as some unexpected development throws all predictions into chaos. For example, Lou Gerstner as head of IBM was most persuasive when he was telling stories about the near future. Here he is in June 1995 talking about the third phase of network-centric computing that will follow the first phase of mainframes and the second phase of PCs:

> Now, what does it take to be successful in that third phase? Well, it takes the industry delivering some very important products. First of all, the products must operate across a very heterogeneous set of hardware and software platforms that today don't work together.
>
> If you're going to have this fully collaborative computing, you must have software that can operate on multiple platforms. And that means it must be open, fully compliant with broad industry standards, and supportive of the full industry range of products.
>
> The second thing it must be is it must be a marriage of the strengths of the desktop—phase two, which is ease of use, ease of application, with the strengths of phase one, which are the reliability, the security, and the robustness of large-scale systems. And so this new model requires a marriage of the strengths of the first two phases.
>
> And the final thing the industry must produce is, these products must work across very small local networks all the way up to cross-border, multi-national global networks including publicly switched networks like telephone company networks.

Gerstner's future story was a persuasive and, as it turned out, a fairly accurate picture of what was about to happen in the world of computers. One reason for its accuracy was that his story was set in the immediate future and in fact was already starting to happen in some places.

A business model is a story that is set in the present or very near future. It helps the sponsors or managers think through how the business will work when it is launched—or understand the dynamic of a business that is already launched.

Of course, if you're telling a story about the long-term future, there's no choice—you have to set your story far in the future. And in that case, you usually need to tell multiple stories—scenarios—to encourage thinking about the various ways in which the future may unfold.

A Shortcut to the Future

Since the issue of a future story's plausibility is related to the length of the causal chain between now and some future state, you can sidestep the issue by telling a springboard story.

As discussed in Chapter Three, the springboard story is a story about the past—something that's already happened. So the story is easy to tell. There's no need to invent anything.

However, the springboard story elicits a future story in the minds of the listeners, who start to imagine what the future could be like if they implemented the relevant change idea embodied in the story in their own contexts. Consequently it's the listeners who do the hard work of inventing the future. Even while the speaker is talking, the audience is soundlessly generating future stories tailor-made to their own situations, and hence grounded in reality. What's more, as the future unfolds, the listeners continuously update the stories they have generated so as to fit the new reality. The springboard story itself doesn't need updating because it doesn't change: it has already happened. As a result, you avoid the yawning gap between the future as envisaged and the future as it unfolds.

Moreover, because the springboard story's listeners invent the future for themselves, they are much more likely to find that future alluring than if some stranger had dreamed it up for them. The springboard story thus sidesteps the problem of telling a compelling future story. Nevertheless, if you need to create a future story, you can take some steps that will improve its prospects of acceptance.

For the Future to Resonate, Make It Evocative

A couple of visions are often quoted as successful examples of compelling future stories, such as Winston Churchill's "We shall fight on the beaches," and Martin Luther King Jr.'s "I have a dream." The fact that they are quoted so often makes one wonder: Why always the same examples? Why not others? The reason becomes evident once you look at these examples in more detail.

First, here's Winston Churchill on June 4, 1940, at the end of a long speech shortly after a large part of the British army had been evacuated from Dunkirk:[13]

> I have, myself, full confidence that if all do their duty, if nothing is neglected, and if the best arrangements are made, as they are being made, we shall prove ourselves once again able to defend our Island home, to ride out the storm of war, and to outlive the menace of tyranny, if necessary for years, if necessary alone. At any rate, that is what we are going to try to do.
>
> That is the resolve of His Majesty's Government—every man of them. That is the will of Parliament and the nation. The British Empire and the French Republic, linked together in their cause and in their need, will defend to the death their native soil, aiding each other like good comrades to the utmost of their strength. Even though large tracts of Europe and many old and famous States have fallen or may fall into the grip of the Gestapo and all the odious apparatus of Nazi rule, we shall not flag or fail.
>
> We shall go on to the end, we shall fight in France, we shall fight on the seas and oceans, we shall fight with growing confidence and growing strength in the air, we shall defend our Island, whatever the cost may be, we shall fight on the beaches, we shall fight on the landing grounds, we shall fight in the fields and in the streets, we shall fight in the hills; we shall never surrender, and even if, which I do not for a moment believe, this Island or a large part of it were subjugated and starving, then our Empire beyond the seas, armed and guarded by the British Fleet, would carry on the struggle, until, in God's good time, the New World, with all its power and might, steps forth to the rescue and the liberation of the old.

The first thing to note is that the speech was effective. Churchill's audience in the House of Commons was initially stunned, and then erupted into a lengthy ovation. The speech was repeated on the radio, and came to symbolize the British attitude to the war.

Second, although the picture that Churchill sketches is an evocative one of the British people resisting the Nazis to the death, fighting them by land, by sea, by air, and so on, Churchill is not telling a story in any conventional sense. Rather, he is painting a set of romantic scenes in the future, which are not linked together in time and space in any coherent way.

Third, the observation that Churchill's speech isn't a detailed story isn't meant as a criticism of the speech. On the contrary, part of the strength of the speech lies in its very lack of specificity. If Churchill had spelled out in detail how the British people were going to fight, he would have been in considerable difficulty, because it was impossible to say in June 1940 how the war would unfold. If he had given any detail, it would have been quickly disproved. So Churchill took the wiser course and refrained from giving any detail. Instead he painted a set of evocative word pictures of the future.[14]

Similarly, Martin Luther King Jr.'s "I have a dream" speech, delivered on the steps at the Lincoln Memorial in Washington, D.C., on August 28, 1963, is notable for its lack of specificity and for the evocativeness of its poetic language:

> I am not unmindful that some of you have come here out of great trials and tribulations. Some of you have come fresh from narrow cells. Some of you have come from areas where your quest for freedom left you battered by the storms of persecution and staggered by the winds of police brutality. You have been the veterans of creative suffering. Continue to work with the faith that unearned suffering is redemptive.
>
> Go back to Mississippi, go back to Alabama, go back to Georgia, go back to Louisiana, go back to the slums and ghettos of our northern cities, knowing that somehow this situation can and will be changed. Let us not wallow in the valley of despair. I say to you today, my

friends, that in spite of the difficulties and frustrations of the moment, I still have a dream. It is a dream deeply rooted in the American dream.

I have a dream that one day this nation will rise up and live out the true meaning of its creed: "We hold these truths to be self-evident: that all men are created equal." I have a dream that one day on the red hills of Georgia the sons of former slaves and the sons of former slave-owners will be able to sit down together at a table of brotherhood.

I have a dream that one day even the state of Mississippi, a desert state, sweltering with the heat of injustice and oppression, will be transformed into an oasis of freedom and justice.

I have a dream that my four children will one day live in a nation where they will not be judged by the color of their skin but by the content of their character. I have a dream today.

I have a dream that one day the state of Alabama, whose governor's lips are presently dripping with the words of interposition and nullification, will be transformed into a situation where little black boys and black girls will be able to join hands with little white boys and white girls and walk together as sisters and brothers.

I have a dream today.

I have a dream that one day every valley shall be exalted, every hill and mountain shall be made low, the rough places will be made plain, and the crooked places will be made straight, and the glory of the Lord shall be revealed, and all flesh shall see it together.

This is our hope. This is the faith with which I return to the South. With this faith we will be able to hew out of the mountain of despair a stone of hope. With this faith we will be able to transform the jangling discords of our nation into a beautiful symphony of brotherhood.[15]

The speech describes a situation in some unspecified future when the nature of race relations is radically different from what it was in 1963. The speech doesn't contain a coherent set of causally linked actions showing how the United States was going to get from where it was in 1963 to the future situation so movingly depicted in the speech. This is not to criticize the speech but rather to suggest that an inherent characteristic of a successful speech about the future is likely to be the lack of specificity and the evocativeness of the language.

Those two examples are from politics. By way of further illustration, here's a less well-known instance of the same phenomenon in the commercial sphere. It's Walt Disney's vision for Disneyland when he was trying to convey to top management and outside investors the vision for this innovative project:

> *The idea of Disneyland is a simple one. It will be a place for people to find happiness and knowledge. It will be a place for parents and children to spend pleasant times in one another's company, a place for teachers and pupils to discover greater ways of understanding and education. Here the older generation can recapture the nostalgia of days gone by, and the younger generation can savor the challenge of the future. Here will be the wonders of Nature and Man for all to see and understand. Disneyland will be based upon and dedicated to the ideals, the dreams and hard facts that have created America. And it will be uniquely equipped to dramatize these dreams and facts and send them forth as a source of courage and inspiration to all the world. Disneyland will be something of a fair, an exhibition, a playground, a community center, a museum of living facts, and a showplace of beauty and magic. It will be filled with the accomplishments, the joys and hopes of the world we live in. And it will remind us and show us how to make those wonders part of our lives.*[16]

Once again the crafter of the vision has used simple but evocative language to conjure up an image of what Disneyland might turn out to be.

All of these visions demonstrate a high degree of linguistic skill in sketching evocative futures. If they are effective, it is because the listeners themselves put flesh on the skeleton: the listeners imagine the detail of how they are going to get to these futures, prompted by the evocative pictures sketched in the vision. The catch is that the crafting of such evocative poetic visions requires consummate artistry. That is why, for most speakers, the springboard story will be a more practical option.

Like the springboard story, an evocative future story has the advantage that as the future actually unfolds with all its unexpected twists and turns, the listeners can remold the narrative in their imaginations on the fly. An evocative narrative is thus continuously updated in the context as it evolves.

Evocative future stories that are told and retold become part of the common mind. It's the unified expression of many voices playing on the same theme. A successful vision is a dream, but it's a dream with a twist: it's a dream that is shared. As the Brazilian proverb goes, when we dream alone, it's just a dream: when we dream together, it's already the beginning of a new reality. Thus, when we share the same dream, we all begin to participate in it.

Avoid Cliché

The effort to craft an evocative, inspiring vision often stretches the drafter's linguistic skills and critical ability to grasp how the resulting language will be viewed by those for whom it is intended. When that process breaks down, you get verbiage like the mission statement mentioned earlier, the one that was cited with approval by Stephen Covey.

Here's another example of a vision statement, this one for an automobile company. It is cited with approval in Gary Yukl's *Leadership in Organizations:*[17]

> We will create an empowered organization to unleash our creativity and focus our energies in cooperative effort; it will enable us to develop and build the best personal vehicles in the world, vehicles that people will treasure owning because they are fun to use, they are reliable, they keep people comfortable and safe, and they enable people to have freedom of movement in their environment without harming it.

Just think about that vision for a moment. It seems more concrete than the first one, but it piles together a set of tired clichés of management jargon: "empowered organization," "unleash our creativity," "cooperative effort," "the best personal vehicles in the world," "vehicles that people will treasure owning," and "freedom of movement in the environment without harming it." If the meaning of any one of these clichés had been unpacked so that the practical implications were made apparent, along with some indication of serious organizational intent to make and implement choices, then the vision would start to have some meaning. But at this level of generality, such a vision is likely to generate in a worker in the production line little but cynicism.

Yukl praises the vision's flexibility, noting that its environmental commitment is compatible with the company's producing gas-guzzling SUVs as well as fusion-powered air cars as in the movie *Back to the Future*.[18] But that's precisely the problem. The vision is infinitely flexible to cover whatever the company might decide to do. It confirms that no hard choices have been made and thus communicates no direction for the future.

Keep It Simple

It's also a good idea to keep the vision simple. One reason for this is that the human capacity to absorb multiple elements isn't unlimited. Research indicates that the mind can hold only seven elements at the same time, plus or minus two.[19] Thus the mental simulations that we spontaneously make of the future are not very elaborate. Gary Klein suggests that there are rarely more than three causal factors, and rarely more than six transition states.[20] Kees van der Heijden reports that the most effective business ideas contain no more than ten elements.[21]

Actual reality may be more complicated, but the story is simplified by chunking together groups of actions. For instance, a computer program might have millions of lines of code, but millions of steps won't fit in the human brain. To understand the program, we group the main actions into a limited number of steps.[22]

So when you're telling a future story, keep in mind the limitation of your listeners' working memory. For the story to be useful, it must be neither too detailed nor too general. The simpler your story is, the more likely that people will comprehend and remember it.

Work Backward from an Image of the Future

When he was director of planning in the Apollo space program, Edward Lindaman discovered that when people create action plans by working backward from a preferred future, they take less time to plan, increase enthusiasm for the plan, and develop a more realistic simulation of the challenge.[23] This insight can be incorporated into corporate planning processes and applied to avoid failure, as well as to achieve success.

Here are some examples of leaders who invited their audiences to work backward from a future state:

- *Choosing a future state: When Jack Welch took over as chairman of General Electric in 1979, he described a simple future state that he believed was essential for GE's success: "We will be #1 or #2" in each sector where the company chose to compete. He proposed getting to this state by the three methods: fix, close, or sell. He exemplified the values of speed, simplicity, self-confidence, and stretch. He promoted radical decentralization—everyone should be a leader. Although his statements were not in themselves fully formed stories, his message prompted the managers and staff of GE to develop stories to make the vision happen. GE in due course became one of the most successful growth companies for the next two decades.*

- *Using a familiar format to communicate a future fiction: Sometimes it's hard to make the future situation plausible. One interesting device to achieve this was used by Melinda Bickerstaff, chief knowledge officer of Bristol-Myers Squibb, to show the importance of knowledge management to the senior executives. She prepared an article describing a situation several years into the future where the firm had successfully implemented knowledge management and gained substantial financial benefits. The article was printed in the distinctive color and style of the* Financial Times—*a favorite newspaper of the top management. The surprise of seeing themselves unexpectedly featured in an article in the* Financial Times *was sufficient to get the executives thinking seriously about the possibility and helped spark a discussion: Why not?*

Make the Future Story Positive in Tone

Like springboard stories (and unlike knowledge-sharing stories), future stories that lead to action are generally upbeat. This is because future stories intend to lead people to a desired future, and this desired future is typically filled with positive characteristics. Listeners will be happier, richer, more fulfilled, better off, whatever.

Nevertheless, negative future stories can also play a role as a kind of burning platform that gets people's attention, shakes them out of their complacency, and forces them to begin thinking of alternatives. Here are some instances where negative stories have been used:

- *"Near-death" experiences:* When a company is facing a real crisis, it's easier to get people's attention. Thus, when Lou Gerstner took over IBM in 1993, the company had lost so much money in the five preceding years that its very survival was in doubt. In a context of dire crisis, Gerstner was able to get people's attention and have them consider basic change they might well have recoiled from had the company been doing well or even just getting by.

- *Y2K:* The stories of impending computer systems meltdown occasioned by entry into year 2000 prompted significant investment in upgrading antiquated systems. Whether the risk of disaster in the looming crisis was overstated, the wide dissemination of early warnings did lead to large-scale preventive action.

Even when the future story is negative, as in these cases, the object is generally to take preventive action so that things end well. Hence, the real object of even a negative future story is to grab people's attention so as to get to a positive future story.

LINK THE FUTURE STORY TO THE LISTENERS' CURRENT MIND-SET

Like all other stories, a future story needs to offer something unusual, something unexpected; otherwise, there's no interest in it. But effective future stories also need to have enough connection with current mental models to make them plausible to a critical mass of the listeners. When listeners can't see the connection between their current worldview and the future story, they will experience the story as unrealistic—as science fiction. It will end up on the shelf without creating much effect. The crux is finding the right balance between the known and the new. Erring on the side of the known will make the story boring. Erring on the side of the new will make the story so outlandish that it is unintelligible.[24]

Linkage can be accomplished by plugging into whatever the audience is already to a certain extent thinking about. Thus, the audience may have in the back of their minds some aspirations that have never been fully articulated. Or they may have some worries that have scarcely been put into words. These nebulous dreams and fears can be the basis for developing useful future stories.

> In a scenario exercise in 1990 for a company involved in the manufacture of machinery for microchip production, a senior manager expressed worry about the depth of a possible recession. By pursuing the implications of what would happen if there was a deeper-than-expected recession, the company began to see that the success of its investment program depended on the emerging recession being shallow. On further review, the company decided that it wasn't willing to gamble its entire future on a shallow recession. As it turned out, the recession was deeper than expected, and the company's foresight enabled it to survive. The credibility of the negative scenario that saved the day, however, rested on at least one senior manager's being already worried about that possibility.[25]

Exemplify the Future State

Given the difficulties of telling a credible future story, keep in mind that the performance of the story can add significantly to the impact. Mahatma Gandhi, for example, not only talked about the future independence India could achieve through peaceful means; he exemplified trustworthiness and moral responsibility in his own frugal, nonviolent lifestyle. Gandhi's fasting and dress became symbols of the self-sacrifice and discipline it takes to change the world.

In the commercial realm, Steve Jobs personifies Apple's mission to produce computers, mp3 players, phones and other electronic gadgets that are considered cool. Jobs exemplifies a "think different" lens through which to view the world. He embodies the mission in his own person through becoming the ideal of the imaginative, tech-savvy, entrepreneur.

Use Role Playing to Develop a Realistic Future Story

Research reveals that experts are not good at forecasting decisions in conflict situations. Such conflicts are complex and often involve several rounds of action and reaction, which makes them difficult to predict. Fortunately, there is an effective alternative: role playing. For conflict situations, research shows that role playing yields future stories that are more accurate than the forecasts of experts.[26]

The role playing needs to take place in a realistic manner. After receiving brief descriptions of their roles, participants read about the situation. Partisans meet with confederates to discuss strategy and act out interactions with the other parties. While encouraged to improvise, participants must stay within their roles. Typically ten independent simulations will be sufficient, but more can be conducted if the decisions vary substantially across simulations. Predictions are based on the frequency with which decisions occur.

Role playing is especially useful in that it can lead to predictions that are not obvious to experts. One paradoxical result, however, is that role playing then generates probable outcomes that are politically unacceptable and hence ignored. For example, the U.S. military used role playing as part of its planning for the Vietnam War and correctly concluded that moderate bombing was the worst strategy the country could follow. Unfortunately, top government officials did not believe the conclusion and proceeded with what seemed reasonable to them.[27]

TELLING DIFFERENT KINDS OF FUTURE STORY

Informal Statements of Intention or Descriptions of Risk

Most future stories are informal in nature and concern intentions or predictions. When the intentions are articulated by people in authority, whether from position or expertise, their stories can have a large impact in the marketplace as other players adjust their conduct to anticipate the new situation.

Plans

A plan is a description of a set of activities that are to take place in some finite future period and may include their timing, costs, benefits, and risks. It is told with a greater or lesser degree of formality. A plan may or may not be expressed in a traditional narrative form. It describes a set of events that are causally linked, particularly actions and their timing and cost, although typically not as a very interesting narrative. Plans deal with what is expected to happen. Interesting stories deal with the unexpected.

Premortems

Once people have developed a plan, they tend to feel too confident in it, particularly if they are not highly experienced. Requests for the authors to review the plan for flaws are generally ineffective: the authors' investigation is half-hearted because they really want to believe in the plan. A premortem can be used to deal with this problem. Planners are asked to imagine that it is months into the future and their plan has been carried out and it has failed. That is all they know. They have to explain why they think it failed. "Of course, it wasn't going to work because . . . ." The idea is to break the emotional attachment people have to the plan by taking on the challenge of showing their creativity and competence by identifying possible sources of breakdown.[28]

Business Models

A business model is a story that explains how an organization will operate. It explains "the theory of the business." It's a story set in the present or near future. The narrative is tied to numbers as the elements in the business model are quantified. The business model answers questions like these: Who is the customer? And what does the customer value? How do we make money in this business? What is the underlying economic logic that shows how we can deliver value to customers at an appropriate cost?[29] Its validity depends on its narrative logic (Does the story hang together?) and quantitative logic (Do the numbers add up?).

Strategies

Strategy has become an ambiguous concept. In its most common application, a strategy is a business model with the addition of the dimension of the competitors. It describes how the organization's activities are different from those of its rivals. A strategy is not about any one core competence, critical resource, or key success factor: it is about the whole system of activities and their interrelationship, not just a collection of parts.[30]

Scenarios

A scenario is a future story covering a longer time period than a business model, which is set in the present or near future. A scenario spells out the long-term implications of either the activities of the organization or the expected context within which the organization will be operating. Multiple scenarios are needed to reflect the uncertainty of the future. Scenarios are to organizations what memories of the future are to individuals. Scenarios are broad in scope and deliberately include a variety of inputs from people inside and outside the particular organization.[31]

Visions

A vision is usually a description of a future state, particularly what the organization will be like when it has achieved its goal. "A vision is about a common goal, not just about what the leader wants. Vision means an ideal and unique image of the future for the common good. It implies a choice of values and something that brings meaning and purpose to our lives."[32] Typically, it is a description or image of the future state rather than a fully fleshed-out story of how the organization will get to that future state.

User Stories

Software developer Mike Cohn in his book, *User Stories Applied*, recommends a standard form for the user story: as a <type of user>, I want <some goal> so that <some reason>.[33] Putting the story in the first person is important, because it draws the team into imagining the client's situation. By saying, "As a such-and-such, I want...," one instantly imagines what it is like to be a such-and-such. For example:

- As a parent, I want a comfortable, affordable home, so that my spouse and I can raise our family.
- As the client of a boutique hotel, I want a comfortable room with a personal feel to it, so that I have an unexpectedly stimulating night away from home.

Other Aspects of Future Stories

Since ancient times, the concept of a perfect world has persisted as a symbol of hope, from the heavenly garden of the ancient Near East through Sir Thomas More's Utopia to the efforts in the past few hundred years to engineer a better society. In general, these efforts, such as Soviet collectivization, the Maoist Great Leap Forward, or Le Corbusier's mass housing projects, were begun with high hopes but ultimately didn't work. One of the most important common factors in these schemes is a high modernist ideology, that is, a belief that it is possible to engineer progress to make the world a better place.

High modernism typically lacks the quality that Homer gave to Odysseus in *The Odyssey: metis*, a Greek word meaning the knowledge that can only come from practical experience. Odysseus was successful because he was ready to adapt to the unexpected twists and turns the future threw at him.[34] So-called scientific theories about engineering a better life typically fail to take into account the indispensable role that practical knowledge, informal processes, and improvisation play in making positive change happen in the face of unpredictability.

Beware the Anti-Story

Because future stories are inherently incredible, they run a significant risk of not being believed. The charge of being unrealistic or science fiction is frequently made. The attack on the message can quickly turn into an

247

attack on the messenger, particularly if the future story puts in question some of the organization's fundamental beliefs.

The launching of a bold and different future story in an organization is in fact likely to be the start of a vast underground river of anti-stories, which will be disseminated widely regardless of the facts, the analysis, or the logic on which the story is based. Therefore, being alert to the appearance of such underground anti-stories can be important. Although the anti-stories cannot be combated by management fiat or by arguments, they can be addressed with springboard stories (Chapter Three) and counterstories designed to tame the grapevine (Chapter Nine).

The Role of Future Storytelling in Innovation

Future stories point to the general direction the organization will take in the future. They can create new concepts and language in the organization, raising the quality of strategic conversation and focusing attention on what is relevant for success. They can make the organization more perceptive of its environment and more adaptive, motivating action and paving the way for innovation.

However, to create and sustain innovation, particularly transformational innovation, future stories are necessary but not sufficient. What is needed is the capability to weave together the full array of narrative tools and use them effectively over a sustained period of time. It is to this challenge that I turn in Part Three.

TEMPLATE FOR CRAFTING A FUTURE STORY

Take these principles into account when constructing future stories:

1. Be clear on the type of future story you are crafting: informal account, plan, premortem, business model, strategy, scenario, or vision.

2. To the extent possible, bring together the people who will be involved in implementing the future story and involve them in crafting the story. If appropriate, use role playing.

3. Understand as much as possible about the current situation, particularly the driving forces that have led up to it and the relative importance of those forces.

4. Consider bringing in outsiders to deepen understanding of the current situation and broaden the horizons concerning alternative futures.

5. Where possible, set the story in the near future, and use examples where "the future has already happened."

6. Keep the story simple and evocative, and avoid clichés.

7. Consider a combination of working backward from an image of the future state and working forward from the present to the future state.

8. Make the future story as positive in tone as circumstances permit.

9. Link the future story to your listeners' current mind-set.

10. Exemplify the future story in your own conduct.

Part 3

———•———

PUTTING IT ALL TOGETHER

SOLVE THE PARADOX OF INNOVATION

Using Narrative to Transform Your Organization

> If at first the idea is not absurd, then there is no hope for it.

Albert Einstein

So far I've been discussing stories as individual tools to solve specific leadership problems. In practice, of course, no leader faces these challenges in isolation. Multiple challenges appear simultaneously: people need to be persuaded, alliances need to be built, the grapevine needs to be tamed, and knowledge needs to be shared, and all at once. Nowhere is this more evident than in the domain of transformational innovation. A great deal has been written on the subject and many solutions proposed. In this chapter, I examine first why the proposed solutions don't work and then how to resolve the problem.

WHY CURRENT APPROACHES DON'T SOLVE THE INNOVATION PARADOX

The need to innovate is now perceived as the key to organizational survival. It's not enough for companies to get better. They have to get different—not just at their periphery through extensions of existing businesses but at their core. Transformational innovation isn't an option; it's a necessity.

As a result, established organizations have to become as good at game-changing innovation as they have been at disciplined execution. Instead of innovation and organizational learning being the responsibility of a few courageous individuals or departments, innovation must become an organization-wide capability—part of the firm's DNA.

The problem doesn't lie in *sustaining innovations*, that is, innovations that target existing customers with better performance than was previously available, either as incremental year-by-year improvements or as technological breakthroughs.[1] Succeeding in sustaining innovation is a question of how well the firm does relative to its competition. Established firms almost always win the battles of sustaining innovation, because incumbents have both the powerful incentives and the deep pockets to be successful.

The paradoxical aspect of innovation arises in what Christensen and Raynor call *disruptive innovations*, which concern new business models that transform the business landscape.[2] Some disruptive innovations involve disruption from below: a way of doing business that is simpler, more convenient, and less expensive and with appeal to new types of customers. In this way, digital photography disrupted print photography. Desktop publishing disrupted traditional publishing. Minicomputers disrupted mainframe computers, and in due course personal computers disrupted minicomputers. Disruptive innovations introduce products and services that initially may not be as good as currently available models but that end up taking over the market.

Disruptive innovation may also involve disruption from above: a more expensive model transforms the business landscape by getting people to think about the domain in a different way, as when Starbucks changed expectations about a cup of coffee. Disruptive innovation is not about doing more of the same but doing something fundamentally different. This is something that most organizations are not currently good at, in large part because the most commonly proposed theories of innovation don't work.

Create a Safe Environment for Innovation

Clayton Christensen and Michael Raynor's book *The Innovator's Solution* is a brilliant analysis of why companies fail to innovate.[3] It explains in convincing detail why corporate managements don't learn about good ideas, and why managers succumb to inherent pressures to run away from the challenge of disruptive competition rather than stand and fight. The decisions made as a result of these pressures make sense in the short run. But in due course they send the organization into an inexorable death spiral.

But while Christensen and Raynor's analysis of the causes of failure to undertake disruptive innovation is immaculate, their proposal for solving the problem is less helpful. The central premise of their thesis—the innovator's solution—is to accept the grim reality that big companies are inherently disinclined to tackle disruptive innovation. A modern organization will crush disruptive new ideas because they represent a threat to management, careers, power structures, customary ways of thinking, client bases, brands, corporate culture.

The authors' solution is to protect genuine innovators and their disruptive change ideas from these hostile forces: corporate leaders should put up a wall between the innovation and the existing hierarchy. Leadership should create an independent business unit, which will provide a safe and protected environment for innovation. There the innovation can flourish without having to fight off the interferences and intrusions and anti-innovation attitudes of the hierarchy.

The approach is seductive but has several flaws. First, it doesn't address innovations that require organization-wide change. At IBM, the shift in focus under Lou Gerstner from selling computer boxes to providing services to networked organizations and e-business was not something that could have been undertaken in an independent business unit. At best, Christensen and Raynor's approach works where the idea is limited in scope and can be launched as a business independent of the parent organization.

Second, even where it is possible to put the innovators in an independent business unit, it is doubtful that they will receive the resources necessary for success. After all, as Christensen and Raynor point out, the parent organization doesn't really want the innovation to succeed.

Even if the innovative independent business unit is successful, the company still faces the issue of what happens next. It doesn't follow that the parent organization will quickly and easily adopt the modus operandi that has been successfully developed in the subsidiary. Christensen and Raynor cite several examples of success, such as Hewlett-Packard's launching of inkjet printing through an independent business unit. But here the change didn't involve any fundamental shift in the way HP does business—it was simply another type of printer. More typical are examples where the parent company is still unwilling to adopt the innovations of the subsidiary. Some of these cases are notorious, like the IBM PC division in the 1980s and the Saturn division of General Motors.

As David Garvin says: "Separate organizations don't work—or at least not for long.... Allowing a different culture to flourish in [a] separate organization eventually leads to repeated power struggles and culture clashes, which members of the mainstream organization invariably win. Interest in the new ventures tends to be cyclical. Brief surges of enthusiasm, triggered by abundant resources and the desire to diversify, are followed by sharp declines. The life spans of both internal venture units and corporate venture capital funds, therefore, tend to be short—on average, only four to five years."[4]

That's the risk with this approach. It's not really the "innovator's solution" as Christensen and Raynor call it. It's actually a "deferring the innovator's solution." At some point, someone has to persuade the parent organization to accept the change.

Christensen and Raynor's solution rests on the hope that if you can build enough commercial success in the marketplace, you have a bigger chance of eventually winning the battle of persuasion. Surely, their argument goes, the hard numbers will win the war. Unfortunately, the track record shows that hard numbers don't win this kind of war. Even with strong commercial success, numbers and reason are not enough to dislodge the forces of stasis and inertia.[5]

Fund Many Innovation Projects

Gary Hamel proposes breeding healthy innovation through a decentral-ized funding system that emulates open markets. Thus, just as in nature many evolutionary experiments precede the emergence of a successful species, so companies should fund many innovation projects and see which ones win out. By giving large numbers of managers throughout the organization the power to allocate budgets for innovation, Hamel hopes to exploit "the wisdom of the many" over the blinkered view of a centralized corporate decision-making process. The decentralized process will thus support genuinely different disruptive innovation, rather than tame me-too look-alike changes:

> *The arithmetic is clear: It takes thousands of ideas to produce dozens of promising stratlets [a swarm of low-risk experiments] to yield a few outsize successes. Yet only a handful of companies have committed themselves to broad-based, small-scale strategic experimentation....*
> *The isolation—and distrust—of strategic experimentation is a leftover from the industrial age, when variety was often seen as the enemy.*
> *A variance, whether from a quality standard, a production schedule, or a budget, was viewed as a bad thing—which it often was. But in many companies, the aversion to unplanned variability has metas-tasized into a general antipathy toward the nonconforming and the deviant. This infatuation with conformance severely hinders the quest for resilience.[6]*

Hamel's approach encounters three problems.

First, he overlooks the reason that centralized decision making is conservative—that it reflects a fear of disruption of entrenched power structures and careers. Line managers throughout the organization expe-rience the same fears. In fact, middle managers usually have more to lose in any basic change than top management does. And so won't they also vote their resources for innovations that bolster their current fief-doms and careers? If they do, the decision making will be more cautious, not less.

Second, Hamel's belief that more resources will resolve the problem of innovation isn't borne out by the facts:

- Christoph-Friedrich von Braun, in his 1997 study "The Innovation War," analyzed thirty Global 500 firms and found almost no correlation between increased R&D spending and improvement in profitability.

- Booz Allen's analysis of global personal care and consumer health care companies showed no clear correlation between R&D spending as a percentage of sales and growth in revenues or profitability.[7]

Profitable innovation, in other words, can't be bought. Simply spending more usually leads to a waste of resources on increasingly marginal projects.

Finally, Hamel's hope is that by funding a variety of ideas, the organization will emulate natural selection and the best ideas will survive and prosper. But will it pan out this way? Once a disruptive idea starts to flourish and becomes more interesting than the normal bread-and-butter work of the organization, it risks becoming a threat to the entrenched interests of the hierarchy. The organization may well welcome the new idea into its bosom, but only to crush it to death. The organization applies its own procedures and processes and attitudes to the new idea and overwhelms it. Donald Sull and Sydney Finkelstein give many examples, such as A&P with its upscale supermarket, Laura Ashley with clothes for professional women, Firestone with radial tires.[8] All of these companies had obvious ideas staring them in the face, which were tested inside the firm and then crushed, precisely because they were successful.

Ultimately Hamel's diagnosis is wrong. The main challenge in innovation is not a problem of generating more ideas. It's figuring out how to take the good ideas and make them happen. To do that, eventually you have to win the battle of persuasion. And not just once, but repeatedly. The problem for management is that the conventional tools of communication—reason, numbers, bullet points—aren't adequate to the task. Unfortunately, even success does not breed success when it comes from unexpected sources in the organizational hierarchy.

Systems Thinking and the Learning Organization

Whatever happened to the learning organization? On rereading Peter Senge's *The Fifth Discipline*, I was struck by how brilliantly he describes the goal of the learning organization: "where new and expansive patterns of thinking are nurtured, where collective aspiration is set free and where people are continually learning how to learn together."[9] Less persuasive, however, is his proposal on how to get to this goal. The critical element, according to *The Fifth Discipline*, is systems thinking—a way of looking at systems as a whole that will enable people to see complex chains of causation and so solve complex problems.

The difficulties? First, getting large numbers of people to adopt systems thinking would itself be a massive challenge of innovation. How could an organization make this happen?

Second, even if systems thinking was widely adopted, it wouldn't necessarily lead to action. Innovation is less about understanding the problem than about getting people to act differently, often contrary to well-established assumptions and practices. Ways around many of the disruptive challenges that have killed businesses were intellectually obvious. The problem was that they weren't adopted with enough energy and enthusiasm.

Third, implicit in systems thinking is an engineering mind-set that is ill adapted to problems involving human beings, their objectives, and their feelings. Habits and emotional attachments aren't based on rational foundations that will lapse simply because intellectual understanding is entrained by systems thinking. For these things to change, people's hearts must change as well as their minds. For this purpose, systems thinking is just thinking—it's operating in the wrong part of the body.

Use Data-Driven Strategic Innovation

Michael Schrage maintains that the key to innovation is data-driven strategic innovation. According to Schrage, it's no longer enough for innovators to be sensitive to potentially provocative correlations. Today's innovators must explicitly generate them en masse. Capital-intensive innovators increasingly structure their research initiatives to ensure that unexpected correlations trigger recognition and review. Correlation becomes the crucible for innovation and insight. According to Schrage, "The future of innovation will increasingly be determined by the future of data-driven statistical techniques."[10]

This approach will doubtless produce some new ideas, and some of the ideas may generate significant revenue—for instance,

- Organizations like GE's aircraft engines division already rely on data-driven techniques to predict the need for maintenance and repairs before significant problems actually happen. Significant savings accrue from this insight.[11]

- In pharmaceutical research, it appears possible that statistical analysis of trials will reveal hidden opportunities in compounds that initially fail as drugs for the entire population.[12]

Data-driven innovation thus will be a useful component of an overall innovation strategy. But it's difficult to agree with Schrage that development of data-driven statistical techniques will be what drives the future of innovation. It will be a component of sustaining innovation but not a very large component of disruptive innovation. It will generate ideas—but not the business-busting ideas that transform a sector in a single stroke.

Use Open Innovation

Another widely discussed approach in innovation theory is open source innovation. According to Henry Chesbrough, "Successful innovators are finding they must complement their in-house R&D with external technologies and offer up their own technologies to outsiders. R&D at large companies is shifting from its traditional inward focus to more outward-looking management—open innovation—that draws on technologies from networks of universities, startups, suppliers, and competitors."[13]

Until recently, R&D was viewed as a vital strategic asset and, in many industries, a barrier to competitive entry. Research leaders like DuPont, Merck, IBM, GE, and AT&T did the most research in their respective industries—and earned the most profits as well. According to Chesbrough, "The change is striking.... Most of the premier industrial research laboratories of the 20th century have retreated from their historic mission of independent scientific discovery because of the low yields they're experiencing."[14]

And here lies the heart of the problem: the research laboratories of large companies are experiencing low yields. Why? Is it because of lack of ideas? Or because of the business-as-usual assumptions that hamper innovation in the big companies? Chesbrough himself answers the question: it's the constraints that firms place on their own research that stifles innovation: "The big toy makers constrain their search by insisting that any new toy bring in $100 million or more in its first year. Even such leading toys as Barbie and Hot Wheels would have failed to bring in a comparable amount when they were introduced in 1959 and 1969, respectively. An insistence on large initial sales condemns the toy manufacturers to merely extending existing brand franchises, or acquiring at a high price new toys successfully launched by smaller innovators."[15]

Similarly in pharmaceuticals, where big companies are struggling despite immense investments in R&D, the perspective of internal R&D must also change: from a focus on finding small molecules to produce a single blockbuster pill that will knock out a major disease for the entire population to more diverse approaches.

This is not to say that open source innovation won't help. Whereas old-school research labs took new technologies from basic science to finished product, open innovation labs can develop technologies that embrace and extend existing intellectual property—even those that might otherwise run into the "not invented here" syndrome.

So open source innovation isn't a bad idea. It's a supplement to the steps needed to resolve the basic problem of innovation, not a solution in itself. The fundamental problem in innovation isn't one of finding more new ideas; it's a matter of establishing a way of running the organization that is open to exploring new ideas and willing to back the most promising of them with resources and talent. To present open source innovation as "the solution" will generally result in a distraction from attacking the core problem, which isn't outside the organization at all. It's right there in the very heart of the organization itself.

Create a Chief Innovation Officer

Another approach to solving the problem of innovation proposed by Debra Amidon in *Innovation Strategy for the Knowledge Economy* is to create the senior position of chief innovation officer (CIO).[16] Given that the existing hierarchy is inimical to innovation, the solution is to create a new high-level position to support innovation.

The idea is interesting, and yet one has to ask: What sort of person would be appointed to such a position? And what sort of incentives would govern his or her actions? What is the likelihood that the CIO would actually tackle the rest of the hierarchy?

One obvious risk is that a CIO would be selected in the image of the existing management mind-set and would encourage innovations that fit the mold that the hierarchy expects—namely, tame me-too extensions of the existing way of doing business, not bold and disruptive revolutionary changes.

Another concern is whether a CIO would be good at sparking heterodox ideas. Powerful people who climb the hierarchy and arrive at the senior positions in large organizations get there because they have been good at maintaining order and focus and discipline. This is good for organizational efficiency and optimization but not always friendly to basic innovation.

The Design of Business

Roger Martin's book, *The Design of Business,* proposes a different approach. There is a need, he says, for a better compromise between the reliability of the supply chain (producing consistent, predictable outcomes) and the innovativeness of the design function (creating new value for customers). Thus, today's organization should achieve a better balance between operations that deliver goods and services and the design function that operates with creativity, with more emphasis on the latter.

The result of the improved compromise, however, is still usually "war in the boardroom," as Al Ries and Laura Ries describe in their book of the same name.[17] The left-brain thinking of the supply chain, supported by traditional management theory, business school teaching, and Wall Street assumptions, tends to crush the creativity of right-brain thinking about new ways to add value for customers.

The design school of innovation is still mainly about innovation "initiatives"—time-limited efforts to solve specific problems—while the rest of the organization continues in its business-as-usual mode of operating that is inimical to innovation. The approach still embodies the fundamental assumption of the twentieth-century management that the default mode of managing is scalable bureaucracy. As a result, it fails to deal with the heart of the problem of innovation.

SOLVING THE PARADOX

In this chapter so far, I've been exploring why the commonly proposed theories of innovation don't work. Is there no way that organizations can succeed in coping with disruptive innovation?

The very fact that none of the leading theories offers a solution suggests that they are looking for it in the wrong place. If innovation is a true paradox, then—as with any other paradox—the resolution must lie in rethinking fundamental assumptions.

Alan Murray gives us a clue in his *Wall Street Journal* article, "The End of Innovation": "Market-leading companies have missed game-changing transformations in industry after industry . . . not because of "bad" management, but because they followed the dictates of 'good' management. They listened closely to their customers. They carefully studied market trends. They allocated capital to the innovations that promised the largest returns. And in the process, they missed disruptive innovations that opened up new customers and markets for lower-margin, blockbuster products."[18] Murray puts his finger on the key issue here: it is the very nature of good traditional management that inhibits innovation.

The solution lies in rethinking the underlying assumptions of traditional management. To generate continuous innovation requires a radically different kind of management that is as good at *both* game-changing innovation *and* disciplined execution. Instead of innovation and organizational learning being the responsibility of a few courageous individuals or departments, we need management in which innovation is an organization-wide capability, a part of the firm's DNA.

My book, *The Leader's Guide to Radical Management*, spells out in detail what this fundamentally different kind of management involves. It entails seven principles and more than seventy practices.[19]

THE SEVEN PRINCIPLES OF CONTINUOUS INNOVATION

The Leader's Guide to Radical Management describes seven basic principles of continuous innovation, along with more than seventy supporting practices.

Radical management is a fundamentally different approach to management, with seven interlocking principles:

1. *The goal of work is to delight clients.* Radical management aims at delighting clients and focuses not on just the marketing department, but on the entire organization on this goal.
2. *Work is conducted in self-organizing teams.* Self-organizing teams draw on the full talents and inspiration of the people doing the work.
3. *Teams operate in client-driven iterations.* Client-driven iterations are key, because delighting clients can be approached only through successive approximations.
4. *Each iteration delivers value to clients.* Client-driven iterations focus on delivering value to clients by the end of each iteration. This forces closure and enables frequent client feedback.

5. *Managers foster radical transparency.* Self-organizing teams working in an iterative fashion, in turn both enable and require radical transparency.

6. *Managers nurture continuous self-improvement.* Continuous improvement means having the entire workforce find better ways to give value to clients.

7. *Managers communicating interactively, through stories, questions and conversations.* An underlying requirement of all of these principles is interactive communication. Unless managers and workers are communicating interactively, using authentic narratives, open-ended questions, and deep listening, rather than treating people as things to be manipulated, none of the above works.

The most important shift is a change in goals. Traditional management of the twentieth-century organization was focused on the simple, linear goal of delivering goods and services to make money. The main method of improving productivity was through achieving economies of scale.

The radically different management that is needed to deliver continuous innovation focuses on the difficult, complex goal of delighting customers; making money is the consequence of the continuous new value that it creates for customers, not the goal.

Merely aiming at delivering goods and services cripples innovation because of the underlying assumption that the firm knows in advance what goods and services need to be delivered. In a rapidly changing marketplace, in which not even the customers themselves know what they really want, the assumption is increasingly unfounded.

When a firm adopts the complex goal of delighting customers, innovation becomes the driving force of everyone and everything in the organization, with adaptation and agility as central preoccupations.

The change in goal changes everything.

The traditional management goal of delivering goods and services can be accomplished in its entirety. Through economies of scale, "the system" enables work to be done progressively more cheaply, albeit with declining returns. Through outsourcing and downsizing, the economies can be continued. Rules can be put in place. Processes can be established. Structures can be built. Mistakes can be eliminated. If mistakes do occur, people can be blamed and punished. In this way, a predictable environment can be built. The system operates as a closed universe. The customer is treated as a thing to be manipulated to buy the products and services generated by the system. The employees are treated as "human resources" (that is, things) to be exploited and discarded as necessary. The entire system is inimical to innovation, because any significant innovation risks destabilizing the simple, linear, finite world that has been created. The continuation of the system becomes an end in itself. For a time, this way of managing worked well enough: in a stable marketplace like that of the 1950s and 1960s, with strong demand, established firms could get away with manipulating customers and treating employees as resources to be mined.

But the world changed. Today the customer is in charge. There has been a fundamental shift in the balance of power between sellers and buyers. Now, unless a firm is inspiring workers to provide a continuous stream of new value for customers, the customers can—and will—go elsewhere. Moreover knowledge workers are unwilling to give their best if they are treated as resources to be mined. As a result, productivity depends on their being treated with respect as adult human beings.

The changes involved in having organizations embrace continuous innovation are substantial. This is more than a minor shift at the periphery. It's more than a new process or structure. It's more than a new management methodology. This is a phase change, even a paradigm shift, to use Thomas Kuhn's expression.[20]

For most organizations, embracing the goal of delighting customers entails a major shift in the complexity of what a firm is undertaking. The goal of a firm becomes difficult and complex rather than simple and linear. Now continuous innovation becomes a central preoccupation of everyone in the organization, rather than a distraction and a destabilizer. Now the firm is involved in continuous experimentation to find out what works and what doesn't in terms of adding new value for clients. Now mistakes are welcomed as an essential element of the learning process rather than being elements that can be eliminated. Now everyone in the organization is focused on what can be done to add more value to customers and clients.

Now structures and rules and processes are formulated so as to enable and reinforce the creativity and energies of the people doing the work rather than undermining them. Now customers and employees are treated as adult human beings with whom the organization has adult-to-adult relationships rather than being treated as "human resources" to be manipulated. Innovation now becomes the driving force of the entire organization. Everyone is responsible for finding new ways to add value to customers. The firm is no longer an end in itself. It becomes "other directed": it is focused on meeting the needs of the customers and stakeholders.

In this radically different mode of managing, the firm still has structures and processes, but the structures and processes create a space to liberate rather than stifle the talents and energies of those doing the work. The structures and processes are designed to create delight customers rather than placate or frustrate them.

Introducing radical management entails significant change. Many organizations have yet to make the shift. But in the end, the economics will be inexorable. The rate of return on assets of U.S. firms is already one-quarter of what it was in 1965. The life expectancy of a firm in the Fortune 500 has declined from around half a century to fifteen years, and is heading toward five years if nothing changes.[21] The dynamics reflected in these remarkable statistics will force a transition to continuous innovation, whether entrenched interests want it or not. The only question is whether it will happen intelligently and quickly, or slowly and clumsily and painfully.

THE IMPORTANT ROLE OF STORYTELLING

For a quick and intelligent transition to the principles of continuous innovation, storytelling will be critical.

First, *persuading the leadership* of organizations to adopt radical management with a new goal for work—delighting clients—will require substantial persuasion. Leadership storytelling, using springboard stories as discussed in Chapter Three, will be central.

Second, the principles of continuous innovation are focused on the goal of *delighting clients.* Those doing the work have to understand the client's story and the story of how their own work contributes to enhancing that story, as discussed in Chapter Five.

A third dimension is that the work is done in *self-organizing teams* of people who are often diverse in terms of both background and status. Attaining collaboration in high-performance teams is likely only if the managers and participants are skilled in the use of story, as discussed in Chapter Seven.

A fourth dimension is *radical transparency*—the systematic communication of impediments to getting the work done. This will typically be done in the form of knowledge-sharing stories, as discussed in Chapter Eight.

A fifth dimension is *the planning of work,* which takes place in the form of user stories. The work program doesn't consist, as in traditional management, in accomplishment of a certain number of "things," such as producing a certain number of products or services or a certain quantity of money. The work program consists of *user stories*, which are stories set in the future, as discussed in Chapter Ten.

In effect, storytelling underlies key aspects of continuous innovation because interactive human-based relationships between organization's leadership, the people doing the work (employees), and the people for whom the work is being done are the engines of productivity and innovation. The leadership involved in creating such interactive relationships is the subject of the final chapter.

A DIFFERENT KIND
OF LEADER

Using Narrative to Become an Interactive Leader

> " To be understood is to be open
> to understanding.
>
> **Vicki Hearne[1]**

In this book, I have been exploring the pathways that words take toward meaning, how the use of those words and meanings in the course of performing narratives lead to actions, and how a family of narrative patterns are effective for different aspects of leadership. The use of narrative opens up leadership capabilities that are not available to someone operating solely in the traditional management mode of command, control, regulation, and optimization.

Implicit in all this is a different idea of what it means to be a leader. It's an interactive mode of leadership that swims in the richness and complexity of living and thrives on the connections between things. Participants grasp the interrelatedness of things in the world—and so are able to connect with the world in new ways. I have been making the case, step by step, that someone who embodies the interactive mode of thinking, speaking, and acting and takes on the new capabilities that

269

narrative enables can accomplish what was inaccessible to someone operating solely in the traditional command-and-control mode.

To this point, I've been looking at leadership through the lens of storytelling. Now I want to look at leadership more directly and state explicitly what kind of leadership I'm talking about. It has several dimensions:

○ ○ ○

- *The interactive leader works with the world rather than against it.* The key is to read the world and let the world do some of the work for you rather than trying to manipulate and control others by imposing various kinds of boundaries, incentives, and disincentives to get compliance with your will. If the traditional manager is a boxer who tries to overpower the world with superior hitting power, the interactive leader is more like a practitioner of judo—someone who can overcome stronger adversaries by catalyzing and channeling his or her energy. As a result, this concept of leadership is independent of hierarchical position and power, and so can be exercised from wherever you are in the organization.[2]

- *Interactive leadership both adds and subtracts elements from the leadership palette.* Interactive leadership supplements the traditional management functions of command, control, regulation, analysis, and optimization by adding new capabilities. But it's also subtractive: it requires setting aside techniques of manipulation and winning regardless of cost that are deployed by the robber barons, hardball strategists, and spin artists discussed in Chapters Five and Six. It's not possible for leaders to exercise manipulative and spinning behavior in one part of their conduct and expect to be accepted as open, truthful, and trustworthy in other domains.

- *Interactive leadership builds on personal integrity and authenticity.* Because you can communicate who you are and what you stand for, others come to know you and respect you for that. Because you are attentive to the world as it is, your ideas are sound. Because you speak the truth, you are believed. Because you treat others as ends in themselves, not merely as means to your own ends, people trust you. Because you make your values explicit and act in accord with those values, your values become contagious and others start to share them. Because you listen to the world, the world listens to you. Because you are open to innovation, happy accidents happen. Because you bring meaning into the world of work, you are able to get superior results.

- *Interactive leadership doesn't depend on the possession of hierarchical authority.* Anyone and everyone who can help clarify the direction or improve the structure, or secure support for it, or offer coaching that improves performance is providing leadership.

- *Interactive leadership benefits from an understanding of the different narrative patterns that can be used to get things done in the world.* This involves telling stories, not talking about storytelling. Competence in narrative theory can lend resonance and depth to your storytelling, but you need not burden the world with the principles of what you are doing. Narrative depends on emotional intelligence, but it also puts emotional intelligence to work to achieve practical outcomes.

- Above all, interactive leadership entails active participation in the world rather than detached observation. And it is to this distinction that I now turn.

LEADERSHIP THAT PARTICIPATES

Employing the interactive mode of leadership means engaging the world with a mind-set of active participation rather than detached observation. The mode of disinterested, objective knowing, removed from moral and social responsibility, has been an animating motif of the modern world. In today's context of rapid change, it is producing diminishing returns. Some issues—the most serious leadership challenges of our time—lie beyond its reach.[3]

Once leaders adopt the interactive mode of thinking and behaving, the world is no longer separate, out there. They escape from the illusion of passionless objectivity, which may aim at clarity but inevitably ends up distorting the world by stripping away the dimension of human viewpoints, emotions, and goals. Objectivity operates as a distancing device. When you are trying to connect with the people you lead, distancing is the last thing you need. One of the great weaknesses of the controlling mode of management is that it pursues its goals under the pretense of providing impregnable certainty and strength.

If you are to achieve appropriate connectedness with the people you lead, you need precisely those capacities for understanding, trust, and respect that the command-and-control mode of management suppresses. Choosing to feel compassion instead of detachment is often ridiculed in business as being insufficiently hard—insufficiently firm, hard-nosed, tough-minded, aggressive, or any of the other alpha male caricatures—and ultimately hard-hearted.

As a comprehensive philosophy, care and compassion are obviously inadequate: sometimes you have no alternative but to stand and resist the enemies of the future. When the house is on fire, you don't stop to have a conversation. But you don't have to pretend that the house is on fire, all day, every day, as a pretext for remaining perpetually in command-and-control mode. In most leadership situations, trust, respect, and collaboration are simply more effective than preemptive domination. As Sun-Tzu pointed out several millennia ago, the skillful leader subdues the enemy's troops without fighting.[4]

LEADERSHIP THAT CONNECTS

To see what I mean by leadership, consider what happens in one of the most frequent and mundane of management interactions: a talk to a group of people. The people might be subordinates, or superiors, or partners or clients, or whatever. Here's what happens when a controlling manager uses narrative, as compared to when an interactive leader makes the same talk.

The controlling manager comes with a message to impart within the context of a larger agenda for achievement. The presentation is typically in the form of an abstract lecture that proceeds independent of the listener. The speaker discourses on the chosen topic based on premises that are entirely the manager's own. They might be about decisions that have been made, or plans that are being announced, or simply news of what has happened. The audience's spontaneous reactions—applause, laughter, disapproval—are essentially irrelevant distractions to the presentation. No one in the audience enters the picture as an active participant unless expressly invited to intervene. Even if people are allowed to ask questions or make comments, it is expected that the comments and questions will be within the overall assumptions of the agenda. The success of the transaction is seen as depending on whether the manager has been able to transmit the message.

For the interactive leader, the situation is very different. This leader comes with a message and an agenda, but also seeks to interact with the audience and learn from their viewpoints. For this purpose, storytelling is an extraordinarily suitable tool. Since all good storytelling begins and ends in listening, the session is inherently participative and interactive.

Even before the presentation has begun, the interactive leader shows an appropriate rapport at the outset to increase the chances of the audience's being responsive. Thus the leader might welcome the audience individually, shaking hands or otherwise physically acknowledging their presence. The leader does this because it's difficult to be utterly unresponsive to someone who is actively signaling responsiveness and reciprocity.

When the interactive leader begins to talk, storytelling is part of the presentation and, as in all other face-to-face storytelling, the reactions of the audience are central. In storytelling, the teller is of necessity attentive to these reactions because they represent essential markers as to how and whether the story is resonating, indicators as to how to proceed from that point onward. The teller adjusts the performance in the light of the reactions observed, and the audience observes that the leader is making adjustments in the performance in response to their reactions. This prompts new reactions from the audience, which lead to new adjustments by the leader. The leader is aware of the audience just as the audience is aware of the leader, and the leader is aware of the audience's awareness of this responsiveness to their reactions. And so on.

It is the presence of the explicitly subjective plane in narratives, and the apparent absence of any such plane in abstract assertions, that contributes to the superior audience responsiveness to narratives over abstractions. In a narrative, we know who's talking and why, and often how the characters view the events, with the result that we can begin to get a handle on the potential human significance of what's being talked about.

So the interactive leader uses a story, and the responsiveness of the audience to the story is contagious. Each listener is very much aware of the reactions of other listeners to the leader. If some listeners start laughing, every listener tends to laugh. The larger the crowd, the greater the likelihood of contagion.

Listening here means not just a passive reception of sounds but rather an active mental state—penetrating, unified, yet focused and permeable, enhanced by the consciousness of the listeners participating in the interaction. The look of the responsive gaze, the frowning brow, the evident delight of a smile—all of these visual cues communicate volumes even though no sound may be heard. In the interaction, a simple and unexpected sense of deep accord forms between the teller and the audience. Whatever the power relations of the teller and the listeners, for the duration of the story, they are simply human beings connected by the act of storytelling.[5]

When the interactive leader invites reactions from the audience, the openness of the presentation has created a mood of possibility. It becomes plausible for the audience not only to offer comments or questions within the given assumptions of the leader but also to offer their own stories, which may have different underlying assumptions from those of the leader, and so the discussion can broaden into areas that would otherwise be impossible to broach. As a result, what begins as a simple talk by the leader to the subordinates can suddenly become an opportunity for new ideas, new possibilities, creativity, and innovation.

The notional presentation under discussion here would be only one incident in a busy leader's day, which may have over a hundred such interactions. By being open and interactive with all the people who fill the day's calendar—subordinates, superiors, board members, clients, partners, investors, analysts—the leader not only gets across the message and the agenda but also is continually opening up new horizons and possible opportunities while encouraging other people's collaboration.

By contrast, the controlling manager spends a day full of the same interactions, but they typically end in adversarial, tension-filled, power-driven outcomes, with few new possibilities or opportunities emerging. On the surface, it's a day of apparent order and focus, as the controlling manager appears to win most of the encounters as a result of superior hierarchical power, but all that submissiveness may be deceptive, as those who perceive themselves as losers continue on, often surreptitiously waiting to fight another day.[6]

Further insights on the nature of interactive leadership can be gleaned from Vicki Hearne's wonderful book on animal training, *Adam's Task*. There she notes that the people who come to visit the animals she works with fall into several categories.[7] First, there are the people with supersized egos, which she calls "Hollywood types": they are self-absorbed and indifferent to where they are and their strutting is essentially irrelevant to the animals. Then there are the "researchers," who are exploring propositions to be tested. These people are contaminated by epistemology. Around dogs, they are "bitees," that is, the people most likely to be bitten as a result of the dogs' frustration with the combination of intrusiveness and unresponsiveness. Finally, there are the "animal trainers," who exhibit soft, acute 360-degree awareness of who they are and who else is there. In the way they move, they offer mute acknowledgment of the presence of the animals and fit into the spaces shaped by the animals. It is precisely this same soft, acute 360-degree awareness that leaders need to exhibit in relation to the people they are seeking to lead.

LEADERSHIP THAT IS LIKE CONVERSATION

The interactive approach to leadership is modeled on the concept of conversation—a dialogue between equals. The relationship between storyteller and listener is symmetrical. The approach proceeds on the assumption that the listener could take the next turn in the conversation.

In an organization, the differences in status between leader and audience may be vast. You may be a boss talking to subordinates. Or a subordinate talking to your boss or bosses. You may be someone with great wealth and power talking to people who have neither, or you may be a supplicant requesting the rich and powerful to change their ways. As an interactive leader, something you can be regardless of overt status, you ignore these differences and talk to your listeners as one human being to another. In so doing, you slice through the social and political barriers that separate individuals from each other.

By contrast, the controlling manager usually exploits differences in status that lead to adversarial relationships. Thus, if you assert, "This innovation is a winner," your listeners' options are to accept or reject the proposition. If they accept it, they are submitting to your authority as an expert, a teacher, a boss, a parent, or whatever. If they reject it or argue with it, then you and they are at once in an adversarial relationship. It's not impossible to maintain a conversation of equals when dealing with someone who adopts a superior hierarchical position, but it isn't easy—there is an inherent tendency to slide into an adversarial relationship of either submission or rebellion.

By contrast, when you tell a story as a leader in the interactive mode, there is no such implication of submission or rebellion. The listeners don't need to accept or reject your story: it is something that the teller and audience relive together. It is a mutually shared experience, something in which the audience actively participates. The normal response is neither acceptance nor rejection but rather to tell another story. It might be a story in the same vein. Or a listener might say, "I have a different take on that!" and tell a story that reflects another point of view. Either way, one story leads to another. It's not a normal response to say, "That story is right" or, "That story is wrong." A story is neither right nor wrong. It simply *is*. In this way, storytelling is naturally collaborative.[8]

LEADERSHIP THAT IS POSSIBLE

At the outset, most of us have to work at being interactive and listening—particularly those who have gotten into the bad habit of looking at the world only from our own viewpoint or of making abstract presentations to which the listeners are essentially irrelevant, and who are at significant risk of becoming our audience's "bitees." If we work at listening, we can make progress. But however we manage it, true listening and interaction appear—paradoxically—at the moment willed effort drops away. We enter a state of flow or effortless effort. At such moments, the self disappears. We are at one with the object of our attention. We dissolve into attentiveness itself.[9]

Are there any CEOs today who are running real companies with interactive leadership? Tom Chappell of Tom's of Maine, Bill George of Medtronic, Herb Kelleher of Southwest Airlines, Tony Hsieh of Zappos, Howard Schultz of Starbucks, and Vineet Nayar of HCL Technologies are sometimes suggested as candidates.[10] The forty or so "idea practitioners" Tom Davenport and Larry Prusak cite in *What's the Big Idea?* would also be candidates as interactive leaders.[11] In any event, further research is needed. The fact that the list of candidates is relatively short may indicate how difficult it is to give birth to this new kind of leadership in the current context.

One possible clue to the conundrum is that there is no ancient Greek hero or god, no long-standing cultural archetype, whose conduct resembles the interactive leadership I'm talking about here. So there's little in the collective psyche that makes it easy for people to understand and slide into this mode of operating. And this may be part of the problem: society is trying to give birth to a new type of the human psyche that would actually encourage good people and innovation and still survive and flourish. Like anything worthwhile, the birth pangs are not painless or easy. Nevertheless the need is there.

LEADERSHIP THAT FITS THE MODERN NEED

Over a quarter of a century ago, Charles Handy noted the tendency in organizations toward bigness and consistency:

> If you are sitting near the top of an organization, responsible in whole or in part for its continued success, or at least survival, there is a strong urge to want to make it bigger and more internally consistent. There are good reasons for each of these tendencies.... The bigger you are, the more able you are to influence your own destiny.... And bigness brings clout.... Bigness brings flexibility and a built-in insurance. A loss in one area can be offset by unusual profits elsewhere.... Consistency is desirable for two reasons. If the future is consistent with one's expectations of it, then planning can be tighter.... Consistency is also forced on organizations from outside.[12]

Bigness and consistency bring with them an organizational culture that Handy calls Apollonian, named after the ancient Greek god Apollo, who was among other things the god of order and rules. According to Handy, "Size ... brings formality, impersonality, and rules and procedures in its train. There is no way out of it. When someone cannot rule by glance of eye and word-of-mouth because there are just too many people, he has to lean on formal systems of hierarchy, information, and control. Similarly, budgets, forms, standardized methods, fixed reporting periods, common documents, and the whole barrage of bureaucracy. The ineluctable logic of efficiency drives organizations toward Apollo and the role culture."[13]

These trends have been accentuated by both globalization and information technology and are now dominant. Yet even as Apollo seems triumphant everywhere, the forces undermining the Apollonian organizational culture are also inexorably at work. "For just as size creates an internal need for Apollonian methods, so the very strengthening of that culture tends to make the total organization less responsive to its environment, less capable of changing, more dinosaur-like than ever—impressive but out of touch and often out of control."[14]

In particular, the managerial burdens of an Apollonian organization in times of rapid change become extraordinary. For the very top of the organization, the traditional management tools—command, control, regulation, analysis, and optimization—are simply too slow and ineffective to reorient the organization to meet the changing needs of the marketplace in a timely fashion.

For the middle and frontline manager, the situation is even worse. "Restrained by the rules and procedures dictated by the pressures for consistency, he must find a way of coping with inconsistency."[15] However, coping with inconsistency was never one of the strengths (or even objects) of the conventional management tools. Indeed, uncertainty for the middle manager derives from the very fact that these tools have become inoperative, since the purposes for which they were devised shift faster than the tools themselves can change. In effect, middle managers have to become leaders rather than managers, creatively generating new goals that can reconcile overall organizational goals with the realities of their units.

People on the frontline—those actually doing the work—also face dilemmas. They can see very readily the tension between the goals of the organization and the realities of what is going on where the work is actually done, and they often have excellent ideas as to how things could be done better. In the formal, role-based organization where command and control predominate, they have no way of making those ideas known and so improving the organization, which trundles on its way, oblivious.

For these dilemmas, the interactive approach to leadership, along with its accompanying narrative tools, is extraordinarily relevant. Suddenly the tasks of getting people to understand and implement complex new ideas, transmitting values, getting people working together, sharing knowledge, and leading people into the future become feasible.

LEADERSHIP THAT IS NOT FOR EVERYONE

Nevertheless the interactive approach to leadership will not appeal to everyone.

It will be of little interest to those who are comfortable in the traditional management mode of command and control. Nor is it likely to attract robber barons, hardball strategists, upwardly mobile lackeys, fawning aides-de-camp, commercial mercenaries, paid-for politicians, or scheming demagogues. Such people have always used inauthentic narrative as a tool of manipulation and control. They have no need to be taught how to tell the quick lie, or how to profit from the devices of the shyster and the shill like foot-in-the-door or bait-and-switch, or how to deceive with political spin, character assassination, and negative campaigning. They need no advice to silence those who dare ask a question or discredit any who are critical of the status quo.[16]

Inauthentic storytelling may work in the short term, but it isn't a sound foundation for any individual, business, or society. If it is tolerated or even encouraged and taught in schools, whether by cunning, carelessness, ignorance, indifference, loss of confidence, or an inability to distinguish right from wrong, or by governmental fiat, then the society is accordingly impoverished, and we are all accountable for the loss.

These people will go on practicing their counterfeit leadership in offices, malls, courthouses, post offices, and parliaments, dangling the threat of layoffs or other disasters over people's heads while increasing the pace and intensity of the work. They will go on using pseudo-empirical studies crafted to contain creative people in cages of quiet desperation. They will seduce newcomers with duplicitous maneuvers. They will go on suppressing human potential, dismissing new ideas, promoting not knowing ahead of knowing, preserving privilege as a suit of armor polished to a shocking glitter.[17] Using these techniques, they may prosper for a period, as they squeeze the last few drops from depleting business models and spend their energy making fresh rationalizations for their dominance.

LEADERSHIP THAT IS RELATIVELY FREE OF EGO

The interactive approach to leadership is not concerned merely with making the deal. This is key, because if who you are gets defined according to the current rate of exchange in a marketplace, then the accommodation you make with the world will distract you, one degree at a time, from what matters. This is how the commercialized version of what it means to be a person brings people under its spell.[18]

True leaders do not lead because they are expecting something in return. They lead because they have something to give. They may get something back, but this is a contingent event, not the goal. They give with a spirit of generosity. They are relatively ego free.

At their best, interactive leaders are willing to bear any suffering, even loss or humiliation, rather than show that their egos are more important than their goal. In this respect, Gandhi, Martin Luther King Jr., and Nelson Mandela have shown us the way. Once opponents realize they cannot intimidate such people, they eventually stop trying. Being relatively ego free will not exempt you from risk. But by removing ego from the game, you change the nature of the game, since the principal lever of those in the control mode is eliminated.

Being relatively free of ego means never exacting revenge. Revenge only strengthens the will to resist. You abandon all notions of a tit-for-tat fight. You don't give as good as you get, since you don't respond in kind. Instead you take the moral high ground of truth and authenticity. Thus anger against the adversary and anger against the self are inseparable. The thrust of the interactive leader is on curing the inner contradictions of those who do not see the future. Your opponents are oppressed by a larger foe—their own fear. You help them deal with this common enemy and teach them to relax their antagonism by showing them through narrative that the prospects are more positive than they apprehend.[19]

LEADERSHIP THAT IS LIKE JUDO

When you take on the role of the interactive leader, aware of who you are, confident of your values, assured of the soundness of your mission, and competent to communicate it through a story, you will acquire supporters. But you will also become an immediate threat to the powers that be, the forces that support that status quo. So what do you do with these opponents? Here are some thoughts.

Above all, you need to feel the importance, the excitement, and the plausibility of your mission. If you don't feel it, no one else will. While you abstain from tilting at windmills, you also choose the biggest possible goal to fight for. Make a war too small, and it's yours alone; no one will join in the action. You ask for everything, because nothing less is worth having. People are more giving if your request challenges them to be heroic. Asking for small things simply makes people feel small. People are drawn to big ideas and big adventures more passionately than to small ones. The interactive leader defines the struggle in terms of a long-range campaign, not isolated skirmishes. No one episode is a defeat if the goal is large.[20]

You don't fight your opponents: you invalidate them. Those who bear the trappings of power don't necessarily have much authority. You behave as if you already possess moral authority. The board of directors may be holding you accountable. Your boss may control your current job. The state may control the army and the police. But they don't have moral authority over you. As a leader, you are an actualist, not an activist. You make your views true in action. You conduct your campaign entirely in the open and at close range. Truth and authenticity are your most powerful weapons. This is the method of resistance. It's not defiance, or subterfuge, or charm, but rather standing on firm moral ground. Resistance is the opposite of compromise. It means not fighting your opponents' battle or even anything like a traditional battle at all. It means enticing the opponents to engage on your ground, in your timing, where your goals determine the outcome.

Thus, in the interactive mode of leadership, dealing with opponents isn't about winning. Winning implies losers, and losers harbor resentment and bitterness that eventually will come back to bite you. You must make your opponents unwitting allies. This means neither hurting them nor eroding their confidence.

Instead you deal with opponents by besting them. Besting leaves opponents unhurt and even inspired. Besting is a mode in which you demonstrate to your antagonist your moral superiority. Through narrative, you offer a clear and inspiring new future—one that motivates everybody.

Thus at the national level, Gandhi bested the British overlords. Martin Luther King Jr. bested the racists. Nelson Mandela bested the apartheid regime in South Africa. Rather than conceiving a simple win against their opponents, they triumphed over them in such a way that eventually everyone could see that this was the way forward.

Besting means not fencing people in—you leave them room to change their minds. You behave as if your opponents are your allies, demonstrating your trust in them and giving them strength to do the right thing. You give them the courage to change by creating heroic expectations for them. The bigger the expectations, the harder they will try to achieve them.

You build a network of support to surround your opponents. A mesh of support is hard to attack because its strength is spread widely. You make sure others know what the network stands for. It becomes the embodiment of your idea. Once your opponents ask, "Who are they?" they are finally taking you seriously. They are no longer detached. They are beginning to see the world through your eyes.

Finally, you end the struggle cleanly, not prematurely. A good ending brings resolution and closure. Thus, at the national level, it eventually becomes clear to the British government that they must hand over India to Gandhi. It eventually becomes clear to the South African government that Nelson Mandela is right: the apartheid regime is unsustainable and must be eliminated. And on a more mundane level, it eventually becomes obvious that e-business is part of IBM's future and that sharing knowledge is crucial to the World Bank's goal of alleviating global poverty. A change in relations occurs as all participants recognize the need for the change.

LEADERSHIP THAT HAS FEELING

Interactive leadership involves passion—another ingredient that is missing from the traditional mode of management. By putting its faith in logic, control, and optimization, command-and-control management has lost sight of the crucial role that passion plays in human action.

By contrast, the interactive approach to leadership thrives on feeling. This is not the demonized sense of feeling that Nietzsche characterized as Dionysian and associated with drunkenness and irrationality.[21] Nor is it the kind of primitive animal instinct that Freud baptized as the id. Most feelings have a rational aspect—as humans, we are happy or angry for a reason, in a context that we understand through narrative. As in all rational activities, we may make a mistake: the reason for a feeling might be the wrong reason, or an emotion may be out of proportion to the cause, but this doesn't disprove that feelings have a rational dimension. Emotions have "a narrative structure which ties together and makes sense of the individual elements of emotional experience .... To make sense of one's emotional life, including its surprises, it is thus necessary to see it as part of a larger unfolding narrative."[22]

Thus, while not jettisoning the value of rational analysis, we also need to recognize the positive, rational dimensions of emotions. Neurological research by Antonio Damasio and others has shown that emotion is integral to the processes of reasoning and decision making. Thus he describes some people he studied "who were entirely rational in the way they ran their lives up to the time when, as a result of neurological damage in specific sites of the their brains, they lost a certain class of emotions and, in a momentous parallel development, lost their ability to make rational decisions." He goes on to point out that these people still have the ability to reason. "[They] can still use the instruments of their rationality and can still call up the knowledge of the world around them. Their ability to tackle the logic of a problem remains intact. Nonetheless, many of their personal and social decisions are irrational, more often disadvantageous to their selves and to others than not."[23]

Damasio concludes that while emotional upheavals can lead to irrational decisions, "emotion probably assists reasoning, especially when it comes to personal and social matters involving risk and conflict.... Well-targeted and well-deployed emotion seems to be a support system without which the edifice of reason cannot operate properly."[24]

The interactive leader uses narrative to mobilize Damasio's "well-targeted and well-deployed emotion" so as to get people into action. Passion is an inherent aspect of narrative because in a story, the listeners relive the narrative in their own minds. It is as if they are there inside the story and so they experience the feelings of the participants. By contrast, the controlling manager typically resorts to abstract analysis and assertions, from which passion is naturally absent.[25]

Another reason that the interactive leader resorts to storytelling is its aural character. The ear enjoys a privileged passageway to the heart, as may be seen in the emotional impact of music. Narratives told face-to-face use the same privileged passageway, which is also amazingly sensitive to the veracity of the content. Thus, research carried out by U.K. professor Richard Wiseman has shown that we can detect lies more accurately from listening to the voice alone. In an experiment in which deliberate lies were told over British television, on radio, and in print, the lies were detected best by the radio audience, next by the newspaper readers, and worst by the television viewers.[26]

Thus the interactive mode of leadership isn't simply about being emotionally intelligent; it's about *acting* with emotional intelligence. If you are emotionally intelligent only in your thoughts while you remain in the traditional management mode of controlling, regulating, and optimizing, then you are unlikely to be successful in engaging the emotions of others. It is generally through narrative that you activate passion and channel the passion in others for constructive purposes. To achieve the proper balance inherent in "well-targeted and well-deployed emotion," you also need to avoid being too much in love with order.

LEADERSHIP THAT AVOIDS "APOLLO RUN AMOK"

Now that Apollonian culture, along with its attendant control mode of management, is everywhere triumphant, the modern workplace often feels as though it has fallen head over heels in love with order. Earlier in this chapter, I discussed the reasons that the Apollonian culture emerged as a result of the forces of bigness and consistency. In fact, the control mode sets out with the best of intentions—that of establishing order out of the potential chaos into which large organizations would otherwise tumble.

But when the love of order becomes extreme, it can undermine the very condition of harmony that it is trying to achieve. The ancient Greeks recognized the phenomenon and—as usual—encapsulated it in a story: the myth of Apollo and Daphne:

Apollo was the god of order and light. He helped ripen crops, destroy pests, and heal illnesses. He was a shepherd god and protected flocks. He was also a builder and the god of colonies and of oracles, and the deity of beauty and music. He was usually depicted as a beardless young man of handsome proportions, and he was often shown with a bow and quiver.

One day in the forest, Apollo saw a beautiful young maiden, Daphne, and fell in love with her. She, however, hated the thought of loving anyone. Her delight was in woodland sports and the spoils of the chase. Many lovers had sought her, but she had rejected them all.

When Apollo saw her hair flung loose over her shoulders, he thought, "If it's as charming as this in disorder, what would it be like if it was arranged?" She rejected his advances, and so he chased her through the woods. She fled, running swifter than the wind.

Even as she continued her flight, Apollo fell even more deeply in love. The wind blew her garments and her unbound hair streamed loose behind her. Apollo grew impatient to catch up with her and picked up the pace.

As he gained on her, he got so close that his panting breath blew on her hair. In her desperation, she called on her father, the river god, to save her. Scarcely had she spoken when a stiffness seized all her limbs. Her breasts were enclosed in a tender bark. Her hair became leaves and her arms branches. Her feet were stuck fast in the ground as roots. Her face became a treetop, retaining nothing of her former self except her beauty. Apollo stood amazed at the transformation.[27]

The myth offers a clue as to the proper balance between passion and order. Excessive pursuit of something can lead to its petrification. In the process of striving for order, you can destroy the very thing you love. The end result for the object of Apollonian attentions is not necessarily death but rather a vegetable state that closely resembles it. The victims of the excess are unable to move. They stay rooted to the ground, immobile.

In the nineteenth century, the idea arose in the writings of Nietzsche that society needed to choose between rules and order on one hand and drunken irrationality on the other. If that were the choice today, it's obvious that anyone would choose the former.

But this isn't the choice leaders of today are facing. It's not a choice between order and irrationality. The more important choice is between an approach of domination and control and one of participation and interaction. Rationality and order can be present in both modes. The question is whether the goal is an order that is subtle and dynamic, based on interactive engagement with others, or an order that is foreordained and sterile and based on command and control.

The ancient Greeks understood this rather better than traditional management. The Greek god Apollo was never an enemy of passion or narrative or interaction. In fact, Apollo was not only the god of order and light but also the god of music and beauty. Whatever the virtues of modern management, no one to date has suggested that they include music or beauty. So it's not Apollo with whom modern management has fallen in love, but rather a demonized version of Apollo, that is, Apollo run amok. We've got the order, but in establishing order, we've lost the music and the beauty.

LEADERSHIP THAT INCLUDES BEAUTY

In fact, of all modern management's sins, one of the least recognized is its neglect of beauty. After all, life was once viewed as beautiful, even though it's hard to recall this when reading management books or looking at the working life of most people today. Wealth doesn't seem to help. As the economy advances, the workplace doesn't become less dreary, with its total focus on analysis, optimization, and the bottom line. If a glimmer of beauty accidentally occurs in a modern organizational setting, it's usually regarded as an embarrassment: it will be dealt with by a rhetoric that has no aesthetic sensitivity to begin with.[28]

But what use is a life of work if there isn't a scintilla of beauty within it? As work consumes more and more of people's waking hours, the systematic draining of beauty from their lives becomes an increasingly graver problem.

Narrative thus has one final contribution to make: restoring beauty to the workplace. With a well-turned phrase, an elegant telling, a story creates the shapeliness of the beginning, middle, and ending. Through the story's tensions and resolutions, both the teller and the audience experience continuing coherent existence. These elements can add beauty to lives that are otherwise bereft of it, like flowers making their way through the cracks in a vast cement pavement.[29]

By contrast, the control mode of management is deadening. You can recognize it in the gray feeling that comes over you when you participate in a departmental meeting, listening to the voice that drones on with announcements of "new findings" that could hardly be more banal, or of the latest reorganization that is so like the previous one, or the fatuous anodynes for managers in distress. These are stagnant waters in which no living thing flourishes.

The dreariness of the modern workplace has been attacked so often that it might seem a waste of time to criticize it further. Yet there are grounds for doing so. While the cause of its ugliness—the controlling approach to leadership—is deadly, it's not dead. Unfortunately, it's horrifyingly active and energetic, like a garrulous bore who won't stop talking. In fact it's this restless energy that suggests the possibility—and even the hope—of change.

For organizations that are run in the control mode, beauty currently has to steal back into departments by way of postcards pinned to cubicle walls, muttered jokes, underground discussions, hurried lunches, or clandestine romances, while management tries to redirect attention toward mounting a never-ending career ladder. The goal is to get people to focus on minuscule salary increments and relative enhancements of standing—a fancier title or a marginally larger workspace.

What is being offered here is an escape route from this mortuary by suggesting a type of leadership that includes meaning as well as beauty. Story responds to our human curiosity to know how the world is connected together and to our longing for shapely forms. We not only look for narrative patterns—we yearn for them. We want to know what happens and also that it will make sense. We suffer the hunger for meaning and cannot resist its satisfaction. Through story we experience the many levels of the self, as well as a deeper coherence of the world.[30]

Through story, we learn to see each other and ourselves, and come to love what we see as well as acquire the power to change it. In this way we come to terms with our past, our present, and our future.

Through story, we can put an end to the worry, the fever, and the fret of trying to live instrumentally. Finally, we can simply be.

INTERACTIVE LEADERSHIP: ITS RELATION TO OTHER LEADERSHIP THEORIES

This chapter describes a kind of leadership that I have called an interactive leadership. It reflects an approach to leadership that includes the capacity to apply, with integrity and authenticity, the full set of narrative tools discussed in this book. In this kind of leadership, every person's perspective is taken into account, and yet an overall moral direction is also evident. This concept of leadership implies no hierarchical power. It sees a leader as someone who has followers, whether any formal authority supports the relationship. The leader may be someone at the top, the middle, or the bottom level of a hierarchy, someone who is aiming to achieve change in an organization—whether a business, a community, or a family. The question being addressed is, What behaviors enable one to acquire followers in pursuit of a cause, whatever the hierarchical situation?

Interactive leadership is contrasted to traditional command-and-control management, which reflects a reliance on hierarchical power and which represents the dominant approach to management today. It is characterized by boss-subordinate relationships, in which the leader is a supervisor who is assumed to have hierarchical power within an organization to hire, fire, reward or reprimand, promote or downgrade employees and allocate their responsibilities. Many of the studies assume this hierarchical relationship as the unstated context, which obviously has a huge influence on what happens, both positive (by way of getting subordinates' attention) and negative (by way of introducing a dimension of inequality that can hinder open dialogue and interactivity).

Both interactive and traditional modes of leading differ sharply from modes of operating based on manipulation and winning at all costs: demagogues, the spin artists whose activities were reviewed in Chapter Five, and the robber barons and hardball strategists discussed in Chapter Six. These people also use narrative techniques, but their narratives are grounded in deception and inauthenticity.

Categories of Leadership

How does the concept of interactive leadership relate to the vast literature on leadership? It's useful to look at the most frequently discussed categories:

○ ○ ○

- *Leadership as a trait:* Early efforts to understand leadership focused on the possibility of enduring personality or character traits that people were born with and that enabled some to become great, but no such traits have been discovered.[31] Although personality tests such as the Campbell Leadership Descriptor and Myers-Briggs Type Indicator are used to assess leadership qualities, no trait has been consistently linked with superior leadership performance. Nor am I suggesting that the ability to tell a story is an innate trait. Some people may be naturally better at telling stories than others. But storytelling is something that all people already perform in a fashion and anyone can get better at.

- *Leadership as a skill:* The concept of interactive leadership is consistent with the idea of leadership being a set of skills that can be learned. Robert Katz has suggested that leadership skills fall into three categories—technical, human, or intellectual.[32] Technical includes the understanding of the subject matter dealt with by the organization. Human includes interpersonal skills and the ability to relate to the people being led. Intellectual includes the ability to understand, analyze, and see the implications of the relationships between potential actions and their consequences. In many leadership theories, the narrative skills of an interactive leader are a missing dimension of the human and intellectual categories. More research is needed on what is involved in upgrading the relevant narrative skills, but abundant anecdotal evidence already shows that they can be learned.

- *Leadership as a style:* Another school of leadership research focuses on the behavior of leaders in terms of repeating patterns of behavior that may be either learned or innate. Blake and Mouton, for instance, developed a managerial grid with two dimensions: concern for results and concern for people.[33] By plotting results on each axis, with scores ranging from 1 to 9, they identified five major leadership styles: authority-compliance (9,1), country club management (1,9), impoverished management (1,1), middle-of-the-road management (5,5) and team management (9,9). The grid is widely used, but despite a massive amount of research, no consistent link has been found between leadership styles and productivity.[34] Of the various styles, interactive leadership has most in common with team management, where work is accomplished by committed people with a common stake in the outcome, which leads to relationships of trust and respect. Interactive leadership constitutes one particular way of achieving an outcome that combines high concern for both people and results.

- *Leadership as situational:* The basic premise of this approach is that different situations demand different kinds of leadership. To be effective, a leader needs to adapt to the demands of the situation. Blanchard mapped behavior on two dimensions: directive behaviors and supportive behaviors.[35] This leads to four leadership styles: delegating behavior (low supportive and low directive), supporting (high supportive and low directive), coaching (high directive and high supportive), and directing (high directive and low supportive). Much of the writing and research in this area deals with management rather than leadership, that is, with straightforward hierarchical situations of supervisors and their subordinates. And while the concept of interactive leadership put forward in this book is obviously highly situational—an interactive leader starts from the existing relationship with potential followers and goes from there—the two-dimensional model that Blanchard offers—supportive versus directive—lacks the conceptual subtlety necessary for understanding or dealing with the complex challenges of genuine leadership interactions that are not buttressed by hierarchical authority.

- *Leadership as motivation:* The goal of this theory is to enhance employee performance and satisfaction by focusing on employee motivation. Different leadership behaviors are identified, including directive leadership (telling subordinates what to do), supportive leadership (helping subordinates get the job done), participative leadership (inviting subordinates to share in decision making), and achievement-oriented leadership (challenging subordinates to perform at high levels).[36] Again, much of the writing and research in this area assumes that the leader has the hierarchical power to determine who gets to decide what, when that is precisely what is in question in the leadership challenges facing organizations today.

- *Leadership as transformation:* Since the publication of James MacGregor Burns's *Leadership* in 1978, attention has shifted toward transformational leadership, which is concerned with emotions, values, ethics, standards, and long-term goals. It involves a process whereby an individual engages with others and creates a connection that raises the level of motivation and morality in both the leader and the follower. Transformational leadership is distinguished from transactional leadership, which focuses on exchanges and deals between leader and followers concerning incentives or disincentives that may be applied in return for an employee's performance; and laissez-faire leadership, which amounts to keeping hands off and letting things ride. Transformational leaders exhibit strong values and ideas and are effective at motivating followers to act in ways that support the overall good; they end up changing both themselves and their followers.[37] Transformational leadership has much in common with the ideas put forward in this book. In fact, interactive leadership is a form of transformational leadership.

What Transformational Leaders Actually Do

The concept of interactive leadership addresses one of the fundamental problems of current theories of transformational leadership: their lack of conceptual clarity. Thus, in the literature to date, theories of transformational leadership tend to focus on traits or personal dispositions that lead to certain kinds of results. Robert Quinn's *Deep Change* sees transformational leadership as a process—as you grow as a person, so does your leadership.[38] Leaders need to constantly be self-aware and to work to become the leader they aspire to be.

What is typically missing in these theories is a specification of what specific leadership behavior leads to what result. It is thus unclear exactly what transformational leaders actually *do* to achieve the results they are said to achieve. This makes it difficult to validate the underlying ideas or to train people to become leaders. It isn't that these writers don't examine leaders' behavior: the problem is that current work in the area usually fails to examine the behavior of leaders in sufficiently fine granularity to identify what exactly is involved. In particular, it tends to overlook the narrative aspect of what is going on.[39]

The fact that narrative is a thread running through everything that a transformational leader does to achieve extraordinary results has thus received insufficient attention. How else could leaders provide succinct and appealing images of what is to be done, except by narrative? How else could leaders help people see meaning in their work except by story? How else could leaders communicate who they are or what their values are, except by narrative? How else could leaders share knowledge, tame the grapevine, or articulate a vision of the future, except by story?

This book has spelled out the specific, identifiable, measurable, trainable behaviors that can be used to achieve the goals of transformational leadership.

NOTES

PREFACE

1. Deloitte Center for the Edge, 2009.

2. Friedman, 2010.

3. Hamel, 2009.

INTRODUCTION

1. Denning, 2000, p. 175.

2. Hearne, 1987, p. 5.

3. Christensen and Raynor, 2003, p. 7.

4. Campbell and Park, 2004.

5. Sirower, 1997.

6. Deloitte Center for the Edge, 2009.

7. Deloitte Center for the Edge, 2009.

8. Deloitte Center for the Edge, 2009.

9. Smith, 2004.

10. For samples from the period November 2003 to June 2004, see my Web site, http://www.stevedenning.com/Storytelling-in-the-News/default.aspx.

11. Kellaway, 2004.

12. McCloskey and Klamer, 1995.

13. For a similar use of this rhetorical device, see Hackman, 2004, p. xi.

14. Luthi, 1982.

15. Senge, 1990, p. 363.

16. Senge, 1990, pp. 10–11.

17. Senge, 1990, p. 11.

18. For example, see Ryan, 2004, and Green, Strange, and Brock, 2002.

19. Strawson, 2004; Charon, 2004.

20. Gabriel, 2000, p. 22.

21. Vincent, 2002, p. 58.

22. For example, see Polkinghorne, 1988, pp. 13–14.

23. This distinction between the internal and external aspects of a story is related to, but different from, the traditional distinction between diegetic and mimetic narration, which goes back to Plato's *Republic* and is discussed in Aristotle's *Poetics*. A diegetic narration is the verbal storytelling act of a narrator. A mimetic narration is an act of showing, or a spectacle. Each of these modes can intrude into a narration dominated by the other (see Ryan, 2004). While diegetic and mimetic narration are to a certain degree alternative modes of performing a story, the internal and external aspects of a story coexist: they are two different ways of looking at the same story.

24. Ryan, 2004, p. 15.

25. Denning, 2000.

CHAPTER ONE

1. Bateson, 1990, p. 34.

2. Orr, 1990.

3. Gardner, 1995; Tichy, 1998; Simmons, 2002.

4. Tyco, 2003, p. 7.

5. Tyco, 2003.

6. Tichy, 1998, p. 174.

7. I am indebted to Tony Quinlan, tony@narrate.co.uk, for supplying me with the example.

8. Welch, 2001, pp. 3–4.

9. Tichy, 1998, pp. 172–188.

10. Block, 2002, p. 2.

11. "Nutty Tales," 2004.

12. Mintzberg, 1973.

13. The only incremental cost is the cost of learning to talk more effectively. Since all human beings spontaneously learn how to tell stories from a young age, the process of upgrading adults' storytelling capacity happens very rapidly.

14. LaClair and Rao, 2002.

15. "The Top 100 Brands," 2004.

16. Osborn and Ehninger, 1962.

17. Kouzes and Posner, 2003, p. 198.

18. Borgida and Nisbett, 1977; Zemke, 1990; Wilkens, 1983; Conger, 1991.

19. Martin and Power, 1982.

20. Hackman, 2004, pp. 236–237.

21. LaClair and Rao, 2002; Denning, 2000.

22. Hackman, 2004, p. 237.

CHAPTER TWO

1. Strunk and White, 1979, p. 66.

2. Thomas and Turner, 1994, p. 3. Storytelling is a an ancient art, and many guides are available. In this chapter, I draw heavily from those parts of the conventional wisdom of storytelling that are of particular relevance to organizational settings, especially Doug Lipman's *Improving Your Storytelling* and Doug Stevenson's *Never Be Boring Again*. Likewise, in terms of adjusting the form of the story itself to the organizational setting, I draw heavily on William Strunk and E. B. White's classic *Elements of Style* and Francis-Noel Thomas and Mark Turner's brilliant *Clear and Simple as the Truth*.

3. Gerstner, 1995a.

4. Thomas and Turner, 1994, p. 41.

5. Thomas and Turner, 1994, pp. 38–39.

6. Thomas and Turner, 1994, p. 36.

7. Thomas and Turner, 1994, p. 57.

8. Thomas and Turner, 1994, p. 47.

9. Thomas and Turner, 1994, pp. 119–120.

10. Thomas and Turner, 1994, p. 14.

11. Thomas and Turner, 1994, p. 14.

12. Strunk and White, 1979, p. 15.

13. Mehrabian, 1971.

14. Hall, 2000.

15. Atkinson, 2005.

16. Kaiser, 1994.

17. Williams and Miller, 2002.

18. Nisbett, 2003.

CHAPTER THREE

1. The conventional wisdom that the way to get people to change is by giving them a reason is reflected in John Kotter's *Leading Change* (1996). Kotter's later book, *The Heart of Change* (2002), continued the theme. The main difference between the two books is that in the later book, he recommends giving people better reasons, an approach that is no more likely to succeed than his earlier recommendation. In *Our Iceberg Is Melting: Changing and Succeeding Under Any Conditions* (2006), Kotter wrote a business fable, implicitly embracing the power of storytelling.

2. Denning, 2000.

3. In 1999 the American Productivity and Quality Center selected the World Bank as one of its best practice organizations in knowledge management. In 2000 the Teleos group chose the World Bank as one of the world's Most Admired Knowledge Enterprises.

4. Mallaby, 2004, p. 415, note 19.

5. Tichy, 1998; Gardner, 2004; Kouzes and Posner, 2002; Heath and Heath, 2007; Simmons, 2000; Loehr, 2007.

6. Day and Jung, 2000.

7. The *Titanic* story is from Levine and others, 2000, p. 89.

8. This familiar way of looking at the world may be an illusion. True life may actually be a muddle, in which we may never get around to formulating clear goals, so we don't set out on any journey in which, after encountering obstacles along the way, we finally attain our goal. But no

matter. This is how we tend to view the world. This is how we "story" the world. And so if you tell a story in this form, the audience will draw meaning from the deep psychological roots of the form. White, 1987.

9. Kim and Mauborgne, 2005.

10. Luthi, 1982, pp. 11–23.

11. Day and Jung, 2000.

12. Hollender and Fenichell, 2004, p. 47.

13. Kearney, 2002, p. 160.

14. Davenport and Beck, 2000.

CHAPTER FOUR

1. Dennett, 1999, p. 418.

2. Rothenberg, 2004.

3. The fractal nature of stories is exploited in the Thematic Apperception Test, which researchers use to assess managerial motivation (McClelland, 1985). The test consists of pictures of people in ambiguous situations. Participants are asked to construct a story about each picture. Because the stories reflect the person's daydreams and aspirations, they can be coded by the researcher to measure underlying needs for power, achievement, and motivation.

4. Dell and Freedman, 1999, p. 3.

5. Hornby, 2001.

6. Mandela, 1990.

7. Mandela, 1990.

8. Block, 2002, pp. 57–58.

9. "The Choice," 2004.

10. As Dan McAdams says, "[Stories] create a shared history, linking people in time and event as actors, tellers and audience. The unfolding drama of life is revealed more by the telling than by the actual events told. Stories are not merely 'chronicles,' like a secretary's minutes of a meeting, written to report exactly what transpired and at what time. Stories are less about facts and more about meanings. In the subjective and embellished telling of the past, the past is constructed—history is made. History is

judged to be true or false not solely with respect to its adherence to empirical fact. Rather it is judged with respect to such narrative criteria as 'believability' and 'coherence'" (1993, p. 28). In asserting that identity is a narrative-based concept, I am parting company with theorists such as Erving Goffman (1959), who see identity in terms of the groups or communities with whom one identifies. The groups and communities with whom you identify are a facet of your identity but not the whole story.

11. Gardner, 2004.

12. Roddick, 2001, p. 33.

13. Katz, 2004.

14. Oz, 2004, p. 23.

15. Taylor, 1991.

16. McAdams, 1993.

17. Maccoby, 2004.

18. Liu, 2004.

CHAPTER FIVE

1. *Harvard Business Review,* cover quotation, Apr. 2010.

2. Landor Associates, 2009.

3. Li, 2010, p. 1.

4. Li, 2010, pp. 231–233.

5. Schultz, 2010.

6. YouTube was created in February 2005 and now has around 120 million users, around a third of the U.S. population. Twenty hours of video are uploaded to YouTube every minute. Facebook is a social networking Web site launched in February 2004 with more than 500 million active users in July 2010. Facebook has more than 6 million page views per minute. Twitter was created in 2006 and now has around 105 million users. In mid-2010, there are around 65 million tweets per day. http://www.penn-olson.com/2010/08/02/15-mind-blowing-facts-about-the-internet-infographic/

7. Li and Bernoff, 2009.

8. Li, 2010, p. 85.

9. Vascellaro, 2010.

10. Ries and Ries, 2002, p. xvi.

11. In June 2010, Johnson & Johnson was facing a congressional investigation into ongoing quality issues with some of its over-the-counter medications: http://www.newsinferno.com/archives/20809.

12. Zyman, 1999, p. 58.

13. Johnson and Jones, 2004.

14. Bhargava, 2008, p. 2.

15. *Bazaar*, Aug. 2010, p. 113.

16. As of August 2010, www.yelp.com shows nineteen reviews with an average of rating of 3 (out of 5). Some customers were highly satisfied, while others were disappointed. The result is an average score.

17. Holt, 2004, pp. 65–93.

18. Landor Associates, 2009.

19. Conley, 2007, p. 144

20. Apple is open in some respects but not in others. Thus, Apple is notoriously open in the partnerships that it develops with firms that manufacture components of its products: its iPhones comprise components from a global catalogue of firms, including Epson, Sharp, Toshiba, and several German firms. But Apple is notoriously closed in dealing with its customers: there are no official blogs, and the dialogue on Facebook and Twitter is markedly one way—from Apple to the rest of the world. Apple can afford to be closed in with customers, because the combination of a charismatic CEO, brilliant designers, world-class products, and a brand that everyone loves is already generating a high-quality dialogue in the marketplace, without Apple having to be involved. So it has taken a strategic decision to monitor the dialog but not to be involved. Li, 2010, pp. 70–71.

21. Levine and others, 2000, p. 100.

22. Levine and others, 2000, p. 100.

23. George, 2003, p. x.

24. George, 2003.

25. Levine and others, 2000, pp. 99–101.

CHAPTER SIX

1. Block, 2002.

2. MacIntyre, 1981, p. 2.

3. Smith, 2004, p. 1.

4. Smith, 2004, p. 1.

5. The position of Stalk and Lachenauer in their *Harvard Business Review* article of April 2004 is less nuanced than in the book they coauthored with John Butman, *Hardball: Are You Playing to Play or Playing to Win?* (2004). In the book, they continue to mock "corporate culture, coddling of customers, leadership, knowledge management, talent management and employee empowerment," while noting that these are "extremely important issues" to be integrated into the overall strategy (p. 6). Since they don't formally retract the macho positions taken in the article, which remains emblematic of a whole school of thought in business, it is the article to which I will refer here.

6. Stalk and Lachenauer, 2004a, p. 64.

7. Mintzberg, 2004b, p. 152.

8. Holmes and Zellner, 2004.

9. Instrumental values can be less strenuous than conventional ethical values. The difference was highlighted in the testimony of Richard Clarke, the White House counterterrorism chief-turned-whistle-blower, before the 9/11 Commission on March 24, 2004. Clarke was asked to explain the apparent discrepancy between his positive account of the Bush administration's terrorism policy in 2002, when he was still employed by the White House, and his critical account of those same policies in his book *Against All Enemies* (2004). At the hearing, former Illinois governor James R. Thompson pressed Clarke, "Which is true?" Clarke, appearing unfazed by the apparent contradiction between his current criticism and previous praise, explained to Thompson, as if addressing a slow student, that he was, like every other loyal employee practicing instrumental

values, highlighting the positive aspects of what the administration had done and minimizing the negative aspects. When Thompson questioned Clarke's morality, Clarke replied: "I don't think it's a question of morality at all; I think it's a question of politics" (Milbank, 2004, p. A01). Instrumental honesty is what we see in what Roger Schank calls "official stories" (quoted in Green, Strange, and Brock, 2002, p. 289).

10. Collins and Porras, 1994, pp. 46–79.

11. Hollender and Fenichell, 2004, pp. 51–58.

12. Zadek, 2004.

13. See, for instance, www.globalreporting.org, www.ceres.org, and www.one-report.com.

14. "Non-Financial Reporting," 2004.

15. Hollender and Fenichell, 2004, p. 47.

16. Greenleaf, 1977.

17. McDonough and Braungart, 2002.

18. Gittell, 2003.

19. Hollender and Fenichell, 2004, pp. 106–120.

20. Vascellaro, 2010.

21. Sztompka, 1999, p. 5.

22. Roddick, 2001.

23. Hollender and Fenichell, 2004, pp. 211–230.

24. Hollender and Fenichell, 2004.

25. Chappell, 1993.

26. Bakan, 2004.

27. Martin, 2010.

28. Karen Dietz, personal communication, 2003.

29. Badaracco, 1997, pp. 97–103.

30. Block, 2002, p. 90.

31. Smith, 2004, p. 85.

32. Pillmore, 2003.

33. Tyco, 2003, p. 19.

34. Clark, 2004, pp. 65–66.

35. 3M Worldwide, 2004

36. 3M Worldwide, 2004. This is a somewhat edited version of the story that appears on the Web site.

37. Matthew 25:14–30.

38. Turner, 1996, p. 5.

39. Clark, 2004, p. 63.

40. Nietzsche, 1967, p. 281.

41. For a fuller discussion of incentives, see Pink, 2009.

CHAPTER SEVEN

1. Garfield, Spring, and Cahill, 1998, p. 13.

2. Hackman, 2004, pp. 51–54.

3. Wenger, 1998.

4. Wenger, McDermott, and Snyder, 2002, p. 43.

5. Hackman, 2004, p. 27.

6. Hackman, 2004, pp. 19–21.

7. Hackman, 2004, pp. 27–28.

8. Katzenbach and Smith, 1994, p. 66.

9. Katzenbach and Smith, 1994, p. 66.

10. Katzenbach and Smith, 1994, p. 66.

11. Senge, 1990, p. 13.

12. Hackman, 2004, pp. 13–14.

13. Katzenbach and Smith, 1994, p. 65.

14. Etzioni, 1996.

15. Katzenbach and Smith, 1994, p. 3.

16. Wenger, McDermott, and Snyder, 2002, p. 12.

17. Hackman, 2004, p. 213.

18. Wenger, McDermott, and Snyder, 2002, p. 12.

19. Wenger, McDermott, and Snyder, 2002, p. 191.

20. Hackman, 2004, p. 28.

21. Kouzes and Posner, 2002, p. 242.

22. Ray and Anderson, 2000.

23. Majchrzak and others, 2004.

24. Brown and Duguid, 2000.

25. Sirower, 1997.

26. Laseter and Oliver, 2003.

27. For a video of part of one such reunion, see "Cultivating the Fire of the Human Spirit," Aug. 2010, http://www.youtube.com/watch?v=ekMOI0-Xy_Y.

28. For an account of the conference, see Brown, Denning, Groh, and Prusak, 2004; the group itself can be found at www.storyatwork.com.

29. To join, visit www.WorkingStories.org, and click on the icon at the bottom of the screen.

30. Wenger, McDermott and Snyder, 2002, pp. 12–13.

31. Wenger, McDermott, and Snyder, 2002, p. 193.

32. Wenger, McDermott, and Snyder, 2002, p. 54.

33. Hackman, 2004, p. 243.

34. Hackman, 2004, pp. 62, 85.

35. Cohn, 2004; Hackman, 2004, p. 86.

36. Hackman, 2004, pp. 23, 27.

37. Gerstner, 1995b.

38. Hackman, 2004, p. 89.

39. Kouzes and Posner, 2002, p. 161.

40. Hackman, 2004, p. 27.

41. Hackman, 2004, pp. 131–132.

42. Personal communication with Valdis Krebs, Nov. 16, 2004.

43. Hackman, 2004, p. 95.

44. Hackman, 2004, pp. 54–59.

45. Hackman, 2004, p. 171.

46. Collins, 2001; Hackman, 2004.

47. Hackman, 2004, p. 195.

48. Hackman, 2004, pp. 168, 177, 180.

49. Collison and Parcell, 2004, p. 97.

50. Collison and Parcell, 2004, p. 131.

51. Collison and Parcell, 2004, p. 147.

52. Gawande, 2002, pp. 29–30.

CHAPTER EIGHT

1. Klein, 1998, p. 182.

2. Brown, Denning, Groh, and Prusak, 2004, pp. 57–61; Gawande, 2002, p. 21.

3. Green, Strange, and Brock, 2002, pp. 292–294.

4. Orr, 1990, pp. 115–116.

5. Klein, 1998, p. 33.

6. For more on *Car Talk,* see Magliozzi and Magliozzi, 2000.

7. Green, Strange, and Brock, 2002, pp. 292–294.

8. Green, Strange, and Brock, 2002, p. 294.

9. Senge, 1990, p. 83.

10. 9/11 Commission, 2004.

11. Klein, 1998, pp. 111–112. This version is somewhat compressed.

12. Klein, 1998, p. 178.

13. Klein, 1998, p. 191.

14. Deutsch, 1997, p. 30.

15. Klein, 1998, pp. 58–62.

16. Christensen and Raynor, 2003, p. 12.

17. Green, Strange, and Brock, 2002, pp. 308–310.

18. Klein, 1998, p. 12.

19. Klein, 1998, p. 112.

20. Pennington and Hastie, 1993.

21. Klein, 1998, p. 183.

22. Brown, Denning, Groh, and Prusak, 2004, pp. 71–74.

23. Klein, 1998, p. 23.

24. Klein, 1998, p. 282.

25. Brown, Denning, Groh, and Prusak, 2004, p. 65.

26. Yannis Gabriel says of much corporate storytelling: "The stories are terse. Hardly a single story bears repetition outside its home territory as a 'good story.' ... A single word may thus be seen as encompassing an entire story." Gabriel, 2000, pp. 21–22.

27. Hirshfield, 1997, p. 119.

28. Schacter, 2001.

29. Green, Strange, and Brock, 2002, p. 294.

30. DeLong, 2004.

31. Haas, 2001.

32. http://www.cognitive-edge.com/blogs/dave/.

33. Sobel, 1996.

34. Klein, 1998, p. 190.

35. Klein, 1998, p. 190.

36. Patterson and others, 2002, pp. 106–109.

37. Csikszentmihalyi, 1996, pp. 208–213.

38. Klein, 1998, p. 195.

39. Chesbrough, 2004.

40. I am indebted to Roberto Chavez of the World Bank for introducing me to this approach.

CHAPTER NINE

1. Henry IV, Part 1, Act I, Scene 2, line 86.

2. In 1999, the American Productivity and Quality Center selected the World Bank as one of its best practice organizations in knowledge management, and in 2000 the Teleos group chose the World Bank as one of the world's Most Admired Knowledge Enterprises. The progress made was

confirmed by the World Bank's own evaluation (Operations Evaluation Department, 2003).

3. Kanter, 2004.

4. Schein, 1988, p. 12.

5. Christensen and Shu, 1999.

6. Philosophers tend toward the complacently mistaken view that know-how is simply another form of knowledge, something that is simply true or false, thereby ignoring the behavioral, technical, aesthetic, ethical, and other criteria that are part of know-how. For example, an introductory text says, "By 'knowledge,' we in each case mean the same. We use that word to endorse opinions, techniques, actions, feelings, and sympathies by endorsing the capacities from which they flow" (Scruton, 1994, p. 327). This maneuver enables philosophers to continue their endless contemplation of what is true or false without having to bother about what goes on in the world of action.

7. Brown, Denning, Groh, and Prusak, 2004, pp. 27–28.

8. Orr, 1990; Geertz, 1973, p. 90.

9. Brown, Denning, Groh, and Prusak, 2004.

10. Geertz, 1973, pp. 84–87.

11. Bianco, 2004.

12. Brown, Denning, Groh, and Prusak, 2004.

13. Guglielmo, King, and Ricadela, 2010.

14. Case and Piñeiro, 2004.

15. Kleiner, 2003

16. Spacks, 1985.

17. Kleiner, 2003.

18. Spacks, 1985.

19. Case and Piñeiro, 2004.

20. From Brown, Denning, Groh, and Prusak, 2004, p. 23.

21. Reissner, 2004.

22. Once the program was in full swing, many people found it hard to believe my descriptions of the initial opposition and were inclined to suspect I was overstating the case. However, an outside observer who had interviewed one of the managing directors at the time reports that my perceptions were accurate: they didn't back knowledge management. See Mallaby 2004, p. 415, note 19.

23. Cary, 2004, p. F1.

24. Case and Piñeiro, 2004.

25. Case and Piñeiro, 2004.

26. Katz, 2004.

27. Hodgart, 1969, pp. 163–168.

28. Contemporary audio recording.

29. Kraus, 1990, p. 77.

30. Saunders, 1999, p. 159.

31. Zax, 2010.

32. The power of social media cuts both ways. In the short term, JetBlue may be able to neutralize a public relations crisis with a satirical post. However the implication in its post that all the other twenty-three hundred flight attendants are happily providing the JetBlue experience can be checked against postings by JetBlue employees on http://www.glassdoor.com, where the picture is at best mixed.

33. Kolbert, 2004.

34. Robbins, 2001, p. 4.

35. Cary, 2004.

CHAPTER TEN

1. Barbalet, 1996.

2. Ingvar, 1985.

3. Geus, 1997, p. 34.

4. Sztompka, 1999, p. 11.

5. Lindaman, 1977.

6. Kouzes and Posner, 2002, p. 111.

7. Tichy, 1998, p. 174.

8. For instance, Noel Tichy's example of Admiral LeMoyne explaining the role of Special Operations Forces to the U.S. Congress (1998, p. 184) is a compelling story—but it isn't a story about the future. It's a story about the past. Similarly, the example of a compelling vision that Annette Simmons gives in *The Story Factor*—a story about the artist van Gogh told by the CEO of a small start-up (2002, p. 16)—is powerful and inspiring, but it isn't about the future. It's a story about the past, even though the idea appealed to the CEO's twenty-something staff's self-perception as "a bunch of crazy lunatic software artists."

9. Covey, 1990, p. 268.

10. Beinhocker and Kaplan, 2002.

11. Kleiner, 1996, pp. 164–180.

12. Roxburgh, 2003.

13. Speech courtesy of the Web site www.winstonchurchill.org.

14. Churchill's speech concludes with an implicit plea for help from the United States, which eventually was forthcoming. In the end, the war was won less by individuals fighting on beaches than by an alliance of countries with superior military might. Nevertheless, the stirring speech helped keep Britain's spirits high as its people tried to find a way to win the war.

15. Downloaded from http://www.mecca.org/rights/dream.html, Nov. 15, 2004. Used with permission.

16. Thomas, 1976, p. 246.

17. Yukl, 2002, p. 284.

18. Yukl, 2002, p. 284.

19. Miller, 1956.

20. Klein, 1998, p. 52.

21. Van der Heijden, 1996, p. 77.

22. Klein, 1998, p. 52.

23. Lindaman, 1977.

24. Van der Heijden, 1996, pp. 119–120.

25. Van der Heijden, 1996, pp. 122–123.

26. Armstrong, 2002

27. Halberstam, 1993.

28. Klein, 1998, p. 71.

29. Magretta, 2002.

30. Mintzberg, Ahlstrand, and Lampel, 1998.

31. Schwartz, 1996.

32. Kouzes and Posner, 2002, p. 125.

33. Cohn, 2004.

34. Scott, 1999.

CHAPTER ELEVEN

1. Christensen and Raynor, 2003.

2. Christensen and Raynor, 2003.

3. Christensen and Raynor, 2003.

4. Garvin, 2004, p. 19.

5. Finkelstein, 2003.

6. Hamel and Välikangas, 2003, p. 59.

7. Kandybin and Kihn, 2004.

8. Finkelstein, 2003; Sull, 2003.

9. Senge, 1990, p. 3.

10. Schrage, 2004.

11. Pool, 2001.

12. Burton, 2004.

13. Chesbrough, 2003.

14. Chesbrough, 2003.

15. Chesbrough, 2003.

16. Amidon, 1997.

17. Ries and Ries, 2009.

18. Murray, 2010.

19. Denning, 2010.

20. Kuhn, 1962.

21. Deloitte Center for the Edge, 2009.

CHAPTER TWELVE

1. Hearne, 1987, p. 107.

2. Brown, Denning, Groh, and Prusak, 2004, p. 8.

3. Stacey, Griffin, and Shaw, 2000.

4. Sun-Tzu, 2002 translation, Book 3.

5. Hirshfield, 1997, p. 4.

6. For a book full of detailed accounts of such adversarial encounters, see *Lifescripts: What to Say to Get What You Want in Life's Toughest Situations*, by Stephen Pollan and Mark Levine. Note that in most of the 109 scenarios laid out in this fascinating book, the end result is an apparent victory for the speaker. However, a careful reading of the interactions suggests that the outcome remains full of tension with an aftermath of bitterness at the exercise of power.

7. Hearne, 1987, pp. 60, 229–230.

8. For more insight on the concept of leadership as conversation, see Buber, 1970 [1923], and Abram, 1997.

9. Hirshfield, 1997, p. 4.

10. For background on the candidates for interactive leadership, see Kim and Mauborgne, 2005; George, 2003; Gittell, 2003; Chappell, 1993; Naya, 2010.

11. Davenport and Prusak, 2003.

12. Handy, 1978, pp. 129–133.

13. Handy, 1978, pp. 129–133.

14. Handy, 1978, p. 133.

15. Handy, 1978, p. 135.

16. Cialdini, 1984.

17. Morrison, 1997.

18. Block, 2002, p. 129.

19. Rubin, 1997, pp. 90–120.

20. Rubin, 1997, pp. 75–76.

21. Nietzsche, 1995 [1872].

22. Goldie, 2002, pp. 4–5.

23. Damasio, 2000, pp. 41–42.

24. Damasio, 2000, pp. 41–42.

25. Bruner, 1986, pp. 20–21.

26. Albert, 1998, p. 17.

27. Bulfinch, 1959 [1855].

28. Hillman, 1998, p. 35.

29. Hirshfield, 1997, p. 9.

30. Hillman, 1998, p. 37.

31. Northouse, 2003, p. 23.

32. Katz, 1955.

33. Blake and Mouton, 1985.

34. Northouse, 2003, p. 75.

35. Blanchard, 1985.

36. House and Mitchell, 1974.

37. Bass and Avolio, 1994.

38. Quinn, 1996.

39. For example, a measuring device that is commonly used in assessing transformational leadership, the Multifactor Leadership Questionnaire (MLQ) developed by Bass and Avolio (1994), purports to measure leadership aspects such as whether "I express with a few simple words what we could and should do" or whether "I provide appealing images about what we can do"; or whether "I help others find meaning in their work." It sheds no light, however, on what are the specific behaviors that transformational leaders use to achieve these outcomes (Northouse, 2003, p. 196).

BIBLIOGRAPHY

Abram, D. *The Spell of the Sensuous: Perception and Language in a More-Than-Human World*. New York: Vintage, 1997.

Albert, J. "Participatory Science and the Mass Media. Free Inquiry, Fall 1998." *Chance News*, Nov. 15–Dec. 10, 1998. http://www.dartmouth.edu/~chance/chance_news/recent_news/chance_news_7.11.html.

Amidon, D. *Innovation Strategy for the Knowledge Economy: The Ken Awakening*. Boston: Butterworth Heinemann, 1997.

Andrew, J., and Sirkin, H. "Innovating for Cash." *Harvard Business Review*, Sept. 2003, pp. 76–83.

Appelbaum, E., Bernhardt, A., and Murnane, R. J. *Low-Wage America: How Employers Are Reshaping Opportunity in the Workplace*. New York: Russell Sage Foundation, 2003.

Armstrong, J. S. "Forecasting in Conflicts: How to Predict What Your Opponent Will Do." University of Pennsylvania, Feb. 13, 2002. http://www.upenn.edu/researchatpenn/article.php?141&bus.

Atkinson, C. *Beyond Bullet Points: Using Microsoft PowerPoint to Create Presentations That Inform, Motivate, and Inspire*. Seattle: Microsoft Press, 2005.

Aufreiter, N., Elzinga, D., and Gordon, J. "Building Better Brands." *McKinsey Quarterly*, Sept. 2003.

Badaracco, J. *Defining Moments: When Managers Must Choose Between Right and Right*. Boston: Harvard Business School Press, 1997.

Bakan, J. *The Corporation: The Pathological Pursuit of Profit and Power*. New York: Free Press, 2004.

Barbalet, J. M. "Social Emotions: Confidence, Trust and Loyalty." *International Journal of Sociology and Social Policy*, 1996, *16*(9/10), 75–96.

Barrera, R. *Overpromise and Overdeliver: How TouchPoint Branding Brings Back Customers Again and Again*. New York: Portfolio, 2004.

Bass, B. M., and Avolio, G. J. *Improving Organizational Effectiveness Through Transformational Leadership*. Thousand Oaks, Calif.: Sage, 1994.

Bateson, M. C. *Composing a Life*. New York: Penguin Books, 1990.

Beinhocker, E. D., and Kaplan, S. "Tired of Strategic Planning?" *McKinsey Quarterly*, 2002.

Berlin, I. *The Hedgehog and the Fox: An Essay on Tolstoy's View of History*. New York: Simon & Schuster, 1953.

Bhargava, R. *Personality Not Included: Why Companies Lose Their Authenticity and How Great Brands Get It Back*. New York: McGraw-Hill, 2008.

Bianco, A. "The Vanishing Mass Market." *BusinessWeek*, July 12, 2004. http://www
.businessweek.com/magazine/content/04_28/b3891001_mz001.htm.

Blake, R., and Mouton, J. S. *The Managerial Grid III*. Houston, Tex.: Gulf, 1985.

Blanchard, K. H. *SLII: A Situational Approach to Managing People*. Escondido, Calif.:
Blanchard Training and Development, 1985.

Block, P. *The Answer to How Is Yes: Acting On What Matters*. San Francisco:
Berrett-Kohler, 2002.

Borgida, E., and Nisbett, R. E. "The Differential Impact of Abstract vs Concrete
Information on Decisions." *Journal of Applied Technology*, 1977, *7*(3), 258–271.

Brook, P. *The Empty Space*. New York: Simon & Schuster, 1968.

Brown, J. S., Denning, S., Groh, K., and Prusak, L. *Storytelling in Organizations: Why
Storytelling Is Transforming 21st Century Organizations and Management*. Boston:
Elsevier, 2004.

Brown, J. S., and Duguid, P. *The Social Life of Information*. Boston: Harvard Business
School Press, 2000.

Bruner, J. *Actual Minds, Possible Worlds*. Cambridge, Mass.: Harvard University Press,
1986.

Bruner, J. *Making Stories*. New York: Farrar, Straus & Giroux, 2002.

Buber, M. *I and Thou* (trans. Walter Kaufmann). New York: Scribner, 1970. (Original
work published 1923.)

Bulfinch, T. *Mythology*. New York: Dell, 1959. (Originally published 1855.)

Burns, J. M. *Leadership*. Thousand Oaks, Calif.: Sage, 1978.

Burton, T. "By Learning from Failures Lilly Keeps Drug Pipeline Full." *Wall Street
Journal*, Apr. 21, 2004.

Campbell, A., and Park, R. "Stop Kissing Frogs." *Harvard Business Review*, July–Aug.
2004, pp. 27–28.

Carter, R. *Mapping the Mind*. London: Phoenix, 1998.

Cary, B. "Payback Time: Why Revenge Tastes So Sweet." *New York Times*, July 27,
2004, p. F1.

Case, P., and Piñeiro, E. "Subversive Aspirations and Identity Work in the Narratives of
a Computer Programming Community." Organizational Storytelling, Seminar 5."
Exeter, England: University of Exeter, 2004.

Chappell, T. *The Soul of a Business: Managing for Profit and the Common Good*.
New York: Bantam Books, 1993.

Charon, R. "Narrative and Medicine." *New England Journal of Medicine*, 2004, *350*,
862–864.

Chesbrough, H. "R&D Through Open Source Innovation." *strategy+business*, Summer 2003.

Chesbrough, H. *Open Innovation: The New Imperative for Creating and Profiting from
Technology*. Boston: Harvard Business School Press, 2004.

Christensen, C. M., Anthony, S., and Roth, E. *Seeing What's Next: Using the Theories
of Innovation to Predict Industry Change*. Boston: Harvard Business School Press,
2004.

Christensen, C. M., and Raynor, M. E. *The Innovator's Solution: Creating and Sustaining Successful Growth*. Boston: Harvard Business School Press, 2003.

Christensen, C., and Shu, K. "What Is an Organization's Culture?" Boston: Harvard Business School, 1999.

Cialdini, R. *Influence: The Psychology of Persuasion*. New York: Morrow, 1984.

Clark, E. *Around the Corporate Campfire: How Great Leaders Use Stories to Inspire Success*. Sevierville, Tenn.: Insight, 2004.

Clarke, R. *Against All Enemies: Inside America's War on Terror*. New York: Free Press, 2004.

Cohn, M. *User Stories Applied: For Agile Software Development*. Upper Saddle River, N.J.: Addison-Wesley, 2004.

Collins, J. *From Good to Great*. New York: Random House, 2001.

Collins, J., and Porras, J. *Built to Last: Successful Habits of Visionary Companies*. New York: HarperBusiness, 1994.

Collison, C., and Parcell, G. *Learning to Fly: Practical Knowledge Management from Leading and Learning Organizations*. Chichester, England: Capstone, 2004.

Conger, J. A. "Inspiring Others: The Language of Leadership." *Executive*, 1991, 5(1), 31–45.

Conley, C. *Peak: How Great Companies Get Their Mojo from Maslow*. San Francisco: Jossey-Bass, 2007.

Court, D. "A New Model for Marketing." *McKinsey Quarterly*, 2004, no. 4.

Covey, S. *Seven Habits of Highly Successful People*. New York: Fireside, 1990.

Csikszentmihalyi, M. *Creativity: Flow and the Psychology of Discovery and Invention*. New York: HarperCollins, 1996.

D'Aurizio, E. "Truth Is, Everyone Lies." *Record* (Bergen County, N.J.), Nov. 22, 2004. http://www.ajc.com/news/content/health/1104/22lies.html.

Damasio, A. *The Feeling of What Happens: Body and Emotion in the Making of Consciousness*. San Diego: Harcourt, 2000.

Davenport, T., and Beck, J. "Getting the Attention You Need." *Harvard Business Review*, Sept.–Oct. 2000, pp. 118–126.

Davenport, T., and Prusak. L. *What's the Big Idea?* Boston: Harvard Business School Press, 2003.

Day, J. D., and Jung, M. "Corporate Transformation Without a Crisis." *McKinsey Quarterly*, 2000, no. 4.

Dell, M., and Freedman, C. *Direct from Dell: Strategies That Revolutionized an Industry*. New York: HarperBusiness, 1999.

Deloitte Center for the Edge. *Measuring the Forces of Long-Term Change: The 2009 Shift Index*. 2009. http://www.edgeperspectives.com/shiftindex.pdf.

DeLong, D. W. *Lost Knowledge: Confronting the Threat of an Aging Workforce*. New York: Oxford University Press, 2004.

Dennett, D. *Consciousness Explained*. New York: Little, Brown, 1999.

Denning, S. *The Springboard: How Storytelling Ignites Action in Knowledge-Era Organizations*. Boston: Butterworth Heinemann, 2000.

Denning, S. *Squirrel Inc.: A Fable of Leadership Through Storytelling*. San Francisco: Jossey-Bass, 2004.

Denning, S. *The Secret Language of Leadership: How Leaders Inspire Action Through Narrative*. San Francisco: Jossey-Bass, 2007.

Denning, S. *The Leader's Guide to Radical Management: Reinventing the Workplace for the 21st Century*. San Francisco: Jossey-Bass, 2010.

Deutsch, D. *The Fabric of Reality*. New York: Penguin Press, 1997.

Dietz, K. "Values and Storytelling." Unpublished paper, Aug. 29, 2003.

Drucker, P. *Management: Tasks, Responsibilities, Practices*. London: Heinemann, 1973.

Dyson, F. *Imagined Worlds* (Jerusalem-Harvard Lectures). Cambridge, Mass.: Harvard University Press, 1998.

Etzioni, A. "The Responsive Community: A Communitarian Perspective." *American Sociological Review*, 1996, *61*(1), 1–11.

Finkelstein, S. *Why Smart Executives Fail: What You Can Learn from Their Mistakes*. New York: Portfolio, 2003.

Fisher, L. M. "How Dell Got Soul." *strategy+business*, Summer 2004.

Fog, K., Budtz, C., and Yakaboylu, B. *Storytelling: Branding in Practice*. Berlin: Springer, 2005.

Forbes.com. "Carty Bows Out at American Airlines." *Forbes*, Apr. 25, 2003. http://www.forbes.com/2003/04/25/cx_vc_0425amr.html.

Forster, S. "Classic Super Bowl Ads Did More Than Just Entertain, They Sold." *Wall Street Journal Online*, Jan. 2002. www.wallstreetjournal.com.

Friedman, T. "Start-Ups, Not Bailouts." *New York Times*, Apr. 3, 2010. http://www.nytimes.com/2010/04/04/opinion/04friedman.html?hp.

Gabriel, Y. *Storytelling in Organizations: Facts, Fictions and Fantasies*. New York: Oxford University Press, 2000.

Gardner, H. *Leading Minds: An Anatomy of Leadership*. New York: Basic Books, 1995.

Gardner, H. *Changing Minds: The Art and Science of Changing Our Own and Other People's Minds*. Boston: Harvard Business School Press, 2004.

Garfield, C., Spring, C., and Cahill, S. *Wisdom Circles: A Guide to Self-Discovery and Community Building in Small Groups*. New York: Hyperion, 1998.

Garvin, D. A. "What Every CEO Should Know About Creating New Businesses." *Harvard Business Review*, July–Aug. 2004, pp. 18–21.

Gawande, A. *Complications: A Surgeon's Notes on an Imperfect Science*. New York: Picador, 2002.

Geertz, C. *The Interpretation of Cultures*. New York: Basic Books, 1973.

George, B. *Authentic Leadership: Rediscovering the Secrets to Creating Lasting Value*. San Francisco: Jossey-Bass, 2003.

Gerstner, L. "IBM Press Conference upon the Purchase of Lotus." June 5, 1995a. http://www.ibm.com/lvg/lotus.phtml.

Gerstner, L. "COMDEX '95." Presentation to COMDEX, Las Vegas, Nev., Nov. 13, 1995b. http://www.ibm.com/lvg/comdex.phtml.

Gerstner, L. Lou Gerstner speeches (untitled). Fall Internet World '96, New York, N.Y., Dec. 11, 1996. http://www.ibm.com/lvg/iw96.phtml.

Gerstner, L. V. *Who Says Elephants Can't Dance? Inside IBM's Historic Turnaround.* New York: HarperBusiness, 2002.

Geus, A. D. *The Living Company: Habits for Survival in a Turbulent Business Environment.* Boston: Harvard Business School Press, 1997.

Gittell, J. H. *The Southwest Airlines Way: Using the Power of Relationships to Achieve High Performance.* New York: McGraw-Hill, 2003.

Goffman, E. *The Presentation of Self in Everyday Life.* New York: Anchor Books, 1959.

Goldie, P. *The Emotions: A Philosophical Exploration.* Oxford, England: Clarendon Press, 2002.

Green, M. C., Strange, J. J., and Brock, T. *Narrative Impact: Social and Cognitive Foundations.* Mahwah, N.J.: Erlbaum, 2002.

Greenleaf, R. *Servant Leadership: A Journey into the Nature of Legitimate Power and Greatness.* New York: Paulist Press, 1977.

Guglielmo, C., King, I., and Ricadela, A. "HP Chief Executive Hurd Resigns After Sexual-Harassment Probe." *Bloomberg BusinessWeek*, Aug. 7, 2010. http://www.businessweek.com/news/2010-08-07/hp-chief-executive-hurd-resigns-after-sexual-harassment-probe.html

Haas, M. "Acting on What Others Know: Distributed Knowledge and Team Performance." Unpublished doctoral dissertation, Harvard University, 2001.

Hackman, J. R. *Leading Teams: Setting the Stage for Great Performances.* Boston: Harvard Business School Press, 2004.

Halberstam, D. *The Best and the Brightest.* New York: Ballantine Books, 1993.

Hall, L. M. "Body Language." 2007. http://www.seductionlabs.org/2007/03/26/body-language/.

Hamel, G. "Moon Shots for Management." *Harvard Business Review*, Feb. 2009, 91–98.

Hamel, G., and Välikangas, L. "The Quest for Resilience." *Harvard Business Review*, Sept. 2003, pp. 52–63.

Handy, C. *Gods of Management: The Changing Work of Organizations.* New York: Oxford University Press, 1978.

Hearne, V. *Adam's Task.* New York: Vintage Books, 1987.

Heath, C., and Heath, D. *Made to Stick: Why Some Ideas Survive and Others Die.* New York: Random House, 2007.

Heifetz, R., and Linsky, M. *Leadership on the Line: Staying Alive Through the Dangers of Leading.* Boston: Harvard Business School Press, 2002.

Hillman, J. *The Soul's Code: In Search of Character and Calling.* New York: Random House, 1998.

Hirshfield, J. *Nine Gates: Entering the Mind of Poetry.* New York: Harper Perennial, 1997.

Hodgart, M. *Satire.* London: World University Library, 1969.

Hollender, J., and Fenichell, S. *What Matters Most: Business, Social Responsibility and the End of the Era of Greed.* New York: Random House, 2004.

Holmes, S., and Zellner, W. "Commentary: The Costco Way." *BusinessWeek*, Apr. 12, 2004. www.businessweek.com.

Holt, D. B. *How Brands Become Icons: The Principles of Cultural Branding*. Boston: Harvard Business School Press, 2004.

Hornby, N. *How to Be Good*. New York: Riverhead Books, 2001.

House, R. J., and Mitchell, R. R. "Path-Goal Theory of Leadership." *Journal of Contemporary Business*, 1974, 3, 81–97.

IBM. "Chairman's Letter." *IBM Annual Report*. 2003. http://www.ibm.com/annualreport/2003/.

Ingvar, D. "Memory of the Future: An Essay on the Temporal Organization of Conscious Awareness." *Human Neurobiology*, 1985, 4, 127–136.

Johnson, J., and Jones, A. "Coca-Cola Shelves Dasani Launch in Europe." *Financial Times*, Mar. 24, 2004.

Kahan, S. *Getting Change Right*. San Francisco: Jossey-Bass, 2010.

Kaiser, D. A. "Interest in Films as Measured by Subjective and Behavioral Ratings and Topographic EEG." Applied Neurosciences Group, 1994. www.skiltopo.com/papers/applied/articles/dakdiss4.htm.

Kandybin, A., and Kihn, M. "Raising Your Return on Innovation Investment." *strategy+business*, Spring 2004.

Kanter, R. M. "The Middle Manager as Innovator." *Harvard Business Review*, July–Aug. 2004, pp. 150–161. (Originally published 1982.)

Katz, M. "Mirth of a Nation: How Bill Clinton Learned to Tell Jokes on Himself—and Get the Last Laugh." *Washington Monthly*, Jan.–Feb. 2004. http://www.washingtonmonthly.com/features/2004/0401.katz.html.

Katz, R. "Skills of an Effective Administrator." Harvard Business *Review*, Jan.–Feb. 1955, pp. 33–42.

Katzenbach, J., and Smith, D. *The Wisdom of Teams: Creating the High-Performance Organization*. New York: HarperBusiness, 1994.

Kearney, R. *On Stories*. London: Routledge, 2002.

Keeley, L. *Taming the New: The Emerging Discipline of Innovation*. Boston: Harvard Business School Press, forthcoming.

Kellaway, L. "Once upon a Time We Had Managers, Not Storytellers." *Financial Times* (London), May 9, 2004. http://www.rics.org.uk/Management/Managementconsultancy/Once+upon+a+time+we+had+managers+-+not+storytellers.htm.

Keller, K. L. *Strategic Brand Management: Building, Measuring and Managing Brand Equity*. Upper Saddle River, N.J.: Prentice Hall, 1998.

Kelley, T., and Littman, J. *The Art of Innovation: Lessons in Creativity from IDEO, America's Leading Design Firm*. New York: Doubleday Currency, 2001.

Kim, W. C., and Mauborgne, R. *Blue Ocean Strategy: How to Create Uncontested Market Space and Make the Competition Irrelevant*. Boston: Harvard Business School Press, 2005.

Klein, G. *Sources of Power: How People Make Decisions*. Cambridge, Mass.: MIT Press, 1998.

Klein, N. *No Logo: Taking Aim at the Brand Bullies*. New York: Picador, 1999.

Kleiner, A. *The Age of Heretics: Heroes, Outlaws, and the Forerunners of Corporate Change*. New York: Doubleday Currency, 1996.

Kleiner, A. "Who's In with the In-Crowd?" *Harvard Business Review*, July 2003, pp. 86–92.

Kolbert, E. "Stooping to Conquer." *New Yorker*, Apr. 19, 2004. http://www .newyorker.com/fact/content/?040419fa_fact1.

Kotter, J. *Leading Change*. Boston: Harvard Business School Press, 1996.

Kotter, J. *The Heart of Change: Real-Life Stories of How People Change Their Organizations*. Boston: Harvard Business School Press, 2002.

Kouzes, J. M., and Posner, B. Z. *The Leadership Challenge*. San Francisco: Jossey-Bass, 2002.

Kouzes, J. M., and Posner, B. Z. *Credibility: How Leaders Gain and Lose it, Why People Demand It*. San Francisco: Jossey-Bass, 2003.

Kraus, K. *Half-Truths and One-and-a-Half Truths: Selected Aphorisms* (H. Zohn, trans.). Chicago: University of Chicago Press, 1990.

Kuhn, T. S. *The Structure of Scientific Revolutions*. Chicago: University of Chicago Press, 1962.

Kumar, N. "Kill a Brand, Keep a Customer." *Harvard Business Review*, Dec. 2003, pp. 86–95.

LaClair, J. A., and Rao, R. P. "Helping Employees Embrace Change." *McKinsey Quarterly*, 2002, no. 4.

Landor Associates. "The Essentials of Branding." In A. G. Bennett (ed.), *The Big Book of Marketing*. New York: McGraw-Hill, 2009.

Laseter, T., and Oliver, K. "When Will Supply Chain Management Grow Up?" *strategy+business*, Sept. 2003.

Levine, R., and others. *The Cluetrain Manifesto: The End of Business as Usual*. Cambridge Mass.: Perseus, 2000.

Li, C. *Open Leadership: How Social Technology Can Transform the Way You Lead*. San Francisco: Jossey-Bass, 2010.

Li, C., and Bernoff, J. *Marketing in the Groundswell*. Boston: Harvard Business School Press, 2009.

Lindaman, E. B. *Thinking in the Future Tense*. Nashville, Tenn.: Broadman Press, 1977.

Lipman, D. *Improving Your Storytelling*. Little Rock, Ark.: August House, 1999.

Liu, E. "Waiting for the Story." *Washington Post*, Sept. 10, 2004, p. A29.

Loehr, J. *The Power of Story: Rewrite Your Destiny in Business and in Life*. New York: Free Press, 2007.

Luthi, M. *The European Folk Tale: Form and Nature* (trans. J. Niles). Bloomington: Indiana University Press, 1982.

Maccoby, M. "Why People Follow the Leader: The Power of Transference." *Harvard Business Review*, Sept. 2004, pp. 76–85.

MacIntyre, A. *After Virtue*. Notre Dame, Ind.: University of Notre Dame Press, 1981.

Magliozzi, T., and Magliozzi, R. *In Our Humble Opinion: Car Talk's Click and Clack Rant and Rave.* New York: Berkley, 2000.

Magretta, J. "Why Business Models Matter." *Harvard Business Review*, May 2002, pp. 87–92.

Majchrzak, A., and others. "Can Absence Make a Team Grow Stronger?" *Harvard Business Review*, May 2004, pp. 131–137.

Mallaby, S. *The World's Banker.* New York: Oxford University Press, 2004.

Manchevski, M., and Raskin, R. "Unhappy Endings, Politics and Storytelling." Dec. 14, 2003. http://www.realitymacedonia.org.mk/web/news_page.asp?nid=2877.

Mandela, N. Address in Cape Town, Feb. 11, 1990. http://www.americanrhetoric.com/speeches/nelsonmandelaprisonrelease.htm.

Mark, M., and Pearson, C. *The Hero and the Outlaw: Harnessing the Power of Archetypes to Create a Winning Brand.* New York: McGraw-Hill, 2002.

Markides, C., and Geroski, P. "Colonizers and Consolidators: The Two Cultures of Corporate Strategy." *strategy+business*, Fall 2003.

Martin, J., and Power, M. E. "Organizational Stories: More Vivid and Persuasive Than Quantitative Data." In B. M. Staw (ed.), *Psychological Foundations of Organizational Behavior.* Glenview, Ill.: Scott, Foresman, 1982.

Martin, R. "The Age of Customer Capitalism." *Harvard Business Review*, Jan.-Feb. 2010, pp. 58–65.

McAdams, D. P. *The Stories We Live By: Personal Myths and the Making of the Self.* New York: Guilford Press, 1993.

McClelland, D. C. *Human Motivation.* Glenview, Ill.: Scott Foresman, 1985.

McCloskey, D. D., and Klamer A. "One Quarter of GDP Is Persuasion (in Rhetoric and Economic Behavior)." *American Economic Review*, 1995, *85*(2), 191–195.

McDonough, W., and Braungart, M. *Cradle to Cradle: Remaking the Way We Make Things.* New York: North Point Press, 2002.

McNally, D., and Spark, K. *Be Your Own Brand.* San Francisco: Berrett-Kohler, 2002.

Mehrabian, A. *Silent Messages.* Belmont, Calif.: Wadsworth, 1971.

Meyer, C., and Kirby, J. "Leadership in the Age of Transparency." *Harvard Business Review*, Apr. 2010, pp. 38–46.

Microsoft. "Microsoft Standards of Business Conduct: Great People with Great Values." May 15, 2003. http://www.microsoft.com/mscorp/legal/buscond/.

Milbank, D. "Clarke Stays Cool as Partisanship Heats Up." *Washington Post*, Mar. 25, 2004, p. A01.

Miller, G. A. "The Magical Number Seven, Plus or Minus Two: Some Limits on Our Capacity for Processing Information." *Psychological Review*, 1956, *63*(2), 81–96.

Mintzberg, H. *The Nature of Managerial Work.* New York: HarperCollins, 1973.

Mintzberg, H. "Enough Leadership." *Harvard Business Review*, Nov. 2004a.

Mintzberg, H. *Managers Not MBAs: A Hard Look at the Soft Practice of Managing and Managerial Development.* San Francisco: Berrett-Koehler, 2004b.

Mintzberg, H., Ahlstrand, B., and Lampel, J. *Strategy Safari: A Guided Tour Through the Wilds of Strategic Management.* New York: Free Press, 1998.

Moeller, L. H., Hodson, N., and Wolfsen, B. "The Superpremium Premium." *strategy+business*, Winter 2004.

Morrison, T. "The Nobel Lecture 1993." In S. Allén (ed.), *Nobel Lectures, Literature 1991–1995*. Singapore: World Scientific, 1997.

Murray, A. "The End of Management." *Wall Street Journal*, Aug. 21, 2010. http://online.wsj.com/article/SB10001424052748704476104575439723695579664.html

Nayar, V. *Employees First, Customers Second*. Boston: Harvard Business School Press, 2010.

Nietzsche, F. *Thus Spake Zarathustra*. London: G. Allen & Unwin, 1967. (Originally published 1883–1892.)

Nietzsche, F. *The Birth of Tragedy*. New York: Dover, 1995. (Originally published 1872.)

9/11 Commission. *The 9/11 Commission Report: Final Report of the National Commission on Terrorist Attacks upon the United States*. Washington, D.C.: General Printing Office, 2004.

Nisbett, R. *The Geography of Thought: How Asians and Westerners Think Differently, and Why*. New York: Free Press, 2003.

"Non-Financial Reporting: Wood for the Trees." *Economist*, Nov. 4, 2004. http://www.economist.com/business/displayStory.cfm?story_id=3364578. A

North Carolina Court System. "Is Winning Really the Only Thing?" Feb. 5, 2003. http://www.nccourts.org/Courts/CRS/Councils/Professionalism/Winning.asp.

Northouse, P. *Leadership: Theory and Practice*. Thousand Oaks, Calif.: Sage, 2003.

Nussbaum, B. "The Power of Design." *BusinessWeek*, May 17, 2004.

"Nutty Tales." *Economist*, June 19, 2004. http://www.economist.com/displaystory.cfm?story_id=2765812.

Operations Evaluation Department. *Sharing Knowledge: Innovations and Remaining Challenges*. Washington D.C.: World Bank, 2003.

Orr, J. *Talking About Machines*. Ithaca, N.Y.: Cornell University Press, 1990.

Osborn, M. M., and Ehninger, D. "The Metaphor in Public Address." *Speech Monograph*, 1962, *29*, 228.

Oz, A. *A Tale of Love and Darkness*. New York: Harcourt Books, 2004.

Patterson, K., and others. *Crucial Conversations: Tools for Talking When Stakes Are High*. New York: McGraw-Hill, 2002.

Pennington, N., and Hastie, R. "A Theory of Explanation-Based Decision Making." In G. Klein and others (eds.), *Decision Making in Action: Models and Methods*. Norwood N.J.: Ablex, 1993.

Pillmore, E. M. "How We're Fixing Up Tyco." *Harvard Business Review*, Dec. 2003, pp. 96–103.

Pink, D. *A Whole New Mind*. New York: Penguin, 2006.

Pink, D. *Drive: The Surprising Truth About What Motivates Us*. New York: Riverhead Books, 2009.

Polkinghorne, D. E. *Narrative Knowing and the Human Sciences*. Albany: State University of New York Press, 1988.

Pollan, S., and Levine, M. *Lifescripts: What to Say to Get What You Want in Life's Toughest Situations*. Hoboken, N.J.: Wiley, 2004.

Pool, R. "If It Ain't Broke, Fix It." *MIT Technology Review*, Sept. 2001.

Quinn, R. *Deep Change: Discovering the Leader Within*. San Francisco: Jossey-Bass, 1996.

Ray, P., and Anderson, S. R. *The Cultural Creatives: How 50 Million People Are Changing the World*. New York: Harmony Books, 2000.

Reichheld, F. E. "The One Number You Need to Grow." *Harvard Business Review*, Dec. 2003, pp. 46–54.

Reissner, S. "Learning by Story-Telling? Narratives in the Study of Work-Based Learning." *Journal of Adult and Continuing Education*, 2004, *10*(2), 99–113.

Ries, A., and Ries, L. *The Fall of Advertising and the Rise of PR*. New York: HarperBusiness, 2002.

Ries, A., and Ries, L. *War in the Boardroom: Why Left-Brain Management and Right-Brain Marketing Don't See Eye-to-Eye—and What to Do About It*. New York: HarperBusiness, 2009.

Robbins, S. "Culture as Communication." *Harvard Management Communication Letter*, Aug. 2001.

Roche, L., and Sadowsky, J. "Stories and Storytelling: An Example of Best Practice of Leadership in a High-Tech Environment." *Business Leadership Review*, n.d. www.mbaworld.com/blrprintarticle.php?article=11.

Roddick, A. *Business as Unusual: The Triumph of Anita Roddick*. London: Thorsons, 2001.

Rothenberg, R. "Kenneth W. Freeman: The Thought Leader Interview." *strategy + business*, Winter 2004.

Roxburgh, C. "Hidden Flaws in Strategy." *McKinsey Quarterly*, 2003, no. 2.

Rubin, H. *The Princessa: Machiavelli for Women*. London: Bloomsbury, 1997.

Ryan, M.-L. *Narrative Across Media: The Languages of Storytelling*. Lincoln: University of Nebraska Press, 2004.

Saunders, D. *20th Century Advertising*. London: Carlton, 1999.

Schacter, D. *The Seven Sins of Memory: How the Mind Forgets and Remembers*. Boston: Houghton Mifflin, 2001.

Schein, E. *Organizational Culture and Leadership*. San Francisco: Jossey-Bass, 1988.

Schrage, M. "Prepared Minds Favor Chance." *MIT Technology Review*, July 1, 2004.

Schultz, H. : "We Had to Own the Mistakes," *Harvard Business Review*, July-Aug. 2010, pp. 180–115.

Schwartz, P. *The Art of the Long View: Planning for the Future in an Uncertain World*. New York: Doubleday Currency, 1996.

Scott, J. C. *Seeing Like a State: How Certain Schemes to Improve the Human Condition Have Failed*. New Haven, Conn.: Yale University Press, 1999.

Scruton, R. *Modern Philosophy: An Introduction and Survey*. London: Pimlico, 1994.

Searls, D., and Weinberger, D. *The Cluetrain Manifesto*. New York: Basic Books, 2000.

Senge, P. *The Fifth Discipline: The Art and Practice of the Learning Organization.* New York: Doubleday, 1990.

Sharf, S. "Lee Iacocca as I Knew Him." *Ward's Auto World*, May 1, 1996. http://waw.wardsauto.com/ar/auto_lee_iacocca_knew/.

Simmons, A. *The Story Factor: Inspiration, Influence, and Persuasion Through the Art of Storytelling.* New York: Basic Books, 2002.

Sirower, M. *The Synergy Trap: How Companies Lose the Acquisition Game.* New York: Free Press, 1997.

Smith, D. K. *On Value and Values: Thinking Differently About We in an Age of Me.* Upper Saddle River, N.J.: Prentice Hall, 2004.

Sobel, D. *Longitude: The True Story of a Lone Genius Who Solved the Greatest Scientific Problem of His Time.* New York: Walker, 1996.

Spacks, P. M. *Gossip.* Chicago: University of Chicago Press, 1985.

Stacey, R., Griffin, D., and Shaw, P. *Complexity and Management: Fad or Radical Challenge to Systems Thinking?* London: Routledge, 2000.

Stalk, G., and Lachenauer, R. "Five Killer Strategies for Trouncing the Competition." *Harvard Business Review*, Apr. 2004a, pp. 62–71.

Stalk, G., and Lachenauer, R., with Butman, J. *Hardball: Are You Playing to Play or Playing to Win?* Boston: Harvard Business School Press, 2004b.

Stevenson, D. *Never Be Boring Again.* Colorado Springs: Cornelia Press, 2003.

Strawson, G. "Tales of the Unexpected." *Guardian*, Jan. 10, 2004. http://books.guardian.co.uk/review/story/0,12084,1118942,00.html.

Strunk, W., and White, E. B. *The Elements of Style.* (3rd ed.) Needham Heights, Mass.: Allyn & Bacon, 1979.

Sull, D. *Revival of the Fittest: Why Good Companies Go Bad and How Great Managers Remake Them.* Boston: Harvard Business School Press, 2003.

Sun-Tzu, *The Art of War.* (trans. L. Giles). New York: Dover, 2002.

Sztompka, P. *Trust: A Sociological Theory.* Cambridge: Cambridge University Press, 1999.

Taylor, S. *Positive Illusions: Creative Self-Deception and the Healthy Mind.* San Francisco: Perseus Books, 1991.

"The Choice." *New Yorker*, Nov. 1, 2004, p. 44.

"The Top 100 Brands." *BusinessWeek*, Aug. 2, 2004. http://www.businessweek.com/pdfs/2004/0431_brands.pdf.

Thomas, B. *Walt Disney: An American Tradition.* New York: Simon & Schuster, 1976.

Thomas, F.-N., and Turner, M. *Clear and Simple as the Truth: Writing Classic Prose.* Princeton, N.J.: Princeton University Press, 1994.

3M Worldwide. "Innovation Chronicles." Oct. 31, 2004. http://www.3m.com/about3m/pioneers/innovChron.jhtml.

Tichy, N. *The Leadership Engine: Building Leaders at Every Level.* New York: HarperBusiness, 1998.

"Top U.S. Corporate Brands." *Forbes Magazine*, 2004. http://www.forbes.com/bbsbrands/2004/03/31/04bbsbrandsland.html.

Turner, M. *The Literary Mind*. New York: Oxford University Press, 1996.

Tyco. "Doing the Right Thing: The Tyco Guide to Ethical Conduct." 2003. http://www.tyco.com/pdf/tyco_guide_to_ethical_conduct.pdf.

Urban, G., and Hauser, J. *Design and Marketing of New Products*. Upper Saddle River, N.J.: Prentice Hall, 1980.

Van der Heijden, K. *Scenarios: The Art of Strategic Conversation*. Hoboken, N.J.: Wiley, 1996.

Vascellaro, J. "Google Agonizes on Privacy as Ad World Vaults Ahead," *Wall Street Journal*, Aug. 6, 2010. http://online.wsj.com/article/SB10001424052748703309704575413553851854026.html?mod=djemalertNEWS

Vincent, L. *Legendary Brands: Unleashing the Power of Storytelling to Create a Winning Market Strategy*. Chicago: Dearborn Trade, 2002.

Walker, R. "The Hidden (in Plain Sight) Persuaders." *New York Times*, Dec. 5, 2004.

Welch, J. *Jack: Straight from the Gut*. New York: Warner Books, 2001.

Wenger, E. *Communities of Practice: Learning, Meaning and Identity*. Cambridge: Cambridge University Press, 1998.

Wenger, E., McDermott, R., and Snyder, W. *Cultivating Communities of Practice*. Boston: Harvard Business School Press, 2002.

White, H. *The Content of the Form: Narrative Discourse and Historical Representation*. Baltimore, Md.: Johns Hopkins University Press, 1987.

Wilkens, A. L. "Organizational Stories as Symbols Which Control the Organization." In L. R. Pondy, P. J. Frost, G. Morgan, and T. C. Dandridge (eds.), *Organizational Symbolism*. Greenwich, Conn.: JAI Press, 1983.

Williams, G., and Miller, R. "Change the Way You Persuade." *Harvard Business Review*, May 2002, pp. 65–73.

Yukl, G. *Leadership in Organizations*. Upper Saddle River, N.J.: Prentice Hall, 2002.

Zadek, S. "The Path to Corporate Responsibility." *Harvard Business Review*, Dec. 2004, pp. 125–132.

Zax, D. "JetBlue Responds to Entire Internet With Single Blog Post," *Fast Company*, Aug 12, 2010. http://www.fastcompany.com/1680940/jetblue-responds-to-entire-internet-with-single-blog-post?partner=homepage_newsletter.

Zemke, R. "Storytelling: Back to Basics." *Training*, Mar. 1990, pp. 44–50.

Zyman, S. *The End of Marketing As We Know It*, New York: HarperBusiness, 1999.

Zyman, S. *The End of Advertising as We Know It*. Hoboken, N.J.: Wiley, 2002.

ACKNOWLEDGMENTS

It is hard to thank all the many people who have contributed to the creation of this book.

Obviously, I am drawing from the rich tradition of storytelling that dates back to Homer and Aristotle, from the vast literature of management and leadership, and from the growing number of practitioners and academics in the field of organizational storytelling. I have done my best throughout the text to indicate the sources of my thinking so that readers can immerse themselves more deeply in these diverse streams of thought.

I would particularly like to thank members of the Golden Fleece Group in Washington, D.C., who have made many worthwhile suggestions to the manuscript and contributed indirectly to my thinking. I learned much of what I know about using story to promote collaboration from Seth Kahan, and I very much appreciate his suggestions for the book. Madelyn Blair has inspired me to think more deeply about the roles of positive storytelling and of future stories. My association with Paul Costello has shaped many of the ideas in this book, particularly the chapter on stories that communicate who you are. Karen Dietz and Alicia Korten were immensely helpful in clarifying my thinking about values. Kelly Cresap and Lynne Feingold have also generously given mke time and insight and made many valuable suggestions to help improve the manuscript.

The book reflects much that I have learned from Dave Snowden in the many activities that we have jointly undertaken around the world. The contributions of Adrian Hosford and Tony Quinlan are much appreciated. Victoria Ward's work has also been of great assistance to me. Working with Svend-Erik Engh and Jane Flarup in Denmark taught me a great deal about the fole of storytelling in different settings.

Mark Morris, Carol Pearson, and Ashraf Ramzi generously shared with me their long experience and expertise in branding and greatly enhanced this aspect of the book. Larry Prusak and John Seely Brown have been very helpful in developing my thinking about storytelling from their different perspectives.

I am deeply grateful to Dr. Con Connell of the School of Management at the University of Southampton for having organized a workshop in December 2004 that discussed the manuscript and to all those who participated in the workshop for their comments and suggestions—Lilly Evans, Yannis Gabriel, Stefanie Reissner, and David Woodward, among many others.

I also appreciate the time and guidance given to me by Jimmy Neal Smith and J. G. "Paw-Paw" Pinkerton, which enabled me to find my way around the world of professional storytelling. Doug Lipman has been immensely helpful in clarifying my thinking about performing a story.

I owe a great deal to Tom Stewart and Paul Hemp for their support and assistance with my article "Telling Tales," which was published in the *Harvard Business Review* of May 2004, where much of the material included in Chapter One first appeared.

I am grateful for the innumerable helpful contributions and suggestions at various meetings, workshops, and conferences in which I have participated and through my web site.

I would like to thank especially Melinda Bickerstaff, Peter Case, Lyn Dowling, Larry Forster, Martine Haas, Valdis Krebs, Erik Piñeiro, Lesley Shneier, and Russ Volckmann.

Finally, I would like to express my appreciation to Kathe Sweeney, Mary Garrett, Erin Moy, Beverly Miller, and the entire Jossey-Bass/Wiley team for their many helpful suggestions and for their commitment to this project.

ABOUT THE AUTHOR

Stephen Denning is the author of eight books, including *The Leader's Guide to Radical Management: Reinventing the Workplace for the 21st Century* (Jossey-Bass, 2010). His book, *The Secret Language of Leadership: How Leaders Inspire Action Through Narrative,* was selected by the *Financial Times* as one of the best books of 2007.

The first edition of *The Leader's Guide to Storytelling: Mastering the Art and Discipline of Business Narrative,* was published in 2005. It was named by the Innovation Network as one of the twelve most important books on innovation in the past several years.

Squirrel Inc.: A Fable of Leadership Through Storytelling was published in 2004. Denning has also published *Storytelling in Organizations* (2004) and *The Springboard* (2000), as well as a novel and a volume of poetry.

Denning consults with organizations in the United States, Europe, Asia, and Australia on topics of leadership, management, innovation, and business narrative. He worked at the World Bank from 1969 to 2000, where he held various management positions, including program director of knowledge management from 1996 to 2000.

In 2000, he was named one of the world's ten most admired knowledge leaders by Teleos, and in 2003, he was ranked as one of the world's top two hundred business gurus by Tom Davenport and Larry Prusak in their book, *What's the Big Idea?*

Denning studied law and psychology at Sydney University in Australia and worked as a lawyer in Sydney for several years. He then earned a postgraduate degree in law at Oxford University.

In 2009, he was a visiting fellow at All Souls College, Oxford University.

Denning's Web site (http://www.stevedenning.com) has an extensive collection of materials on radical management, leadership, innovation, knowledge management, and business narrative.

INDEX

Page references followed by *t* indicate a table.

Branding narrative: based on organization values, 124; communicated within the firm, 123–124; customer stories on social media, 109–110; description of, 28, 33*t*; organizational examples of social media for, 110–111; template for crafting, 125; 20th century marketing model for, 111–118; 21st century marketing model for, 118–124. *See also* Corporate culture; Organization brand

Brent Spar oil rig, 130

Bristol-Myers Squibb, 241

British Royal Astronomical Society, 198

British Telecom, 75–77, 130

Bubbles/infant delivery story, 186–187

Budweiser, 117

Building trust narrative: by communicating who you are, 27–28, 33*t*; how to tell your story, 99–104; with a new audience, 90; understanding the importance of the, 89–91; where you tell your story, 104–107; why you tell your story, 91–99. *See also* Credibility

Built to Last (Collins and Porras), 129–130

Burns, James MacGregor, 292

Bush, George W., 98, 105, 218

Bush, George W. H., 217

Business design, 262–263

Business models, 245

C

Cahill, S., 151

Campbell Leadership Descriptor, 291

Capellas, Michael, 80

Car Talk (radio show), 183–184, 193

Carroll, Dave, 109

Case, P., 215

CDC Web site, 18, 20

Champions for change, 223

Change: IBM and making the case for, 82; impact of storytelling for implementing, 36; official and emerging stories gap during, 213–215; pitched battles over, 223–226; rational case for, 224; springboard stories used to initiate, 9, 62–88; study of computer programming community during, 215; transformational leadership as embodying values of the, 107. *See also* Innovation; Transformational change

Change idea: finding example of accomplished, 65–67; have springboard story fully embody the, 70–71; having clear and worthwhile, 64–65; link springboard story to the, 77–79

Chappell, Kate, 133

Chappell, Tom, 133–134, 277

Chesbrough, Henry, 260, 261

Christensen, Clayton, 254, 255, 256

Churchill, Winston, 25, 235–236

"Cinderella" (fairy story), 81

CIO (chief innovation officer), 262

Cirque du Soleil story, 71–72

Clark, Evelyn, 10, 141, 145

Cliché, 239–240

Clients: expectations of, 167–168; goal of work as delighting, 264, 268; iterations driven by, 265. *See also* Customer stories

Clinton, Bill, 100, 104, 217–218

Clinton, Hillary, 217

Clio (Renault ad series), 116–117

The Cluetrain Manifesto (Searls and Weinberger), 124

Coaching story telling, 106

Coca-Cola, 114–115

Cohn, Mike, 246–247

Collaboration: hierarchy concept in discourse of, 163–164; meaningful experience of high-performance, 156–157; shared values as basis of, 158–159; strategies for nurturing, 170–179; template for nurturing, 180; work patterns of, 161–163; work situations benefiting from, 160–161. *See also* Fostering collaboration narrative; Work groups

347

In Chapter Nine, excerpts from Case and Piñeiro's study of a computer programming community are used with permission.

In Chapter Ten, the excerpt from Lou Gerstner's speech at the Lotus Press Conference, New York, New York, June 5, 1995, is reprinted with permission from the IBMCorporate Archives.

In Chapter Ten, the excerpt from Winston Churchill's speech "We Shall Fight on the Beaches," presented to The House of Commons, June 4, 1940, is reproduced with permission of Curtis Brown Ltd., London, on behalf of The Estate of Sir Winston S. Churchill.

In Chapter Ten, excerpts from "I Have a Dream" are reprinted by arrangement with the Estate of Martin Luther King Jr., c/o Writers House as agent for the proprietor, New York, New York. Copyright © 1963 Martin Luther King Jr., copyright renewed 1991 by Coretta Scott King.

In Chapter Ten, information from an interview with Melinda Bickerstaff is used with permission.

In Chapter Eleven, the excerpt from Lou Gerstner's speech at *Fall Internet World '96*, New York, New York, December 11, 1996, is reprinted with permission from the IBM Corporate Archives.